DATE DUE

JUN 3 0 1993		
JAN 0 5 1998		
MAY 2 6 1998		
NOV 1 6 1999		

#47-0108 Peel Off Pressure Sensitive

THE PERSONALITY OF
THE HORSE

CIRCUS HORSES. John Marin. *Courtesy, The Metropolitan Museum of Art: The Alfred Stieglitz Collection, 1949.*

THE PERSONALITY OF THE HORSE

EDITED BY BRANDT AYMAR
AND EDWARD SAGARIN

BONANZA BOOKS

NEW YORK

This 1983 edition is published by Bonanza Books,
distributed by Crown Publishers, Inc.

Manufactured in the United States of America

Library of Congress Cataloging in Publication Data
Main entry under title:

The Personality of the horse.

    1. Horses—Literary collections. 2. English
literature. 3. American literature. I. Aymar,
Brandt. II. Sagarin, Edward, 1913–
PR1111.H6P47 1983   820'.8'036   82-24446
ISBN: 0-517-037858

j i h g f e d

ACKNOWLEDGMENTS

We wish to thank the authors, publishers, and literary agents for granting us permission to use the following works in this book:

AMERICAN MERCURY for "The Horse Who Would Not Be Scratched" by James
Holledge, from the *American Mercury*, February, 1960.
APPLETON-CENTURY-CROFTS for "Levant" by Hugh Johnson from *Century Maga-
zine*, copyright 1911, The Century Company, and for "A Stranger to the Wild"
by Charles G. D. Roberts from *Century Magazine*, December, 1906.
THE ATLANTIC MONTHLY for "The Black Mare" by MacGregor Jenkins from *The
Atlantic Monthly*, July, 1935.
MRS. GEORGE BAMBRIDGE, DOUBLEDAY AND CO., INC., and the MACMILLAN CO.
OF CANADA for "The Maltese Cat" by Rudyard Kipling.
S. OMAR BARKER for his poem "The Mustang Bay" from *Songs of the Saddlemen*,
copyright 1954 by S. Omar Barker.
HERBERT ERNEST BATES for "Lanko's White Mare" from *Seven Tales and Alex-
ander* by Herbert Ernest Bates, copyright 1929 by H. E. Bates.
ERNEST BENN LIMITED, London, for "Horses" from Dorothy Wellesley's *Selected
Poems*.
JOHN BIGGS, JR., for his story "Corkran of the Clamstretch" from *Scribner's Maga-
zine*, December, 1921.
WALTER VAN TILBURG CLARK for his story "The Rise and the Passing of Bar" from
The Virginia Quarterly Review, Winter, 1943.

CAROLINE CLEMENT, Estate of Mazo de la Roche, for "The Pony That Would Not Be Ridden" and "Justice for an Aristocrat," both from *The Sacred Bullock* by Mazo de la Roche.

MRS. ARTHUR DAVISON FICKE for two poems by Arthur Davison Ficke, "Loreine: A Horse," which originally appeared in the *Saturday Review*, and "Caroline: A Horse."

FINE EDITIONS PRESS for the two poems, "The Huckster's Horse" by Julia Hurd Strong and "Old Major" by Bianca Bradbury.

VARDIS FISHER for his story "The Scarecrow" from his book *Love and Death*, published by Doubleday and Co., Inc., 1959.

FRED GIPSON for his story "Sad Sam," which appeared in *Southwest Review*, Autumn, 1946.

HARPER AND BROS. for "The Doctor's Horse" from *Understudies* by Mary E. Wilkins.

SIR ALAN HERBERT, THE PROPRIETORS OF *Punch*, MESSRS. METHUEN AND CO., LTD. (Canada), and DOUBLEDAY AND CO., INC. for the poem "The Racing-Man" from *Tinker Tailor*, copyright 1922 by A. P. Herbert.

HILL AND WANG, INC. for "Champions of the Peaks" from *The Hunting Horn and Other Dog Stories* by Paul Annixter. Copyright © 1957 by Paul Annixter.

HOUGHTON MIFFLIN COMPANY for "The War God's Horse Song," a poem from *The Navajo Indian* by Dane and Mary Roberts Coolidge.

BRUCE HUMPHRIES, INC. for "Mission for Baby" by I. N. Drinkard from *Anthology of Best Original Short Stories* by Robert Oberfirst, copyright 1953 by Robert Oberfirst. Also for the poem "Horses" from *Yours for the Asking* by Richard Armour, copyright 1947 by Bruce Humphries, Inc.

J. B. LIPPINCOTT COMPANY for "The Corralling of Flicka" from *My Friend Flicka* by Mary O'Hara, copyright 1941 by Mary O'Hara. Published by J. B. Lippincott.

WILLIAM MORRIS AGENCY, INC. for the story "Crusader" by Stuart Cloete, copyright 1943 by Stuart Cloete.

G. P. PUTNAM'S SONS for "Northwind" by Herbert Ravenel Sass from *The Way of the Wild* by Herbert Ravenel Sass.

FRANK SULLIVAN for "Love Makes the Filly Go" from *A Pearl in Every Oyster* by Frank Sullivan.

MRS. JOSEPH TENENBAUM for "Horses Are Horses" from *Mad Heroes* by Joseph Tenenbaum.

UNIVERSITY OF NEBRASKA PRESS for "The Colt" by Wallace Stegner from the *Southwest Review*.

THE VIKING PRESS for "The Gift" from *The Red Pony* by John Steinbeck, copyright 1933, 1960 by John Steinbeck.

The editors wish to express their appreciation to Barry L. Sheer for his valuable assistance in the compiling of this anthology.

CONTENTS

ILLUSTRATIONS

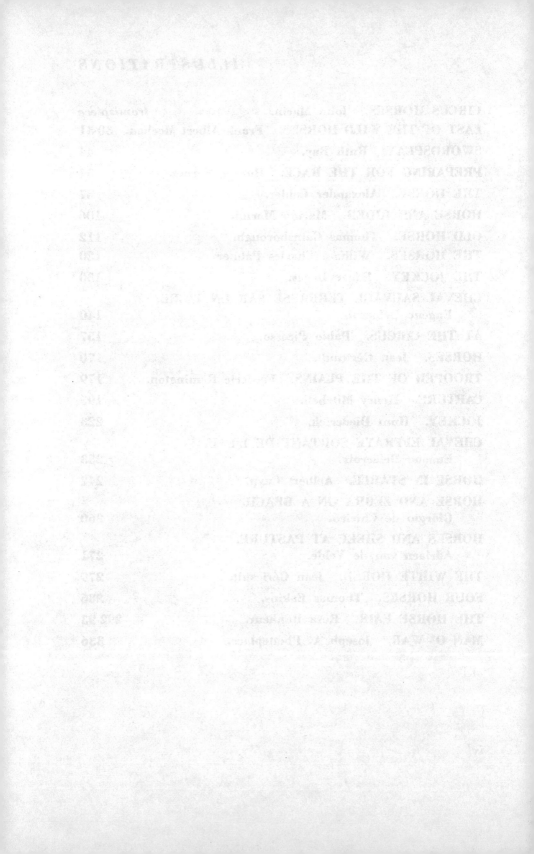

There are many who say one should not speak of a horse as having *personality*. For the word "personality" surely suggests, if it does not require, that one is speaking about a group of traits and characteristics found in human beings. This human being is a person, and no matter how many of these traits might be found in a horse, he is not (and doubtlessly would not want to be) a member of the human race.

Thus, man (sitting on his high horse, one might say) has taken an entire group of traits which are, alas, only rarely encountered in his fellow men, and called the individual who has these highly desirable and most enviable characteristics (such as kindness, sympathy, gratitude, and warmth) *humane*. Robert Burns, bemoaning man's cruelty, has referred to "man's inhumanity to man." But Jonathan Swift, who chose the horse to contrast with man so that nobility could be contrasted with ignominy, would have retorted: Not inhumanity, but humanity. This is what it means to be human.

In the same way, man takes such traits that give a living creature his individuality and calls this "personality." Not "horsonality," mind you, but "personality"!

However, although the horse is not a person, and perhaps never dreams of an afterlife in which he would be reincarnated as a human, individuality of character he has, and this individuality gives him a personality. This personality has been imputed to him by painters, storytellers, poets, sculptors, and folklorists just as long as man has had the horse as friend, companion, and co-worker in the arduous job of living in an all-too-hostile world.

Horses have been fascinating to man for centuries. If one were to collect the poetry, novels, and short stories, and add to them the paintings and the mythologies of many peoples, one would require a many-volumed encyclopedia. Many writers have approached their material from the viewpoint of man's relationship to the horse. Some have tried to see life from the horse's point of view. Some of them have even told their stories out of the horse's mouth. It is with the latter two categories that this anthology is concerned.

To tell the story out of the horse's mouth, to imagine what is going on inside this strange, silent, mysterious animal, calls for all the ingenuity of the creative writer. And yet, is this not his task whenever he enters the domain of imagination, to relate what is going on as seen from a view he has not himself experienced?

In so doing, the writer is arranging the infinite observations and experiences around him in some artistic order. Whether he chooses another human being through whom he communicates what he sees and how he orders it, or whether he chooses forms of life other than his own species, he cannot escape from this artist's burden. So that, when it is the horse about whom he is writing, he is actually writing about people and himself, using the horse to depict the world as he sees it. Thus one could say about these stories depicting the personality traits of horses that one could not imagine more penetrating portraits of human beings!

The writers collected in this work knew much about the horse, for they saw and depicted horses that were faithful, savage, warlike, unconquerable, selfish, martyred, heroic, valiant, sympathetic, compassionate, patient, gracious, beloved, remorseful.

But these are characteristics that no author could find in a horse if he had not searched for and found (or failed to find) them in human beings. It would be difficult to imagine a warmer and more heart-rending story of compassion than that of Jody for Gabilan in John Steinbeck's "The Red Pony," but one has not read this story in its fullest meaning if one does not see and feel the reciprocating love, the fondness of Gabilan for Jody as much as the reverse. As a further example, Frank Sullivan in "Love Makes the Filly Go" tells us more about romance, jealousy, and the whims and wiles of males and females chasing one another than authors have related in dozens of novels fifty times the length of this story. It is the use of the horse that gives the author the opportunity to sit back and majestically laugh at himself, at stallions and fillies, at men and women, at life itself, yet to see this world all the more seriously because he is able to dismiss it with laughter.

On the other hand, one turns to Wallace Stegner's "The Colt" to find the hobbling and handicapped Socks, loved all the more by the boy who feels guilt-ridden for what has befallen the animal; yet what is this poignant and tragic portrait all about if not a reciprocating and mutual dependency that ties two beings to each other, even though one may not be human?

What these writers have done is to show that, even when the works are written from the human viewpoint, there is an implicit horse's viewpoint in them, and the reverse: when the stories are horse-centered, they are really talking about people.

This, in a word, is what we, the anthologists, have found in searching through the world of equine literature, gathering writings and art that depict the personality of the horse as man sees it and imagines that it must be.

All introductions are too long, so it is now time to stop horsing around and to urge you to gallop into the enjoyment of what follows.

B.A. and E.S.

THE PONY THAT WOULD
NOT BE RIDDEN
by Mazo de la Roche

He was cobby and round and well fed, he was kind and sweet-tempered and strong—but nobody wanted him! He spent his days and his nights in a field where sheep were pastured, on the side of a hill. Other hills rose one after another to the purple hills of Wales in a glorious panorama, but Lord Ronald saw only his hill, the small black-faced sheep that grazed on its shaggy side, and the benevolent hump of the hayrick from which he pulled whenever he chose a wisp of sweet-tasting hay. He would stand with his stocky legs well planted, a wisp of hay dangling from the side of his mouth, and stare tranquilly at his own hill, his companions the sheep, and the kindly hump of the rick. Only one thing was lacking to him and that was a pair of legs he used to know.

Between himself and these legs there had existed a fond intimacy. They had talked to him in a language he could understand, though sometimes he had pretended not to. There had been hands too, thin young girl's hands, on whose smooth palms he had mumbled with his sensitive upper lip for sugar. The voice that belonged to these legs and hands had been high and clear. Sometimes a silky mane had mingled with his own.

He had no definite longing for these but the memory of them sometimes stirred in him, vaguely but deeply, though it was two years since they were lost to him. He had a grand appetite. It was this that Farmer Goslett resented. There he was, a useless animal, eating the good hay and oats that might have fattened the young bullocks. The pony was mischievous, too. In the long idle days he was often up to tricks that made for trouble. More than once he had forced an opening in the hedge, through which the sheep scattered themselves along the road and were chased by dogs. Another time he got himself caught in some barbed wire and there was a vet's bill.

He was a nuisance and he was an expense and he was no earthly use. Goslett did not know what to do about him. He had come by him in this way.

A family from South Africa had taken the dower house on a nearby estate for a term of years. There had been several school-boys in the family and a little girl of eight. She was a delicate little thing but full of life. She was eager for a pony of her own and gave her father no peace until he bought one for her. The parents had been anxious to find a thoroughly reliable pony and it had been Goslett himself who had put this little Lord Ronald in their way. He was a handsome pony with a kind of sturdy nobility in his lines and he was guaranteed not to misbehave. He never had. He and the little girl became a familiar sight on the roads, he rounded and sturdy, she ethereally thin, her lank dark hair clinging about her neck and shoulders. She had a long, pointed face, large, rather startled-looking blue eyes, and a mouth always ready to widen in a broad smile that showed two rows of lovely little teeth.

She was almost always smiling when she rode. She looked as happy as a foal in a spring meadow, but the servants in the house said that her governess found her a handful and that she sometimes had tantrums that upset the whole household. Perhaps she had them because her health wasn't good. Every now and again she had a bout of illness. The neighborhood had so taken her delicacy for granted that everyone was shocked when one morning, after the family had lived four years in the dower house, the news came that she had died the night before.

For four years she had cantered and galloped across the fields and along the roads on her pony. She had grown from a little thing of eight to a long-legged child of twelve. There had been something about her that had caught the eye and held it. When she was gone people spoke tenderly of her and it was some time before she was forgotten.

Her parents could not endure the house. They left their

sons in England and went back to South Africa. They were not missed nearly so much as their child was.

The father had given the pony to Goslett because he had wanted to make sure of a kind home for him. Goslett said that his own young daughter would be glad to have him for riding to school. He thought to himself that he might make good use of him for light work on the farm.

But the first time that Lord Ronald felt Mary Goslett's fat legs pressed to his sides he refused to move. She coaxed and petted him, but he hated the feel of her fat hands on his neck. When she spoke to him in her strong Herefordshire accent he quivered with displeasure. Her father and the laborer who worked for him shouted to her to give him a taste of the whip. Mary did, but Lord Ronald stiffened himself against the blows and did not budge. Not with ears laid back and an expression of willful mulishness, but simply as though he could not bring himself to move.

Then they coaxed him with sugar and carrots, the two men pushed him from behind, but nothing would induce him to move. They tried him again the next day and the next and the next, but neither beatings nor all the tricks they heard of from the neighbors were of any use. He stood like the shapely statue of a pony, immutable as granite, impervious to pain or cajolery. Mary Goslett was bitterly disappointed. She had liked the idea of showing off before the other children at the parish school, riding back and forth on the pony.

The village children jeered at her. "The pony won't have naught to do with you, Mary. Him's used to little lady ridin' him!"

When Goslett put the pony between shafts it was just the same. He planted his feet on the ground and nothing could move him. In other ways he was perfectly docile, trotting back to his friends the sheep after each trial with a gentle beam in his eyes, whether his sides were ridged with welts or the sweetness of sugar lay on his tongue.

It became a joke among the neighbors that Goslett's pony felt itself so far above him that it refused to do his bidding. In spite of his usual good sense he began to resent what seemed the pony's feeling of superiority. He said to his wife:

"It's damned swank, and no mistake. I've a mind to lather him till he drops where he stands."

"No," she answered, "his heart is just chronic with longing for his young lady and he won't tolerate any other rider. It's a rare disappointment for our Mary but you mustn't beat him any more. Folk will only laugh at you."

Lord Ronald was not beaten again, but Goslett now made up his mind to sell him. He took him to a horse fair at a distance where no one had heard of his stubbornness. He had groomed him until he shone. His mane and tail were bright with energy. His large blue-brown eyes had a friendly beam in them. There was none other such handsome pony at the fair.

But it was the same old story. When the would-be purchaser mounted him Lord Ronald turned into a statue that nothing could bring to life until once more the saddle was empty. Then he turned his glowing eyes from face to face, his velvet nostrils quivered against the damp air, and his small hoof pawed eagerly, as though he would be off.

"What d'ye think I want?" cried the would-be purchaser. "A hobbyhorse?"

Goslett was deeply chagrined. He led Lord Ronald home with his heart full of resentment. He turned him into a field and ignored him for the rest of the summer.

But when autumn came he again tried to master the pony. He had no success and again he led him to fairs and advertised him for sale. Lord Ronald was becoming well known. It put the horse dealers, farmers, and hostlers in good humor just to see him.

"Hullo, Jack!" they would call. "Give us a ride on hobbyhorse!" Or—"'Ere comes the favorite! What odds be you offering, Goslett?"

Goslett got to hate the pony. He would have given him away, but nobody wanted him.

Now, two years after Lord Ronald had come into his possession, a gypsy offered to buy him. He had been passing in his cart and had seen the pony standing shapely and alert gazing across the hills. He had got out of the cart and gone to the farm gate and leant on it, chirruping and talking in his gypsy lingo to the pony. He had made some inquiries about him, learned how he would allow no one to ride him. Now he stood with Goslett at his side, looking him over. His slender dark hands moved over Lord Ronald's muscular body like two brown monkeys intent on mischief. His soft eyes looked up sideways into Goslett's face.

"I'll buy him of you," he said, and he offered a sum so low that Goslett could have knocked him down for his cheek. This pony, this handsome Scottish pony with his powerful loins, his lovely shoulders, his coat that was like polished steel, when he was groomed, though now it was muddy and burrs clung in his mane, to be sacrificed as a gift to a sly gypsy.

" 'Tis no use buying him," growled Goslett. "He'd not go for ye. He'll go for no man."

"He'll go for me," said the gypsy.

Goslett turned his slow gaze on him. He said:

"I'll not have him treated cruel."

The gypsy showed his pointed teeth. "I know a trick or two," he said. "But I'd not hurt him."

"You don't know him. Get on his back and you'll see what I mean. He's stubborn to the bone. No trick of yours would budge him. But I don't want him hurt."

"You want to keep him for the rest of his days, eating his head off, eh?"

The gypsy smiled impudently into Goslett's face. Then he placed his hands on Lord Ronald's back and sprang, light as a panther, mounting him. He laid his slim body along the arch of the pony's neck and whispered in his ear.

The effect was startling to Goslett. Lord Ronald rose, as though touched by some secret spring in his inmost being, and stood erect on his hind legs. He stood so more than straight that it seemed he must fall backward at the next moment. He and the gypsy were turned into an equestrian statue of granite, wild, stark, almost terrifying.

"By gum! You've done it!" muttered Goslett. "You've made him move!"

Slowly, like a trained horse, Lord Ronald lowered himself until once more he stood on his four legs. He was trembling and sweat had turned the color of his hide from steel to iron.

"Now you've done so much, why don't ye make him go with ye?" demanded Goslett. "A lot of good he'll be to ye, standin' on his hind legs like a circus pony!"

The gypsy slid to the ground. "Time enough later on. But you see I can make him move. He knows he's met his master."

"Well," growled Goslett, sullenly, "I'll take your offer. And I say you're a queer pair and I wish you luck with each other."

The gypsy promised to come back in three days with the money. Other gypsies were coming then with their caravan and they would take Lord Ronald away.

Goslett would be glad to see the last of the pony but he wished he might have got rid of him in some other fashion. He had disliked the way he had broken into a sweat and trembled when the gypsy was on his back. He felt that he had almost sooner put a bullet through him and bury him in the pasture than see him led off by the gypsy. Still—money was money and in these hard days he needed it all too badly.

He and the gypsy stood talking a moment in the trampled mud outside the gate before they went their different ways, the gypsy dark and slender, a neckerchief tied about his throat, driving off in his cart, the farmer fair and thickset, his sturdy calves encased in leather leggings, trudging off with his sheep dog following at his heels. Neither turned to look back at Lord Ronald.

He stood watching their departing figures, his large eyes dilated, one hoof pawing nervously at the frosty grass, the hairs of his mane and tail seeming separately alive.

The road ran through the farm and the laborer was now crossing it carrying the noonday feed for the poultry which were in the meadow next Lord Ronald's pasture. As the laborer crossed the road with his bucket he was met by a flock of white leghorns that surged about him like a wave. They chanted their joy in his coming and a group of turkeys came, trailing their dark feet and crying plaintively for their share. The ducks left their pond across the road and rocked after the farmhand, all but two who slumbered with heads tucked under wings among the reeds at the edge of the pond.

Lord Ronald was usually fascinated by the feeding of the poultry, putting his nose over the hedge and whickering to the man to make haste with the meal for himself and the sheep. But now he stood unmoved by the clatter of the hens or by the oncoming sheep that bundled themselves down the hillside toward the hayrick like a wind-blown patch of fog. Every now and again a tremor of fear shook him.

At last the man came and put down meal for him and for the sheep. The behinds of all the flock were turned to Lord Ronald. Their little black legs were rigid under their gray bodies, their black faces thrust into the meal. The man called.

"Coom along then, pony! S'all I give yer feed to the sheep?"
But he would not go.

All day the fog cloaked the countryside. The hills might have
been plains for all that was visible of them. Out of the fog came
the sounds of the hens and the sheep and the breathless gurgling
of a little stream that hastened through the hoary grass.

The pony had not made a fresh hoofprint since the gypsy
had slid from his back when the sun freed itself from the mantle
of fog and showed a crimson disc beyond the mountains of
Wales. The sky turned a pale blue like a tranquil lake and birds
came from every tree and hedge to seek a grain of sustenance
before the night.

But the night did not bring darkness. The full moon sailed
out on the clear lake of the sky. Lord Ronald's shadow was black
as a bat beside him. He bent his head to look, as though for the
first time in his life he were conscious of it. The shadow turned
away its head and the pony trembled in fear. An owl flew out of
the hedge and began to strut up and down in front of him, dropping its wings and making low, tremulous sounds.

A thin hand touched his mane, then slid up over his cheek
to his forelock. Fingers began delicately to draw out the burrs
that clung there. As the burrs were dropped they did not fall
straight to the ground but drifted, as though on a breeze, out of
sight. Lord Ronald lowered his head and pressed it toward the
fluttering hand. He gave a sharp whicker of delight.

Now he felt a bridle being put on him with a touch so
caressing as to be almost unbearable. A bit was slipped into his
mouth from which he sucked a new and dazzling power. He
pawed the ground. He could scarcely wait for the thin legs to
bestride him. He felt their taut pressure. He felt the familiar lift
to the bridle and they were off!

The sheep ran to the farthest corner of the meadow, bun-
dling themselves close together, baaing in consternation. This
was not the pony they knew. This was a strange steed that flashed
across the pasture scarcely seeming to touch it. As he flew he
gave a neigh that echoed like a trumpet among the hills.

On the hills the russet bracken was crisp and the most delicate outlines shone in silver. On and on the humped hills un-
folded themselves to the black mountains of Wales. The moon
rose and sank. . . .

"That there pony's off his feed," observed the farm laborer next day.

" 'Twill do him no harm to fast a bit," answered Goslett, but he went that afternoon to have a look at him.

Lord Ronald stood just where the gypsy had left him. It seemed that he had not moved from the spot where his small hoofs were planted. He gave his usual look of beaming intelligence at the farmer. His nostrils were red as though he had been racing.

" 'Tis a pity you've such a bad nature," said Goslett, "for you're handsome, and no mistake."

He thought that the laborer must have pulled the burrs from his mane and groomed the mud away, and he was surprised.

The next day the pony still refused to feed and stood in the selfsame spot. Goslett was glad that the gypsy was coming tomorrow to take him away.

But when tomorrow came and they went to the pasture he was not there. The fog was heavy and they plodded through it searching every corner, peering for breaks in the hedge. The sheep followed them in a body. There was a strange light in their yellow eyes, as though they knew something they wanted to tell.

THE UNVANQUISHED HORSE

THE BRONC THAT WOULDN'T BUST

Anonymous

I've busted broncos off and on
Since first I struck their trail,
And you bet I savvy broncos
From nostrils down to tail;
But I struck one on Powder River
And say, hands, he was the first
And only living bronco
That your servant couldn't burst.

He was a no-count buckskin,
Wasn't worth two bits to keep,
Had a black stripe down his backbone,
And was woolly like a sheep.
That hoss wasn't built to tread the earth;
He took natural to the air;
And every time he went aloft
He tried to leave me there.

He went so high above the earth
Lights from Jerusalem shone.
Right thar we parted company
And he came down alone.
I hit terra firma,
The buckskin's heels struck free,
And brought a bunch of stars along
To dance in front of me.

I'm not a-riding airships
Nor an electric flying beast;
Ain't got no rich relation
A-waitin' me back East;
So I'll sell my chaps and saddle,
My spurs can lay and rust;
For there's now and then a digger
That a buster cannot bust.

THE COMPETITIVE HORSE

THE RISE AND THE PASSING OF BAR
by Walter van Tilburg Clark

Bar inherited the remuda when he was less than two years old, and still tolerated by his sire, Nomad. Nomad's was a shameful death for a great leader and the winner of eight duels. After a long run from two Indian riders into the hot hills north of the reservation, he became careless in the dusk, plunged his right foreleg into a gopher hole and snapped it with a small explosion. Sage, the aging broodmare, whimpered around him, shying from his thrashing, but finally led the helpless remuda on. It was starlight when they found the bitter spring towards which Nomad had aimed. They drank slowly, grazed, and slept on the meadow in the mouth of the canyon. Sage fretted Bar as he drank, but he did not understand, and she took the sentry post herself.

Bar stood alone in the box canyon above the well, but could not sleep. The stars moved slowly and together over the canyon, and once the coyotes talked in the far dark. The remuda was silent below him, each with one hind leg relaxed. A little after midnight his restlessness became a moving command, and he picked his way down to the trail, turned south, and opened into a swinging trot. Only Sage saw him go.

First dawn made a secret light over the great plateau before Bar slackened his pace. He stopped four times on one brush-covered dome girdled by the trail, and cast with his tail up, and took the wind. When his excitement escaped in a high, vibrating blast, it was answered at once from above him. He swung, whinnying again, and ascended in long, driving strides, his scanty mane and tail of youth bannered behind him. On the summit he drew up in martial pose. Across the dome, huge in the colorless light, his long mane sailing, his plume sweeping brush, stood Nomad, on three legs. The fourth was queerly bent, and bore no weight. Bar shrilled and stepped nervously, filled with dread of this master, feeling again the nips and shoulder blows Nomad had used daily to remind him he was a stripling. As he drew to battle, this dread was like seed barbs in him, yet he cantered proudly along a crescent aimed to come home against Nomad's strong shoulder. It was a lofty and impudent approach, but also more, for when Nomad trumpeted again to check him, he broke into a gallop. Nomad shifted on the one great foreleg, so that the charge glanced off, and when Bar spun back, reared and broke his rise with a blow which nearly threw him, but Nomad could not follow up. They sounded and milled, Bar parading, Nomad pivoting slowly in the center with his neck stretched out. Bar struck diagonally at the bulging shoulder, and Nomad could not meet him with weight, and his teeth clacked in air. Bar continued the light flank attacks, slashing with his teeth, sometimes driving a rear hoof against the great barrel as he went away. Only once, overconfident from a dozen free sallies, he was slow to swing off, and was struck by both teeth and forehoof, so that his hindquarters winced under, and then nearly sank. Then he was consistently cautious, attacking fleetly in passing, and awaiting his break. It would come. Already Nomad, weary from enduring the broken leg, breathed like the rattle of drums, and rose more slowly against each charge. The smell of his fear began in the air, even over the trampled sage. It was a slow battle, but over by sunrise. There came finally the charge that Nomad could neither avoid nor meet in time, and then Bar did not swerve. Nomad squealed furiously, but fell, the broken leg refusing, and screamed so the wide valley echoed across. Bar whirled and crashed his hind hoofs against the great head struggling snakelike to come up, and the scream broke, and then the echo after it, in separate agony. Bar trampled in the dark skull, and when the first sun showed on the peaks in the west, stood and sounded his triumph, his hoofs stained crimson to the fetlock.

Sage was too wise to bear green triumph unchecked. The remuda was gone from the spring, and only two red steers were there, drinking slowly in the dancing heat. When Bar nickered, they raised dripping muzzles and stared at him glassily, their ears twitching against flies, and again drank. A strength Bar had never had perceived was fallen away, leaving him without will. He circled on the meadow and the slopes, pausing and whinnying like a colt. The spring was beyond the range he knew, and the desire increased to return to familiar land, to the naked hills south, and the trails along the lake cliffs. At noon he was passing under the battle dome again. He saw the great, loose wings of a vulture settling above, and heard a small squabbling as it sank from sight.

Through four days he raced, with growing panic, on the old trails, seldom grazing, and never sleeping. His ribs emerged, his hardened wounds ached, and he became crazy with weariness, seeing the remuda on shimmering dry lakes, or far down valleys where there was nothing. When he was unable to run steadily, he turned north again towards the sour spring, stopping often to rest and pull at the yellow bunch grass. He took three days for the journey, and curiously went over the battle hill. Nomad's bones were already a nearly odorless white arch, and the military ants foraged in fragments of hide. He came to the spring at sunset of the seventh day, and the remuda was there.

His vexation returned, and he selected the yearling Rocky as his victim. When he blared, the remuda lifted startled heads and then scattered watchfully. Rocky nickered and cast in short, aimless runs because Bar blocked the open below him. But when Bar lifted toward the colt, Sage lumbered between them, and when he swung right to pass, bared her teeth and nipped him. He twisted aside, posed, and challenged again, but on descending scale and only to save his pride. Then he went up to the spring and drank, and returned to graze apart from the others, who lifted their heads with sudden jerks whenever he moved out of sight. Rocky grazed most nervously of all, and always near Sage.

For two days Sage heavily resisted Bar's efforts to put the remuda on the trail. Once, when he bullied it into motion, blocking each turn with ears laid back, Sage appeared to surrender, galloped into the lead, and with turning head watched Bar working the rear, as she had watched for Nomad's orders. At the first Y, however, she swung into a pass to the left, and an hour later brought them down through the rattling shale to the spring again. Bar gave up, and contented himself with lookout excursions to near heights. The next day, in the shadowy cold before sunrise, Sage took the trail south, walking, and watching over her shoulder. Bar fumed and delayed, but at last drove the others up in a thundering bunch. Sage broke into the trail trot, and the remuda drew into file and became intent upon making distance. Sage continued to watch Bar, and for the first time he felt the urge of duty rather than pride, and chivied constantly along the flanks, or surged up to lookouts. When he drew abreast of Sage, she slowed to a walk or stopped, and the remuda fell apart to individual grazing. Before evening, Bar understood that he must work the rear only, and create no confusion of leadership.

In the following days Sage led over all the home trails, and Bar watched her steadily, learning to work by her lead, to select his lookouts, to chivy the remuda according to their natures, and give them the rest they needed. There was yet the master maneuver, which must await chance.

The chance came early in an afternoon in summer, while the remuda went south on a wagon road beside the shallow lake east of the big lake mountains. The air was still, and dust hung over the slow march and settled languidly behind. The only movement on the lake was of reflected heat waves on reflected chalk mountains. Insects clacked and sang in the brush. When Sage nickered gently in this silence, the remuda stopped and looked about with lifted heads. Then they all watched the tiny mark under its puff of dust far ahead. Something from the past nudged in Bar. The remuda spread into the brush, and alternately grazed and looked. Bar stirred uneasily about the edges, but Sage continued the grazing walk towards a fork, whence a wavering white trail climbed up through the gray and disappeared over a saddleback in the mountains between the lakes. At the fork they saw that the dust was made by three Indian riders in sombreros, two men and a boy. Bar began to chivy the remuda, but Sage balked, and they fanned out and resumed their nervous grazing. Bar shrilled lightly in protest, but stopped chivying, and

Sage went on. The Indians turned up into the brush and sep-
arated widely, but still walked their mounts. Where a fainter
trace went northwest from the saddleback road into the mountains, Sage stopped again. Most of the excited remuda pressed
past her onto the saddleback road, but three turned into the
trace and began to trot. Bar swung, plume raised, to chivy them
back. The Indians lifted their ponies into a lope and began to
cry shrilly, "Yippee, yippee, yippee." Sage nipped the horses on
the road into a lope also, Rocky on their rear, but swung against
Bar and the other three. Bar blared at her, but she forced them
back into the trace, and then, with her ears flattened, drove him
up into the lead. He had never seen her so furious. He broke into
a gallop, but kept swinging to watch her. When she stopped, he
started to double, but she charged him again. Then he understood, and opening into a long lope, led the three up the trace,
swinging only his head to watch Sage. She turned and went back
through the brush in a heavy, weaving gallop. Before the main
remuda, tiny with distance, disappeared over the saddleback, its
dust streaming east in the wind from the big lake, she was leading
again. The Indians stopped yipping, reined in one at a time, drew
slowly together and turned back down towards the wagon road.

Bar kept his charges up to the lope until they came into a
concealing pass, then trotted, and when the pitch steepened, let
down to a steady, heaving walk. At the summit the expanse of
the great lake opened below, rimmed with white rock. White,
pointed islands stood up in the haze in the far north. During the
descent manes and tails blew over to the cliff wall. An hour later
the remuda was joined on the shore, and Bar had learned the
split flight.

Sage taught Bar his place in the generation of the remuda
also. When he attempted to seal his succession to Nomad upon
her, she repulsed him, twice gently, but the third time savagely
and finally. The stately, eight-year-old roan, Blue, who had been
Nomad's last favorite, also resisted him for two seasons. He selected, then, the trim and virginal sorrel, Fan, as his delight,
though proving her election not by monogamous neglect of the
others, but by delicate commonplaces, by protecting choice
grazing bits for her, letting her drink first at the wells, and never
nipping her when he chivied. All the mares, Sage helping viciously, taught him to let alone even the meekest mare when she

was closed against him and already in love with the foal to come. And in spring, when the desert was sweet with tiny blossoms and flowering bushes, though snow still lay in the creases of the hills, he learned another limitation of his power.

The remuda, ragged from winter, drank snow water in a ravine. There had been a light rain at noon. The diffused sunlight made blue shadows of the new aspens, and high over the canyon, thin, windy vapors melted into azure. When they were cropping, a heavy bay mare, for whom they had stopped often on the trail, lifted her head as if stung, and nickered. Head lowered, but still nickering, she walked slowly down from the remuda. When Bar, irritated by her complaints, would have chivied her back, Sage thwarted him. He blew, and ran in circles, but Sage blocked each sally until the mare had gone slowly out of sight around the north wing of the canyon. At sunset Bar wanted to herd the remuda to a windbreak miles from the water, his habit when close to the reservation, but Sage prevented this also.

The bay mare returned in mid-morning, thin, and walking slowly, with many waits for the new foal. At sight of the erratic dwarf, Bar turned restlessly about and whistled. He reared and dropped and began to dance with light, rhythmic thunder in an arc towards the flank where the foal pressed. This rage was a new kind, squeamish and curdling, so that his lips curled back and his ears flattened without his knowing it. The tired mare extended her head at him with the same expression. But before he could reach her, Sage attacked him furiously and without warning, and when he wheeled again to come in, turned her heels to him, kicking repeatedly, so that he shied away. His murderous seizure returned several times during a day of uneasy grazing and short, fitful runs, but Sage blocked him each time. The remuda remained near the creek for three days, until the bay mare and her foal could travel. Thereafter Bar had few such rages, though he remained uneasy at each foal.

In the years before Sage resigned, Bar also learned battle. His first challenge came at a strange time, and from an unknown. The remuda was moving south at quick-trot under a gray sky, and kept behind a ridge for shelter from a northwest wind full of the smell of snow. There was already a thin snow on the desert, through which brush and rocks protruded with startling individuality. There is only one fear before a blizzard. Bar neglected his lookouts and drove the file steadily before him. The colors showed proudly on the snow, his own iron gray with the black bar along the spine and the black plumes, old Sage's dapple, the many bays, bright Fan, the roan Blue, Rocky, black as his sire and starred, the buckskin mare Tinto, and Cloud, Bar's son by Tinto, a queer powder-gray colt with white crest and plume and one white eye, the dark pupil of which gave him a wild and evil look. Even in this lee the wind wrapped their tails to their haunches and blew their manes ahead like flags.

The first challenge was diminutive as the whining of an insect, yet Bar winced, as if from Nomad's teeth. Then he blared and chivied the remuda to a gallop, and swung back from it to stand listening. The second blast came with the wind, high and prolonged, and Bar discovered the enemy. He stood silhouetted on the ridge, his full mane and tail blown about him like smoke. Bar turned his head and saw the remuda going away well, and turned back and sounded his defiance. The intruder blared once more, dropped from the ridge, and raced in a long diagonal down slope. He was a long-backed harlequin pinto with short legs which fled under him nimbly, and so big a head on a short neck that he seemed to run without lift, like a coursing dog. Bar could not meet this dropping charge at a standstill. Sounding nervously, he swung away in a half circle, plume lifted. The pinto swerved out of the line of charge into the flat and stopped, head high. Bar charged first, but at once the pinto matched his advance. When they closed, and Bar reared, squealing, to crush, the pinto ran under, making a long incision, like a rip of a hot point, in Bar's flank. He swung back before Bar could pivot and gouged his haunch and struck once with a forehoof. He was much shorter than Bar, but his chest and shoulders were heavy, and his small hoofs wickedly rapid and sharp. Mature and mettled, and quicker in every maneuver, he nearly reversed against Bar his own victory over Nomad. Bar, rearing and hammering at each charge, was repeatedly marked and bruised. The thin snow about the trample was pencilled by flying streaks of his blood. It was perhaps a slip that saved him from defeat. Querulous with rage and growing fear, he reared once with his hind hoofs badly set, and fell against the pinto. His own fall checked, he recovered first, and as the pinto tried to double out, struck him behind the shoulder, bowled him over and hammered twice before the pinto rolled free and scrambled away to his feet. After that he met each charge on the level, slashed the harlequin often, and gradually took the offensive. Shunted off by the great weight, the harlequin in his turn began to rear and flail, twisting his head to get under Bar's teeth to his neck. In these tactics he was not Bar's equal. His white neck and shoulders blossomed and grew running streamers of red. Bar's fury became a desire to annihilate. He pressed so constantly, shouldering, hammering, biting, that at last the pinto looked only for escape, and cried dread at each clash. Finally, only half rising against Bar's rearing drive, he ducked under the great forehoofs and made his break, running for the open with streaming tail. Bar followed heavily. The pinto turned like a rabbit, drove up the slope zigzag, and dropped from sight. From the ridge Bar saw him, like a little constellation of black stars, far out on the level and flying west, and abandoned the chase with a last high bugle of contempt.

The slight second combat came in his fourth year. It broke on a clear night on the north shore, when Rocky, too long with the remuda, climbed Fan as she drank. Their commotion was loud in the still darkness. When Bar sounded, Rocky splashed off to the shore, but only half met the first charge, with a false challenge that rang in the stone island, and then fled up through the boulders. Bar closed on his haunch five times, and each time Rocky squealed like a mare or a scared colt. Bar's anger waned. He stopped and sounded once more. Rocky's shadow swam small across the stars in the northeast, and he was gone.

Later Bar ejected Cloud, though not so easily.

After the first split remuda, Bar brought his charges off safely from three other human encounters, and began to feel easy about men. The fourth adventure, however, shook him into permanent caution. Fortunately for the remuda this occurred when Sage, steadily opposing Bar's efforts to induct Fan, had promoted Blue to brood mare, and when she was established, had taken her own weakness off one night into the black hills to die.

There had been a dry spring after a winter of little snow, and both water and grass were gone from the home range. The remuda had gradually moved into a region unknown even to Nomad, the higher mountains northwest of the lake, where there were meadow ponds in which the water grass stood and the little frogs piped in the evenings, and where the midday air was full of the smell of rosin. Slowly, through the summer, they grazed southward and early in a September morning were coming down a canyon through stones and aspen leaves, with the sun in their faces. For some minutes the air had made Bar uneasy, but it was motionless, and the creek under them covered other noises. The uneasiness did not mature.

At the mouth of the canyon Blue stopped and swerved back, throwing the remuda into disorder. Bar came down the side angrily, but also checked. In a clearing, walled below by cottonwoods, was a gray barn, and a split-rail corral holding four jumping stands. At the corral fence stood two men in leather chaps, talking. One of them had one foot up on a rail, and was smoking a cigarette, which made the smell Bar had disliked. Two saddled ponies stood behind the men. The men saw the remuda, and at once the one heeled out his cigarette and they ran for the ponies, speaking short words in a changed way.

Bar felt behind him the stiff climb and the traps of the blind ravines, and that there was no time to chivy. Shrilling his order, he broke down slope into a wild gallop. Blue slithered on the creek bank, clambered, and came down after him, and then the remuda, with Cloud the second, who had two white eyes, tailing. Bar drummed onto a road through the cottonwoods, slacked until Blue closed, and rolled forward thunderously. The dust of their start hung in the canyon mouth. They flashed into sunlight past a long screened porch where people jumped up and called out, again fled under big trees, and emerged onto a long, grassy lane going down hill before them between a fence and thick brush along the creek. The human crying faded back, but then down through it came the yip-yipping of the first two riders. A colt broke from line and crashed among the willows, shrilling his dismay. Bar swung out, also crashing heavily, shrilled at Blue, and when the flight had swept past, furiously drove the colt out and down into place, then spun back, and when he saw the riders break into the sun, challenged tremendously. Coming down on the rear, flags lifted for battle, he swung repeatedly to measure the interval. The riders were afraid in the narrow lane, and the remuda pulled away. When the shining lake opened below them, under a long slope of boulders and brush, suddenly the lane emptied into a white cross road. Blue swung to the right, confused, and the remuda pooled in a cloud of floury dust. Bar swept past, sounding, leaned left into the familiar north, and went away, and the remuda broke after him. When Blue had come up, and the file formed, Bar fell off to the rear, and even then felt a flash of jealousy that Cloud was tailing so well.

A mile north, Bar went up sentinel on the left flank. The two riders were coming, their mounts running well, and far behind them two others, small under their dust, burst from the lane, and then many together under a big cloud. Bar trumpeted anger at this harassment, but then was afraid of so many, and tore down again into the road and goaded the remuda to greater speed.

Where the road forked east around the end of the lake to home range, Bar, seeing the leaders still coming, and one of the second pair gaining, pressed forward along the right flank, shrilling at Blue, who understood now and swung east. Bar plunged through the center of the file, Cloud saw and chivied the pooling behind him, and the remuda was split. On a rise well north of the fork, Bar swung out to look again, the others following Fan on over. Blue's herd, running easily under its pennant, neared the stone islands, and was unpursued. On the north road the two riders came more heavily, the third close on them, the fourth far back. The many had drawn up at the fork, milling and watching. Bar raced back into the lead in triumph.

But the next lookout showed three running together, the fading fourth still following, and from the next the fourth was out of sight behind a roll of the desert, but the three still came, strung out, and the foremost seemed even to have gained on the remuda. Bar bullied his failing charges to a renewed effort. When he went up again there was only the one pursuer in sight, but he had clearly gained. Behind that swell Bar, with flattened ears, broke his little herd and sent Fan east with Cloud to tail, and with only two veteran mares, pressed north again at a gallop. When the following post, which was high, showed him the back riders, fading and past Fan's turn, but the leader running freshly, and so close Bar could see his mount, a tall black with a star, he felt dismay, as at a ghost of Nomad, and then led too hard. The mares were unable to stay with him, and in the cover of a deep wash, he shunted them east also, towards a rock pile like those by the lake, but brown and rounder with more centuries of weather, and waited alone, casting anxiously.

When the black came over, his rider yelled at seeing Bar so

close, but then had to work, for the black reared and challenged. Bar knew him then for Rocky, the last son of Nomad, and trumpeted too, and when the rider had put Rocky down, led north freely, not trying to lengthen his short lead, but drawing the thin man on the stallion farther from all the turns of the remuda.

At noon he went off through the brush towards the low hills on the northeast, and when Rocky, the rider making his weaving less fluid, lost ground, blew scorn and slackened his pace. Selecting his pass, he ran north away from it, intending to cut back, sprint on the slope, and lose them in the pass. He felt his first fear since the mares had been passed, when Rocky did not follow directly, but widened an angle to intercept the cutback and steal the lead. He swung about and stood, mane flying before him in the rising afternoon wind, which exploded dust on the knolls and far south made a thin, staggering column of dust. The rider pulled Rocky to a walk. Bar swung towards the pass, and Rocky loped to intercept him. Bar slacked off, and Rocky walked at him again. Bar posed, and nickered his irritation. This new, intangible force shouldered him wherever he moved. He turned and ran north again. Rocky followed, but slowly, and Bar thrilled with confidence again, sounded it, and stretched.

An hour later, the pursuit long out of sight, he crossed a saddleback, dropped to the flats, and ran south among the spasms of dust. He made many checks, but nothing appeared, and at last he trotted and began to regather the remuda in his mind. On a sandy rise he walked, but at its crest spun back in dismay, for Rocky stood close below, and the eyes of the thin rider stared up. Bar sensed their freshness as he cast right and left for the open and was always blocked, and at last turned up into the betraying pass and climbed without restraint. Clear distance was his only hope against this phantom of a greater horse that thought ahead of him. From the summit he fled down and north again in the late sunlight, against his yearning to go south, and did not slacken until he had made a rise nearly at his first crossing. From there, shaken by his breathing, he saw Rocky and the rider, tiny in the red light and nearly out to the road again. He sounded, and the figurine lifted a sombrero in token of defeat. Bar recrossed the hills, went slowly south in the dark, and picked up the two mares at dawn. It was sunset of the second day before the full remuda was joined, north of the shallow lake.

In time, Bar's domination became absolute. He drove Cloud
the second from the remuda less than a month after the long
chase, eliminated two others before they were old enough to offer
contest, and tolerated a third, the pinto Paint, because he remained small. In his tenth year, Blue felt her weakness beginning,
and selected the quiet buckskin, Snow, as her understudy, but on
the remuda's first move after Blue's death, Bar forcibly installed
Fan, the last of his charges who remembered Nomad, and there
was no longer even a silent question of his complete control. Yet
vestiges of his early humiliation under Sage made him jealous of
his power, and he began to develop the crotchets of an aging
autocrat, becoming sharp and sudden even with foolish colts, and
punishing the most trivial deviations with wicked severity. The
subservient Fan afforded the remuda no defense against any of
his whims. When he was fifteen, still giving little physical indication of this slow failing, an unknown buckskin made the first
challenge against him in years, and though Bar beat him off, he
could not break him, and was weary and evil tempered for days,
harrying the feckless Paint without mercy. It was under a new
kind of enemy, however, that the remuda first clearly perceived
his aging.

They were standing in the winter sun on the north shore,
their sterns to the wind which fretted the lake, and in the blast
did not immediately recognize the sound as new. Finally they
lifted their ears, and then milled gently. Bar scouted out, nickering, and Fan, because the drone seemed to come from everywhere, could not lead off. Nothing had ever taught them to fear
sky or to expect such speed, and when at last they saw the monoplane because it gleamed in the instant of banking towards them,
they milled wildly, and then, at its incredibly swift enlargement
and increase of voice, became witless and exploded in all direc-
tions up the slope. Bar also felt the panic, but even more the
insubordination, and spun and reared, but could not even hear
his own challenge, and lost the foe over him before he could
reach once, and then saw its great shadow sweep upslope over
the scattering mares and wink off on the crest. Running and
blaring, he turned the mares, but before they were joined the
monoplane, which had circled behind the ridge and the islands
to the west, came at them again from the water. Four times it
circled and dove roaring, and then, when even Bar broke towards

the islands, followed little groups of two and three far beyond the ridge, to the east, to the north, to the west, and only at dusk fled away again over the chapped waters into the southwest, leaving the wind alone. It required four days to reform the remuda, and Paint brought home more than Bar, who even then was so spent that for a week he made their movements too short and slow to please them.

The first actual break in his control came three months later, in the long veils of spring rain in the big open to the north. There the remuda again heard the drone, and began to mill widely in spite of Bar's summons. When he began to lead southeast at a run, however, they followed at once, though bunched. The monoplane swooped down over them twice from the rear, but having headway they only swelled apart a little at each dive and then drew together again. The first losses were four new foals, one driven under in the opening rush, and the others left behind. One of the mares was blind with panic and kept on with the remuda, but three swung back to their foals and were sheared off the course by a third roaring dive. When that roar receded to a drone, Bar went up on a low swell to call in the wandering. The remuda lost headway behind the uncertain Fan, and at the next dive, swept past her, disintegrating. Before Bar could pick them up, the plane changed tactics, circled wide into the south, and came back at the herd head on, and it broke wildly. Bar, rearing when the plane dove at him, so that it was forced to lift, galloped in great circles, blaring, and made short sorties after single mares, but each time the malicious enemy, roaring down close over its shadow, turned them again, and they scattered beyond hope. Then it charged repeatedly on Bar alone, until his great heart gave and he ran heavily north, shying away each time from its din and pummeling draft, and it did not leave him until the last sunlight shone through the rains over long shadows, miles north of the old sour spring.

He never recovered the full remuda. When he gave up, after a week of weary ranging, eight mares, two foals, and Paint, besides the dead, were missing. From then on his age began to show dreadfully, and he often fell asleep in the sun or wandered slowly off by himself. It was in his heart that he must find Paint, slay him, and unite the remuda, but even this knowledge was a burden.

As it was, he did not have to find Paint. Three weeks after the remuda had been broken, the pinto came in alone. Bar's moment of the desire to kill passed. Paint offered no defense, but waited with his head down. His neck and flanks were torn, and where his left eye had been was only a festered swelling. The summer flies crept in his wounds. Bar drove him off without battle or triumph.

It was September before the full remuda was joined again. Bar's herd had watered at dawn in a canyon north of the deserted mine, and were grazing downslope towards the lake. One of the younger mares first lifted her head and nickered gently, and then all stood listening. From the high trail on the cliff to the north came the faint and fluctuating sound of multiple trotting and the rattling of pebbles. Bar's heart beat heavily between hope and dread, but when Fan neighed and was answered, and the little herd turned north, he checked them with a flash of the old authority, and beat out alone, head up and banners flying. A repeated challenge from the heights echoed like brass in the canyons, and scared four white pelicans from the shore out over the glassy water. Bar pressed up to a rocking gallop. The newcomers waited on the trail down from the cliff to the inner end of a canyon. Snow stood at their head. Bar slowed and circled, sounding, and blew again, very high and long, when he saw the challenger drop from the trail straight down under dust, and knew him, even at that distance, as Cloud the first. He lifted and rolled forward again.

They met midway between the remudas, on a great delta of gravel from the cliffs. Huge and widely separate boulders stood like monuments upon the delta. The upper field was still in the shadow of the cliffs, but the arena was in sunlight, and the two stallions brought long shadows with them, across the fixed shadows of the boulders. It was a long battle, but after the first few minutes its issue was clear. Cloud was nearly as big as his father, and newly come into the mettle Bar had lost. Bar staked all in a first fury, and Cloud met it and survived, turning as many charges as turned him, and won the offensive. Then Bar, waiting, lifting only slightly against the attacks, his breath coming in whistles, looked the old champion. In the searching light his bones made shadows and ancient scars showed through the thinning coat. Cloud was himself too massive to use destroyer tactics well, and tried to make each shock full, feeling his impetus gradually take toll. Twice, slipping his head under, but caught by the neck, he found the old stallion's teeth worn and easily bearable.

For two hours of pausing, circling, charging over the same arena, the battle continued in an increasing dance of heat. Then Bar, no longer actively defending, but too exhausted and embittered to feel fear, simply bore the steady hammering of his young foe. Yet he would not fall, but with his feet planted wide, turned his front slowly, kept his long head snaked out with the lips curled back, and in the pauses balanced there, waiting, one side of his head and neck shining with blood, his body hung with a net of blood. Cloud's temper sagged against this stubborn weight. He attacked wearily, and the battle became so slow that Bar's blood made patches rather than flung marks upon the sand and gravel. In the end the veteran's legs failed him, and Cloud, in a flurry of hope, drove him against a great boulder and hammered him to his knees. Then Bar wished to escape. It was not fear, but a dull yearning, like irresistible sleepiness, to avoid further punishment. After two beaten tries, he heaved himself to his feet again, and Cloud, spent in that burst, let him go, only chivying him southward by stages, tormenting him until he stood, then freeing him again. On the ridge of the peninsula south of the old mine, the new master, white banners flying and white eye shining, sounded a final, shivering triumph, and swung back to take up his command.

Diminutive on the descending track, Bar went very slowly south past the white stones like a sphinx and the brown island like a pyramid in the blue water. He stopped often to rest, but without raising his head.

THE VICTIMIZED HORSE

WILD HORSE JERRY'S STORY
by Sarah Elizabeth Howard

Wild horses were often captured to fill out the "remuda" or "cavvy" for the working cowboy, who needed several changes of mount in a day. Some of the methods used are described in the following matter-of-fact verse.

> All over this unsettled country, bands
> Of wild and unowned horses roam, each band
> Protected and controlled by one strong male.
> This stallion will allow no rival near,
> And weaker males are often found alone,
> Upon the plains. Terrific fights sometimes
> Ensue, when two aspire to leadership.
> I followed once, for forty hours or more,
> A band that was becoming very tired;
> We chanced to pass upon the plains, one of
> These lone and beaten males. He seemed at once
> To know his hated rival's strength was gone,
> And saw his chance to take the band from him.
> They fought for mastery for more than half
> A day, and reared, and struck, and bit, and fell
> Upon their knees and wrestled terribly,
> Until the lonely horse the leadership
> Assumed,—made victor by his greater strength.
> The man who captures these wild animals
> Must test his patience and endurance well.
> When I discover where they range, I make
> My camp as near them as I can and still
> Be near a good supply of water; then,
> I place my men and extra horses there—
> In camp—and ride out toward the wary band.
> You know all horses cling to their old range,

LAST OF THE WILD HORSES. Frank Albert Mechau. *Courtesy, The Metropolitan Museum of Art: George A. Hearn Fund, 1938.*

And will not leave it unless driven off,
And then, when free, return. This instinct,—when
I only follow them enough to keep
Them moving,—causes them to circle some,
And makes it quite an easy thing for me
To have a new fresh horse from camp when mine
Is tired. Wild horses are intelligent,
And harder to surprise than antelope.
They see me when a mile away, and stand
And watch me for awhile, and when they learn
That I am nearing them, they run to some
Far hill and watch again. When they decide
That they are followed, then, the work begins.
They then will start and run for twenty miles,
Or more. I do not try to follow near
To them, but ride the way they went until
They notice me, and run again, and so
Allow them little time to eat, or sleep.
I always let them drink; they then become
More gentle and less active, too. I do
Not try to crowd them day and night, but try
To get them used to seeing me. A day
Or two, I work like this, and then ride near
To them, and in a measure can direct
Their course. The yearlings tire out first and want

To stop. One time, a leader tried to drive
Me back; as he came near to me I threw
Some rocks and hit him just behind the ear;
I felled him several times; at last, he kept
Away, but still showed fight. Three days and nights
I've followed these wild creatures, without sleep,
Excepting that I dozed a little as
I rode. The horses were so weary that
They could not travel fast, or far; I drove
Them very carefully into a strong
Corral, so made that it did not betray
It was a trap for them. If I had urged
Them then, they would have scattered, and my work
Would all have been in vain. The largest herd
I ever caught, was thirty. Men have stunned
And captured animals they coveted,
By "creasing" them; they wound with rifle ball
A certain cord upon the horse's neck,
Which causes him to fall unconscious; then,
They bind their prize, and hold him prisoner,
And while they cure the wound, they tame the horse.
It often happens that the bullet strikes
A vital point, an inch below the mark,
And then the noble creature murdered falls—
A victim of man's cruelty and greed.

THE HANDICAPPED HORSE

THE COLT
by Wallace Stegner

It was the swift coming of spring that let things happen. It was spring, and the opening of the roads, that took his father out of town. It was spring that clogged the river with floodwater and ice pans, sent the dogs racing in wild aimless packs, ripped the railroad bridge out and scattered it down the river for exuberant townspeople to fish out piecemeal. It was spring that drove the whole town to the river bank with pike poles and coffeepots and boxes of sandwiches for an impromptu picnic, lifting their sober responsibilities out of them and making them whoop blessings on the C.P.R. for a winter's firewood. Nothing might have gone wrong except for the coming of spring. Some of the neighbors might have noticed and let them know; Bruce might not have forgotten; his mother might have remembered and sent him out again after dark.

But the spring came, and the ice went out, and that night Bruce went to bed drunk and exhausted with excitement. In the restless sleep just before waking he dreamed of wolves and wild hunts, but when he awoke finally he realized that he had not been dreaming the noise. The window, wide open for the first time in months, let in a shivery draught of fresh, damp air, and he heard the faint yelping far down in the bend of the river.

He dressed and went downstairs, crowding his bottom into the warm oven, not because he was cold but because it had been a ritual for so long that not even the sight of the sun outside could convince him it wasn't necessary. The dogs were still yapping; he heard them through the open door.

"What's the matter with all the pooches?" he said. "Where's Spot?"

"He's out with them," his mother said. "They've probably got a porcupine treed. Dogs go crazy in the spring."

"It's dog days they go crazy."

"They go crazy in the spring, too." She hummed a little as she set the table. "You'd better go feed the horses. Breakfast won't be for ten minutes. And see if Daisy is all right."

Bruce stood perfectly still in the middle of the kitchen. "Oh, my gosh!" he said. "I left Daisy picketed out all night!"

His mother's head jerked around. "Where?"

"Down in the bend."

"Where those dogs are?"

"Yes," he said, sick and afraid. "Maybe she's had her colt."

"She shouldn't for two or three days," his mother said. But just looking at her he knew that it might be bad, that there was something to be afraid of. In another moment they were both out the door, both running.

But it couldn't be Daisy they were barking at, he thought as he raced around Chance's barn. He'd picketed her higher up, not clear down in the U where the dogs were. His eyes swept the brown, wet, close-cropped meadow, the edge of the brush where the river ran close under the north bench. The mare wasn't there! He opened his mouth and half turned, running, to shout at his mother coming behind him, and then sprinted for the deep curve of the bend.

As soon as he rounded the little clump of brush that fringed the cutback behind Chance's he saw them. The mare stood planted, a bay spot against the grey brush, and in front of her, on the ground, was another smaller spot. Six or eight dogs were leaping around, barking, sitting. Even at that distance he recognized Spot and the Chapmans' airedale.

He shouted and pumped on. At a gravelly patch he stooped and clawed and straightened, still running, with a handful of pebbles. In one pausing, straddling, aiming motion he let fly a rock at the distant pack. It fell far short, but they turned their heads, sat on their haunches and let out defiant short barks. Their tongues lolled as if they had run far.

Bruce yelled and threw again, one eye on the dogs and the other on the chestnut colt in front of the mare's feet. The mare's ears were back, and as he ran, Bruce saw the colt's head bob up and down. It was all right then. The colt was alive. He slowed and came up quietly. Never move fast or speak loud around an animal, Pa said.

The colt struggled again, raised its head with white eyeballs rolling, spraddled its white-stockinged legs and tried to stand. "Easy, boy," Bruce said. "Take it easy, old fella." His mother arrived, getting her breath, her hair half down, and he turned to her gleefully. "It's all right, Ma. They didn't hurt anything. Isn't he a beauty, Ma?"

He stroked Daisy's nose. She was heaving, her ears pricking forward and back; her flanks were lathered, and she trembled. Patting her gently, he watched the colt, sitting now like a dog on its haunches, and his happiness that nothing had really been hurt bubbled out of him. "Lookit, Ma," he said. "He's got four white socks. Can I call him Socks, Ma? He sure is a nice colt, isn't he? Aren't you, Socks, old boy?" He reached down to touch the chestnut's forelock, and the colt struggled, pulling away.

Then Bruce saw his mother's face. It was quiet, too quiet. She hadn't answered a word to all his jabber. Instead she knelt down, about ten feet from the squatting colt, and stared at it. The boy's eyes followed hers. There was something funny about . . .

"Ma!" he said. "What's the matter with its front feet?"

He left Daisy's head and came around, staring. The colt's pasterns looked bent—*were* bent, so that they flattened clear to the ground under its weight. Frightened by Bruce's movement, the chestnut flopped and floundered to its feet, pressing close to its mother. As it walked, Bruce saw, flat on its fetlocks, its hooves sticking out in front like a movie comedian's too-large shoes.

Bruce's mother pressed her lips together, shaking her head. She moved so gently that she got her hand on the colt's poll, and he bobbed against the pleasant scratching. "You poor broken-legged thing," she said with tears in her eyes. "You poor little friendly ruined thing!"

Still quietly, she turned toward the dogs, and for the first time in his life Bruce heard her curse. Quietly, almost in a whisper, she cursed them as they sat with hanging tongues just out of reach. "God damn you," she said. "God damn your wild hearts, chasing a mother and a poor little colt."

To Bruce, standing with trembling lip, she said, "Go get Jim Enich. Tell him to bring a wagon. And don't cry. It's not your fault."

His mouth tightened; a sob jerked in his chest. He bit his lip and drew his face down tight to keep from crying, but his eyes filled and ran over.

"It is too my fault!" he said, and turned and ran.

Later, as they came in the wagon up along the cutbank, the colt tied down in the wagon box with his head sometimes lifting, sometimes bumping on the boards, the mare trotting after with chuckling vibrations of solicitude in her throat, Bruce leaned far over and tried to touch the colt's haunch. "Gee whiz!" he said. "Poor old Socks."

His mother's arm was around him, keeping him from leaning over too far. He didn't watch where they were until he heard his mother say in surprise and relief, "Why, there's Pa!"

Instantly he was terrified. He had forgotten and left Daisy staked out all night. It was his fault, the whole thing. He slid back into the seat and crouched between Enich and his mother, watching from that narrow space like a gopher from its hole. He saw the Ford against the barn and his father's big body leaning into it pulling out gunny sacks and straw. There was mud all over the car, mud on his father's pants. He crouched deeper into his crevice and watched his father's face while his mother was telling what had happened.

Then Pa and Jim Enich lifted and slid the colt down to the ground, and Pa stooped to feel its fetlocks. His face was still, red from windburn, and his big square hands were muddy. After a long examination he straightened up.

"Would've been a nice colt," he said. "Damn a pack of mangy mongrels, anyway." He brushed his pants and looked at Bruce's mother. "How come Daisy was out?"

"I told Brucie to take her out. The barn seems so cramped for her, and I thought it would do her good to stretch her legs. And then the ice went out, and the bridge with it, and there was a lot of excitement. . . ." She spoke very fast, and in her voice Bruce heard the echo of his own fear and guilt. She was trying to protect him, but in his mind he knew he was to blame.

"I didn't mean to leave her out, Pa," he said. His voice squeaked, and he swallowed. "I was going to bring her in before supper, only when the bridge . . ."

His father's somber eyes rested on him, and he stopped. But

his father didn't fly into a rage. He just seemed tired. He looked at the colt and then at Enich. "Total loss?" he said.

Enich had a leathery, withered face, with two deep creases from beside his nose to the corner of his mouth. A brown mole hid in the left one, and it emerged and disappeared as he chewed a dry grass stem. "Hide," he said.

Bruce closed his dry mouth, swallowed. "Pa!" he said. "It won't have to be shot, will it?"

"What else can you do with it?" his father said. "A crippled horse is no good. It's just plain mercy to shoot it."

"Give it to me, Pa. I'll keep it lying down and heal it up."

"Yeah," his father said, without sarcasm and without mirth. "You could keep it lying down about one hour."

Bruce's mother came up next to him, as if the two of them were standing against the others. "Jim," she said quickly, "isn't there some kind of brace you could put on it? I remember my dad had a horse once that broke a leg below the knee, and he saved it that way."

"Not much chance," Enich said. "Both legs, like that." He plucked a weed and stripped the dry branches from the stalk. "You can't make a horse understand he has to keep still."

"But wouldn't it be worth trying?" she said. "Children's bones heal so fast, I should think a colt's would too."

"I don't know. There's an outside chance, maybe."

"Bo," she said to her husband, "why don't we try it? It seems such a shame, a lovely colt like that."

"I know it's a shame!" he said. "I don't like shooting colts any better than you do. But I never saw a broken-legged colt get well. It'd just be a lot of worry and trouble, and then you'd have to shoot it finally anyway."

"Please," she said. She nodded at him slightly, and then the eyes of both were on Bruce. He felt the tears coming up again, and turned to grope for the colt's ears. It tried to struggle to its feet, and Enich put his foot on its neck. The mare chuckled anxiously.

"How much this hobble brace kind of thing cost?" the father said finally. Bruce turned again, his mouth open with hope.

"Two-three dollars, is all," Enich said.

"You think it's got a chance?"

"One in a thousand, maybe."

"All right. Let's go see MacDonald."

"Oh, good!" Bruce's mother said, and put her arm around him tight.

"I don't know whether it's good or not," the father said. "We might wish we never did it." To Bruce he said, "It's your responsibility. You got to take complete care of it."

"I will!" Bruce said. He took his hand out of his pocket and rubbed below his eye with his knuckles. "I'll take care of it every day."

Big with contrition and shame and gratitude and the sudden sense of immense responsibility, he watched his father and Enich start for the house to get a tape measure. When they were thirty feet away he said loudly, "Thanks, Pa. Thanks an awful lot."

His father half-turned, said something to Enich. Bruce stooped to stroke the colt, looked at his mother, started to laugh and felt it turn horribly into a sob. When he turned away so that his mother wouldn't notice he saw his dog Spot looking inquiringly around the corner of the barn. Spot took three or four tentative steps and paused, wagging his tail. Very slowly (never speak loud or move fast around an animal) the boy bent and found a good-sized stone. He straightened casually, brought his arm back, and threw with all his might. The rock caught Spot squarely in the ribs. He yiped, tucked his tail, and scuttled around the barn, and Bruce chased him, throwing clods and stones and gravel, yelling, "Get out! Go on, get out of here or I'll kick you apart. Get out! Go on!"

So all that spring, while the world dried in the sun and the willows emerged from the floodwater and the mud left by the freshet hardened and caked among their roots, and the grass of the meadow greened and the river brush grew misty with tiny leaves and the dandelions spread yellow along the flats, Bruce tended his colt. While the other boys roamed the bench hills with .22's looking for gophers or rabbits or sage hens, he anxiously superintended the colt's nursing and watched it learn to nibble the grass. While his gang built a darkly secret hideout in the deep brush beyond Hazards', he was currying and brushing and trimming the chestnut mane. When packs of boys ran hare and hounds through the town and around the river's slow bends, he

perched on the front porch with his slingshot and a can full of
small round stones, waiting for stray dogs to appear. He waged
a holy war on the dogs until they learned to detour widely around
his house, and he never did completely forgive his own dog, Spot.
His whole life was wrapped up in the hobbled, leg-ironed chestnut colt with the slow-motion lunging walk and the affectionate
nibbling lips.

Every week or so Enich, who was now working out of town
at the Half Diamond Bar, rode in and stopped. Always, with that
expressionless quiet that was terrible to the boy, he stood and
looked the colt over, bent to feel pastern and fetlock, stood back
to watch the plunging walk when the boy held out a handful of
grass. His expression said nothing; whatever he thought was
hidden back of his leathery face as the dark mole was hidden in
the crease beside his mouth. Bruce found himself watching that
mole sometimes, as if revelation might lie there. But when he
pressed Enich to tell him, when he said, "He's getting better,
isn't he?" He walks better, doesn't he, Mr. Enich? His ankles
don't bend so much, do they?" the wrangler gave him little encouragement.

"Let him be a while. He's growin', sure enough. Maybe give
him another month."

May passed. The river was slow and clear again, and some
of the boys were already swimming. School was almost over.
And still Bruce paid attention to nothing but Socks. He willed so
strongly that the colt should get well that he grew furious even
at Daisy when she sometimes wouldn't let the colt suck as much
as he wanted. He took a butcher knife and cut the long tender
grass in the fence corners, where Socks could not reach, and fed
it to his pet by the handful. He trained him to nuzzle for sugar-
lumps in his pockets. And back in his mind was a fear: In the
middle of June they would be going out to the homestead again,
and if Socks weren't well by that time he might not be able to go.

"Pa," he said, a week before they planned to leave. "How
much of a load are we going to have, going out to the homestead?"

"I don't know, wagonful, I suppose. Why?"

"I just wondered." He ran his fingers in a walking motion
along the round edge of the dining table, and strayed into the
other room. If they had a wagonload, then there was no way

Socks could be loaded in and taken along. And he couldn't walk thirty miles. He'd get left behind before they got up on the bench, hobbling along like the little crippled boy in the Pied Piper, and they'd look back and see him trying to run, trying to keep up.

That picture was so painful that he cried over it in bed that night. But in the morning he dared to ask his father if they couldn't take Socks along to the farm. His father turned on him eyes as sober as Jim Enich's, and when he spoke it was with a kind of tired impatience. "How can he go? He couldn't walk it."

"But I want him to go, Pa!"

"Brucie," his mother said, "don't get your hopes up. You know we'd do it if we could, if it was possible."

"But, Ma. . . ."

His father said, "What you want us to do, haul a broken-legged colt thirty miles?"

"He'd be well by the end of the summer, and he could walk back."

"Look," his father said. "Why can't you make up your mind to it? He isn't getting well. He isn't going to get well."

"He is too getting well!" Bruce shouted. He half stood up at the table, and his father looked at his mother and shrugged.

"Please, Bo," she said.

"Well, he's got to make up his mind to it sometime," he said.

Jim Enich's wagon pulled up on Saturday morning, and Bruce was out the door before his father could rise from his chair. "Hi, Mr. Enich," he said.

"Hello, Bub. How's your pony?"

"He's fine," Bruce said. "I think he's got a lot better since you saw him last."

"Uh-huh." Enich wrapped the lines around the whipstock and climbed down. "Tell me you're leaving next week."

"Yes," Bruce said. "Socks is in the back."

When they got into the back yard Bruce's father was there with his hands behind his back, studying the colt as it hobbled around. He looked at Enich. "What do you think?" he said. "The kid here thinks his colt can walk out to the homestead."

"Uh-huh," Enich said. "Well, I wouldn't say that." He inspected the chestnut, scratched between his ears. Socks bobbed, and snuffed at his pockets. "Kid's made quite a pet of him."

Bruce's father grunted. "That's just the damned trouble."

"I didn't think he could walk out," Bruce said. "I thought we could take him in the wagon, and then he'd be well enough to walk back in the fall."

"Uh," Enich said. "Let's take his braces off for a minute."

He unbuckled the triple straps on each leg, pulled the braces off, and stood back. The colt stood almost as flat on his fetlocks as he had the morning he was born. Even Bruce, watching with his whole mind tight and apprehensive, could see that. Enich shook his head.

"You see, Bruce?" his father said. "It's too bad, but he isn't getting better. You'll have to make up your mind. . . ."

"He will get better though!" Bruce said. "It just takes a long time, is all." He looked at his father's face, at Enich's, and neither one had any hope in it. But when Bruce opened his mouth to say something else his father's eyebrows drew down in sudden, unaccountable anger, and his hand made an impatient sawing motion in the air.

"We shouldn't have tried this in the first place," he said. "It just tangles everything up." He patted his coat pockets, felt in his vest. "Run in and get me a couple cigars."

Bruce hesitated, his eyes on Enich. "Run!" his father said harshly.

Reluctantly he released the colt's halter rope and started for the house. At the door he looked back, and his father and Enich were talking together, so low that their words didn't carry to where he stood. He saw his father shake his head, and Enich bend to pluck a grass stem. They were both against him; they both were sure Socks would never get well. Well, he would! There was some way.

He found the cigars, came out, watched them both light up. Disappointment was a sickness in him, and mixed with the disappointment was a question. When he could stand their silence no more, he burst out with it. "But what are we going to *do?* He's got to have some place to stay."

"Look, kiddo." His father sat down on a sawhorse and took him by the arm. His face was serious and his voice gentle. "We can't take him out there. He isn't well enough to walk, and we can't haul him. So Jim here has offered to buy him. He'll give you three dollars for him, and when you come back, if you want, you might be able to buy him back. That is, if he's well. It'll be better to leave him with Jim."

"Well . . ." Bruce studied the mole on Enich's cheek. "Can you get him better by fall, Mr. Enich?"

"I wouldn't expect it," Enich said. "He ain't got much of a show."

"If anybody can get him better, Jim can," his father said. "How's that deal sound to you?"

"Maybe when I come back he'll be all off his braces and running around like a house afire," Bruce said. "Maybe next time I see him I can ride him." The mole disappeared as Enich tongued his cigar.

"Well, all right then," Bruce said, bothered by their stony-eyed silence. "But I sure hate to leave you behind, Socks, old boy."

"It's the best way all around," his father said. He talked fast, as if he were in a hurry. "Can you take him along now?"

"Oh, gee!" Bruce said. "Today?"

"Come on," his father said. "Let's get it over with."

Bruce stood by while they trussed the colt and hoisted him into the wagon box, and when Jim climbed in he cried out, "Hey, we forgot to put his hobbles back on." Jim and his father looked at each other. His father shrugged. "All right," he said, and started putting the braces back on the trussed front legs. "He might hurt himself if they weren't on," Bruce said. He leaned over the endgate, stroking the white blazed face, and as the wagon pulled away he stood with tears in his eyes and the three dollars in his hand, watching the terrified straining of the colt's neck, the bony head raised above the endgate and one white eye rolling.

Five days later, in the sun-slanting dew-wet spring morning, they stood for the last time that summer on the front porch, the loaded wagon against the front fence. The father tossed the key in his hand and kicked the doorjamb. "Well, good-by, Old Paint," he said. "See you in the fall."

As they went to the wagon Bruce sang loudly,

Good-by, Old Paint, I'm leavin' Cheyenne,
I'm leavin' Cheyenne, I'm goin' to Montana,
Good-by, Old Paint, I'm leavin' Cheyenne.

"Turn it off," his father said. "You want to wake up the whole town?" He boosted Bruce into the back end, where he squirmed and wiggled his way neck-deep into the luggage. His mother, turning to see how he was settled, laughed at him. "You look like a baby owl in a nest," she said.

His father turned and winked at him. "Open your mouth and I'll drop in a mouse."

It was good to be leaving; the thought of the homestead was exciting. If he could have taken Socks along it would have been perfect, but he had to admit, looking around at the jammed wagon box, that there sure wasn't any room for him. He continued to sing softly as they rocked out into the road and turned east toward MacKenna's house, where they were leaving the keys.

At the low, sloughlike spot that had become the town's dump ground the road split, leaving the dump like an island in the middle. The boy sniffed at the old familiar smells of rust and tar paper and ashes and refuse. He had collected a lot of old iron and tea lead and bottles and broken machinery and clocks, and once a perfectly good amber-headed cane, in that old dump ground. His father turned up the right fork, and as they passed the central part of the dump the wind, coming in from the northeast, brought a rotten, unbearable stench across them.

"Pee-you!" his mother said, and held her nose. Bruce echoed her. "Pee-you! Pee-you-willy!" He clamped his nose shut and pretended to fall dead.

"Guess I better go to windward of that coming back," said his father.

They woke MacKenna up and left the key and started back. The things they passed were very sharp and clear to the boy. He was seeing them for the last time all summer. He noticed things he had never noticed so clearly before: how the hills came down into the river from the north like three folds in a blanket, how the stovepipe on the Chinaman's shack east of town had a little conical hat on it. He chanted at the things he saw. "Good-by, old Chinaman. Good-by, old Frenchman River. Good-by, old Dumpground, good-by."

"Hold your noses," his father said. He eased the wagon into the other fork around the dump. "Somebody sure dumped something rotten."

He stared ahead, bending a little, and Bruce heard him swear. He slapped the reins on the team till they trotted. "What?" the mother said. Bruce, half rising to see what caused the speed, saw her lips go flat over her teeth, and a look on her face like the woman he had seen in the traveling dentist's chair, when the dentist dug a living nerve out of her tooth and then got down on his knees to hunt for it, and she sat there half raised in her seat, her face lifted.

"For gosh sakes," he said. And then he saw.

He screamed at them. "Ma, it's Socks! Stop, Pa! It's Socks!"

His father drove grimly ahead, not turning, not speaking, and his mother shook her head without looking around. He screamed again, but neither of them turned. And when he dug down into the load, burrowing in and shaking with long smothered sobs, they still said nothing.

So they left town, and as they wound up the dugway to the south bench there was not a word among them except his father's low, "For Christ sakes, I thought he was going to take it out of town." None of them looked back at the view they had always admired, the flat river bottom green with spring, its village snuggled in the loops of river. Bruce's eyes, pressed against the coats and blankets under him until his sight was a red haze, could still see through it the bloated, skinned body of the colt, the chestnut hair left a little way above the hoofs, the iron braces still on the broken front legs.

SWORDSPLAY. Ruth Ray. *Courtesy, Grand Central Art Galleries: Collection of Mr. William G. Robertson.*

THE IMMORTAL HORSE

THE WAR GOD'S HORSE SONG
Translated from the Navajo by
Dane and Mary Roberts Coolidge

I am the Turquoise Woman's son.
On top of Belted Mountain
Beautiful horses—slim like a weasel!
My horse has a hoof like striped agate;
His fetlock is like a fine eagle plume;
His legs are like quick lightning.
My horse's body is like an eagle-plumed arrow;
My horse has a tail like a trailing black cloud.
I put flexible goods on my horse's back;
The Little Holy Wind blows through his hair.

His mane is made of short rainbows.
My horse's ears are made of round corn.
My horse's eyes are made of big stars.
My horse's head is made of mixed waters
(From the holy waters—he never knows thirst).
My horse's teeth are made of white shell.
The long rainbow is in his mouth for a bridle,
            And with it I guide him.
When my horse neighs, different-colored horses follow.
When my horse neighs, different-colored sheep follow.
            I am wealthy because of him.

            Before me peaceful,
            Behind me peaceful,
            Under me peaceful,
            Over me peaceful,
            All around me peaceful—
            Peaceful voice when he neighs.
            I am everlasting and peaceful.
            I stand for my horse.

THE JEALOUS HORSE

LOVE MAKES THE FILLY GO
by Frank Sullivan

Zuleika's head drooped and she gazed upon the world with a
jaundiced eye. Stifling a sob, she nibbled a shred of wood from
a stanchion. It soothed her lately to eat wood.

It would have seemed to the casual observer that no filly at
Saratoga had less reason to chew wood than Zuleika. Everything
that makes for the happiness of the average horse was hers. She
was only two, yet she was the bright particular star, the ex-

pectancy and rose of the stable of Eric Dwindle, youthful heir to
the Dwindle headache-powder millions. Fame, fortune, family,
beauty, youth, health—all were hers. Except the one thing she
wanted more than anything else in the world.

Love was denied Zuleika.

On the racing programs she was described as a "Br f, 2,"
but so dazzling a creature as Zuleika cannot be dismissed by calling her a "Br f, 2," and letting it go at that. "Br f, 2" gave no hint
of the sheen of her coat, a coat the color of a cup of coffee—very
best grade—to which a tablespoonful of heavy cream had been
added, or possibly two tablespoonfuls. It gave no idea of the
bewitching curve of her jugular groove, throat latch, and windpipe. It gave no hint of the elegance of her neatly turned fetlock,
nor did it convey one whit of the charm of her muzzle, kneepan,
hock, gaskin, or croup.

Not only in love but in love beneath her station. Not only in
love beneath her station but vainly in love beneath her station.
Spurned by a harrow puller. That was the pass to which the
proud filly who was the favorite in the approaching Posterity
Stakes had come. She sighed and took another nibble of soft
pine.

A month previously, Zuleika had come to Saratoga heart-
whole and fancy-free. It was on a morning shortly after her arrival that she first saw Dan. She was having her usual morning
workout. He was pulling a harrow around the track.

She paid no attention to him. He was just another horse.
Perhaps not even that, for Zuleika, in the unthinking arrogance
born of the knowledge of her own superior position in the social
scale, might at that moment have questioned the right of a
harrow puller to be termed a horse in the finer sense of the word,
as exemplified by herself and the members of her set.

The second time she saw Dan, he struck her eye. She noticed
that he stood out from all the other horses on the racecourse, and
not a few of the men. There was something fine and clean and
true about him. The third time she saw him their eyes met. An
electric something passed from her fetlock to her withers, and she
knew that she was hopelessly in love.

After that day, she was disturbingly aware of Dan's nearness
when he was near, and of his farness when he was far. They spoke
no word to each other, yet such is the magical telegraphy of love,

she knew that he knew, and she knew that he knew that she knew. And he knew too.

Zuleika broke the ice one July morning by nodding. Dan bowed courteously in return. Slowly their love ripened into friendship. Every morning a little chat; quite formal, confined to trivia about the weather, the condition of the track, and suchlike small talk. It wasn't much, but it was better than nothing.

Her new-found happiness showed in her work. She skimmed about the course like a bird, breaking track records as casually as though they were champagne goblets crashed into the fireplace by hussars toasting the Czar. Uncle Bill Spellacy, her trainer, was beside himself with joy, although not aware of the cause of her delirium. A lovable old fellow, Uncle Bill had been around horses almost since the invention of the spavin, and he knew them backward. He had his heart set on Zuleika winning the Posterity, not only for her sake but because he wanted it to be a proper swan song for his own career. He planned to retire at the close of the Saratoga meeting and devote his remaining years to his hobby, automobile racing. Above all, he wanted Zuleika to show her heels in the Posterity to The Vamp, the champion that had swept all before her in the West and had now come East to scalp Zuleika.

After a time, Zuleika began to find friendship rather dull stuff. Courteous whinnies about the condition of the track are all right as far as they go, but they don't go far when a filly is in love. The condition of the track was a matter of indifference to Zuleika at the moment. What she wanted was to pillow her muzzle on Dan's broad withers and hear him whisper into her ear the three words that would make her the happiest equine in the world.

The trouble was he would never say them. He was a harrow puller, but he was proud. He knew his place. In a month, Zuleika would be leaving Saratoga, moving on to fresh triumphs at Belmont Park. She might never see him again. Perish this intolerable thought! She decided to act.

One morning after a night spent pacing her stall, she faced Dan on the track.

"Dan," she said.

"Zuleika."

Her name, on his lips. Her heart leaped into her windpipe.

"Dan, I have something to say to you."

"Zuleika." He made as if to interrupt.

"Dan," she hurried on, pawing the earth nervously. "We—you—I—things can't go on like this."

"Zuleika, please."

"No, hear me out, Dan. I love you." She hung her head in pretty confusion. "There. You have made me say it." She smiled up at him. "I knew you never would, so I pocketed my pride."

"Zuleika."

"Yes, Dan."

"I wish you had not spoken."

"Why?"

"It can never be."

For a moment there was silence. It was she who spoke first.

"You mean there is another?" asked Zuleika quietly.

Dan seemed to be in the throes of a severe inward struggle. He pawed the earth. His eyes rolled. He twitched and shuddered, and his tail swished violently. He spoke.

"Yes," he said, "there is."

Zuleika's color changed from brown to bay.

"I see," she said, keeping a stiff upper lip. "I'm sorry—I—your actions had led me to believe—I thought that we—"

"Zuleika," said Dan.

Suddenly she turned on him.

"Stop calling me Zuleika!" she cried. "I hate you! I hate you!" With that, she fled.

"Zuleika!" cried Dan.

In her workout the next morning, Zuleika did six furlongs in 3.26 2/5, which was a new unofficial track record for the slow-motion pictures. Uncle Bill Spellacy followed her to her stall in dismay.

"Gosh-all-Friday, Zuleika, what's the matter with you?" he cried.

For answer, she pillowed her head on his comfortable shoulder and burst into a storm of weeping.

"Oh, Uncle Bill, I'm so miserable."

"Tell Uncle Bill about it," said Mr. Spellacy, for, as we have seen, he understood horses.

She told him about Dan. Uncle Bill whistled softly.

"Mr. Dwindle must not hear a word of this," he said.

"Who?"

"Mr. Dwindle. Your owner."

"You mean the little fellow with no chin? The one that's afraid of us horses?"

"Yes."

"Oh, him."

Zuleika had known that someone owned her and the rest of the stable, but had never given the matter much thought.

"He'll be furious if he finds out," said Uncle Bill. "He's socially ambitious, you know, and he's at a point now where a *mésalliance* on the part of himself or any of his horses might bar the doors of Newport, Tuxedo, and Palm Beach to him forever. And you pick this moment to fall in love with a harrow puller!"

"I'll not hear a word against Dan," said Zuleika, with spirit.

"I understand, honey," said Uncle Bill. "I've been in love myself. I can see her now. It was back in '78. She was as fair—"

"Uncle Bill," said Zuleika, "do you think by any chance it's The Vamp he's in love with?"

"Oh, posh!" said Uncle Bill. "He don't even know her."

"Is that so? Well, I've seen them talking together several times since she got here."

"It's probably platonic. I'll find out. Now, Zuleika, don't you worry. Everything will come out all right. The important thing now is for you to go out there Saturday and win that Posterity, Dan or no Dan."

"I'm sorry, Uncle Bill; I shan't win the Posterity."

"Not win the Posterity! Zuleika, what are you saying?"

"I can't help it, Uncle Bill. I don't feel it—here."

She bent her lovely head toward her heart.

"I don't think I shall ever win anything again," she said sadly.

Uncle Bill saw there was no use trying to reason with her at that moment. He withdrew.

"Drat!" he swore to himself as he left her stall. "Won't win the Posterity. Chewing wood. In love with a harrow puller. And he spurns her."

Uncle Bill began to get mad!

"Why, the insufferable bounder! What does he mean by spurning Zuleika? Where is he? I'll see about this!"

Uncle Bill went in search of Dan. He found him trudging

down the backstretch, pulling his harrow. There was the hint of a droop to the splendid shoulders, a weary look in the fine eyes.

"May I have a word with your horse?" Uncle Bill asked Dan's driver.

"Certainly, certainly," said the driver, recognizing the famous trainer.

"In private, if you don't mind," Uncle Bill requested.

"Oh, pardon me," said the driver, withdrawing to a discreet distance.

"Your name is Dan?" asked Uncle Bill.

"Yes, sir, it is."

"I am William Spellacy, the famous trainer."

"I know."

There was a simple dignity about the horse that impressed Uncle Bill in spite of himself.

"I am not going to mince matters, Dan," said Uncle Bill. "I'll be brief and to the point. Is what I hear about you and my Br f, 2, Zuleika, true?"

"Yes, it is."

"You turned her down, eh?"

"I wouldn't put it that way, Mr. Spellacy."

"Ain't she good enough for you?"

"Not good enough for me! Zuleika!"

Dan laughed—a hollow, mocking laugh of despair.

"By Jove," thought Spellacy, "here is a horse that has suffered."

"Mr. Spellacy, I love Zuleika."

"Then why—"

"She is dearer to me than life itself."

"But you told her—"

"I made up that story on the spur of the moment. I did it for her sake. There is no other filly. There never has been. There never will be. There never could be. There never—"

"I know," said Uncle Bill. "You decided she and you were as far apart as the poles and that your love could lead only to tragedy."

"Yes. I couldn't give her all—that." With a swish of his tail, Dan indicated the palatial Dwindle stables in the distance.

Uncle Bill found himself liking the harrow puller a great deal.

"I understand, Dan," he said, and there was a suspicious dewiness in his eye. "I was in love myself once. It was in '78. She—"

"Zuleika is destined for great things, Mr. Spellacy," said Dan. "While I am only a harrow puller."

"She loves you."

"I know," said Dan brokenly.

"Don't take it too hard, Dan. I remember, that time I was in love—"

"I thought I was acting for the best," said Dan sadly. "I tried to do the decent thing. But I see it all now. I was wrong in my stubborn pride. I have been a fool—a fool. Has she mentioned my name, Mr. Spellacy?"

"Yes, she has."

"What did she say?" asked Dan eagerly.

"If she never sees you again, it will be too soon, she says."

Dan smiled.

"Even in her despair at what she thinks is the loss of my love, she has not forgotten her sense of humor," he said.

"She keeps chewing wood," said Uncle Bill, "and she says she won't win the Posterity."

"Zuleika not win the Posterity! Nonsense! Why, she's got to win the Posterity!"

"Allows as how she won't," said Uncle Bill. "Says she don't feel it—here. You're to blame, of course."

Dan groaned.

She thinks you're in love with The Vamp," said Uncle Bill.

"Me, in love with The Vamp! Why, I scarcely know her. Just pass the time of day with her occasionally. . . . Say!"

Suddenly Dan became lost in thought. He remained there for a moment. When he reappeared, he was excited.

"Mr. Spellacy, Zuleika is going to win that Posterity. Listen."

"It won't work," said Uncle Bill, when Dan had finished detailing his plan.

"It will," said Dan. "I know Zuleika, and it will work."

"Do you really think so?"

"I know so, Mr. Spellacy."

"Well, what can we lose?" mused Uncle Bill.

"I tell you we won't lose."

"Dan, I'll do it."

"Good for you, Mr. Spellacy. Now you'll have to arrange matters so that I can do my part. My time isn't my own, as you know. I am more or less a slave to this harrow. We haven't much time. Three days. The Posterity is being run Saturday."

"I'll fix everything," said Uncle Bill. "I'll arrange to get you Saturday afternoon off."

Uncle Bill and Dan went about their mysterious plans and Zuleika remained in the wood-chewing trance in which we found her at the beginning of our story.

Saturday afternoon found a tremendous crowd assembled at the famous old racecourse. One writer, describing the scene, stated without hesitation that it was a record-breaking throng. A second, not to be outdone, characterized the event as a gala occasion. Racing was freely referred to as the sport of kings.

The grandstands, paddocks and lawns were filled with devotees of the sport of kings in holiday mood. The clubhouse was crammed with the cream of society. In one box alone—that of Mrs. C. Dettrington Tufft, the soap heiress—there were four princesses, each one of them every inch a princess, too; so that, assuming the height of the average well-nourished princess to be five feet eight and a half inches, you had two hundred and seventy-four inches of simon-pure princess in that one box alone. The situation was almost as exciting in other boxes.

A half hour before the Posterity post time, Zuleika was led to the copse in the paddock where she was to be saddled. She had always been a great favorite of the crowd, because of her born showmanship. She liked the acclaim of the multitude, and usually showed it by prancings, curvetings, spirited neighings, and graceful postures, interspersed with an occasional kick, often planted —with a disregard for authority which was part of her charm— on the person of some august racing official.

Today it was obvious that she was not herself. Her head drooped. She surveyed the gay scene with an aloof melancholy and her tail hung listlessly at its mooring. Not once did she kick anyone, although several splendid opportunities presented themselves. At one moment Tommy Spree, the millionaire playboy, was having his picture taken with his seventh fiancée for that year, within three feet of Zuleika's hoofs, and she never rose to the bait. On seeing this, many of her fans shook their heads sorrowfully and rushed off to wager their all on The Vamp.

Uncle Bill Spellacy hovered about nervously. He seemed to be waiting for something to happen.

In the clump of birches where The Vamp was being saddled, the scene was quite different. Here all was gaiety and confidence. The Vamp was a handsome filly, and a large crowd had gathered about her as she held court in her clump. And among those prominent in the crowd was Eric Dwindle! Race fans were electrified when they heard him say, distinctly and with enthusiasm, "By Jove, she looks like a winner to me. Yesterday I didn't think she had a chance."

Instantly the word spread throughout the racecourse that Eric Dwindle had conceded the defeat of Zuleika. Pandemonium reigned and the stewards were considering an official rebuke to Dwindle for such unsportsmanlike and premature surrender, when it developed that Mr. Dwindle had joined The Vamp's court under the impression that she was Zuleika.

"All horses look alike to me; I never could tell one from another," he explained, laughing, as he was led over to Zuleika's copse.

Uncle Bill continued nervous. He was standing first on one leg, then on another, like a stork waiting for a call. He cast frequent glances toward The Vamp's clump. Then he suddenly saw something that moved him violently. The crowd around The Vamp had cleared momentarily. Uncle Bill's face lit up. He turned hastily to Zuleika and whispered, quickly but casually, "Wonder who that handsome work horse is, talking to The Vamp." He had to say it twice before Zuleika lifted her head and gazed languidly toward The Vamp's corner.

She stiffened. Something seemed to have happened to Zuleika; something not unlike, let us say, a thousand volts of electricity.

"It's Dan!" she managed to snort, in Uncle Bill's ear.

"Is that Dan?" said Uncle Bill innocently. "He's not a bad-looking horse, for a harrow puller. I guess you were right about The Vamp, Zuleika."

Zuleika's answer was to look about her carefully, get the range, and plant a carefully aimed kick on Mr. Dwindle with such force that only an intervening wallet saved him from a permanent dent. Uncle Bill was overjoyed. It was the first sign of

PREPARING FOR THE RACE. Horace Vernet. *Courtesy, The Metropolitan Museum of Art: Bequest of Catharine Lorillard Wolfe, 1887.*

animation Zuleika had shown since the day of her showdown with Dan.

The bugle sounded for the parade to the post. The Vamp passed, escorted by and engaged in animated conversation with Dan. Zuleika tossed her head unconcernedly and looked straight through them both. Uncle Bill winked at Dan, who winked at Uncle Bill.

On the way to the post, Zuleika was suddenly her old gay self. Eric Dwindle trained his field glasses on her, decided she must be The Vamp, and whispered to Uncle Bill a concession of Zuleika's defeat. Uncle Bill smiled. Sports lovers who had wagered their all on The Vamp after noting Zuleika's failure to kick Mr. Spree gazed upon the rejuvenated Zuleika with delight and scurried off to rewager their all on her. Her odds dropped like a barometer before a monsoon.

At the post she was the life of the party. She would show Dan how little she cared. She popped her jockey off twice, with a graceful arching of her back. She kicked the assistant starters whenever possible, and plunged the starter, Mr. Delehanty, into a frenzy by her antics. She broke away once and capered halfway around the course. See if she cared!

At last that tenth of a second came when they were all quiet for a fifteenth of a second. Mr. Delehanty hastily pressed a button and shouted, "W-o-o-mp!" or something that sounded like that. The barrier flew up. The gong sounded. And the age-old cry of the turf rang through the historic park: "They're off!"

And so they were. All except one. Zuleika. She had been left at the post.

A groan went up from the record-breaking throng. But it was too late now for them to re-rewager their all on The Vamp. Zuleika stood, cool as a cucumber. A cloud of dust in the distance indicated the rest of the horses. A slight commotion in front of the clubhouse marked the spot where Uncle Bill Spellacy had sunk to the ground in a swoon. Other Zuleika fans joined him almost immediately. Dan had ceased winking.

"Who's that left at the post?" inquired Mr. Dwindle.

"The Vamp," replied a tactful, though mendacious, friend.

Mr. Delehanty had been mopping his brow in relief. He emerged from behind the bandanna and saw Zuleika. He had thought he had got them all off to a good clean start. She leered at him mischievously. With a cry of baffled rage, Mr. Delehanty seized a club, leaped from the starter's platform and made for her, but she was too quick for him. With a flirt of her tail she was off. Her jockey, taken unawares, had just time to grab her mane and hang on for dear life. A roar went up from the crowd. Approximately a hundred more race fans swooned.

"She's off!" "She's gaining!" "Come on, you Zuleika!" "She's caught 'em!" and then, "She's passed 'em!" as Zuleika, with no great effort, overtook her colleagues and, passing wide on the turn, saluted The Vamp with a smile of scorn. In another few seconds Zuleika was out in front, running alone.

"She's leading by a furlong!" shouted a fan.

"Who is?" demanded Eric Dwindle anxiously.

"The Vamp," lied a disgruntled sports lover in the next box, and it must have been a petty gratification he derived from the ensuing spectacle of poor Mr. Dwindle sliding from his chair in a syncope. Others continued to faint as the excitement waxed.

Zuleika, a furlong and a half ahead of her rivals, spied a bed of fresh young daisies. With a suddenness that sent her jockey sliding into her mane, she stopped, thrust her head inside the rail and began to munch daisies leisurely. A roar went up from the crowd. The rest of the field swept by. Zuleika nodded casually at them, and threw a wickedly sweet smile at The Vamp. The Vamp threw back a look that should have cremated Zuleika.

Emory Minton, the racing expert who was broadcasting the event, was rapidly coming to a boil.

"What a race, ladies and gentlemen," he told the vast radio audience. "Oh, boy! I wish you folks could just see this race. Probably never been a race like this in the history of the American turf. It's more like the type they have in England. Oh, boy! Zuleika's stopped. The rest of the field is a furlong ahead. Looks like the rest of the field would win easy. What's that? Zuleika's off. Yes, there she goes. She's off. Look at that colt—I mean that mare—I mean that filly—go! What a race! People are fainting around here like flies. O-o-p, there goes Mrs. Sneeden Twedd of Newport. What a nose dive she took! There goes Alicia Serrington Caulfield, the twine heiress, out like a light, followed by her fiancé, Lord Twigg of Twigg. Let's see what's going on out there on the track. Where's Zuleika?"

Zuleika, replete with daisies, had started after her comrades again and was tearing around the turn into the backstretch. The Vamp, well ahead of the field, cast troubled glances behind to locate Zuleika. The rest of the horses seemed confused but kept on running. At the turn into the stretch, Zuleika was again abreast of the pack. A second later, she was neck and neck with The Vamp. The crowd roared.

"What a race!" screamed the broadcaster. "I wish you folks could see this race. I don't know what's happening. They're in the stretch. Zuleika and The Vamp are neck and neck. It's a duel. Hup, what's that? Zuleika's down! The Vamp tripped her! Zuleika's jockey has landed safely on top of a furlong pole. Folks, it looks like The Vamp's race. Zuleika's up! No, she's down! She's up! She's down! She's up! She's gone back to get her jockey. He's up! He's on! She's off! She's running on three legs! She's gaining! She's caught 'em! She's neck and neck with The Vamp again. They're fighting it out down the last furlong. There will now be a brief pause for station announcements. . . ."

"Bing, bo-ong, bo-o-ong. Ladies and gentlemen, this is Station WWT at Saugerties, New York. This program is also broadcast internationally by W3Z2M. The time is now eleven seconds before five, by courtesy of the McGrath Sun Dial Company. We now return you to the Saratoga race track, where Emory Minton is broadcasting a description of the sixty-fourth annual running of the historic Posterity Stakes."

". . . and here they come, folks! Zuleika and The Vamp fighting it out at the finish—a-a-nd the winner is—"

The vast radio audience heard no more from Emory Minton that day. The strain had been too much. He had fainted.

As Zuleika and The Vamp crossed the finish line, no roar went up from the record-breaking throng. No roar could. The most exciting race that had ever taken place in the history of the American turf had taken its toll. Everyone had fainted.

Everyone except Uncle Bill Spellacy and a few peculiar men who had sat all through the race with their backs to the horses, doing crossword puzzles. They were the members of the famous Keep Your Shirt On Club, stoics who made it a practice to attend all major sports events without getting hysterical. At championship prize fights they were invariably to be found in ringside seats arranging their stamp collections while the reigning heavyweight champ was being knocked out. At World Series games it was their custom to hire two or three of the best boxes and play chess during the crucial innings.

Only Uncle Bill actually saw the finish. Having been the first to swoon, he was the first to revive, just in time to see Zuleika sweep across the finish line a length ahead of The Vamp.

He rushed to the track as Zuleika limped back.

"Zuleika!" he shouted. "You did it, old girl! . . . Why, Zuleika, you're hurt!"

"It's nothing," said the Br f, 2, sliding quietly to the ground in a faint.

When she came to, Dan was bending over her.

"You!" she said weakly but scornfully.

"Zuleika, I can explain everything," interposed Uncle Bill hastily. And he did. He told her the true state of Dan's feelings toward her, and of the harrow puller's willingness to sacrifice himself for her. He told her how Dan's interest in The Vamp had been simply a clever ruse to play on Zuleika's jealousy and goad her into winning the Posterity.

"And you must admit it worked," said Uncle Bill happily.

"Is all this true?" said Zuleika, lifting her great brown eyes to Dan.

"It is, Zuleika."

"Then you do love me?"

"You are more to me than life itself."

"Oh, Dan, I am the happiest horse in the world."

"Mr. Dwindle," said the veterinarian who had been examining Zuleika's leg during this scene, "this filly will never race again. Bowed tendon. You won't have to shoot her, but you'll have to turn her out to grass for the rest of her days."

"That's all right with me," said Mr. Dwindle cordially. "I'm never going to race again either. What's the use? I can't tell one horse from another. They don't like me. They're always biting me, or kicking me, or neighing right in my face. They call it neighing but I call it laughing. And there's something about a horse's neigh that sends cold shivers up my spine, like people cracking their knuckles, or rubbing pencils across glass. At the races I never can tell who's winning; I'm always looking through the wrong end of these confounded field glasses. The game just isn't worth the candle as far as I'm concerned. . . . Spellacy, you said you were going in for automobile racing when you got back to New York."

"That was my intention, sir."

"I'm going along with you. At least automobiles don't whinny."

"Uncle Bill," said Zuleika, "does this mean I won't have to race again?"

"I'm afraid it does, honey."

"You're afraid?"

"Yes. When The Vamp tripped you, I guess she finished your racing career, all right."

"And I can stay here in Saratoga with Dan for ever and a day?"

"I don't see why not."

"Well, then, all I can say is, bless The Vamp's kind old heart. Dan!"

"Yes, dear."

"Where's that harrow of ours?"

And the record-breaking throng, which by this time was practically 100 per cent revived, roared.

THE BELOVED HORSE

THE RED PONY
by John Steinbeck

At daybreak Billy Buck emerged from the bunkhouse and stood for a moment on the porch looking up at the sky. He was a broad, bandy-legged little man with a walrus mustache, with square hands, puffed and muscled on the palms. His eyes were a contemplative, watery gray and the hair which protruded from under his Stetson hat was spiky and weathered. Billy was still stuffing his shirt into his blue jeans as he stood on the porch. He unbuckled his belt and tightened it again. The belt showed, by the worn shiny places opposite each hole, the gradual increase of Billy's middle over a period of years. When he had seen to the weather, Billy cleared each nostril by holding its mate closed with his forefinger and blowing fiercely. Then he walked down to the barn, rubbing his hands together. He curried and brushed two saddle horses in the stalls, talking quietly to them all the time; and he had hardly finished when the iron triangle started ringing at the ranch house. Billy stuck the brush and currycomb together and laid them on the rail, and went up to breakfast. His action had been so deliberate and yet so wasteless of time that he came to the house while Mrs. Tiflin was still ringing the triangle. She nodded her gray head to him and withdrew into the kitchen. Billy Buck sat down on the steps, because he was a cowhand,

and it wouldn't be fitting that he should go first into the dining room. He heard Mr. Tiflin in the house, stamping his feet into his boots.

The high jangling note of the triangle put the boy Jody in motion. He was only a little boy, ten years old, with hair like dusty yellow grass and with shy polite gray eyes, and with a mouth that worked when he thought. The triangle picked him up out of sleep. It didn't occur to him to disobey the harsh note. He never had: no one he knew ever had. He brushed the tangled hair out of his eyes and skinned his nightgown off. In a moment he was dressed—blue chambray shirt and overalls. It was late in the summer, so of course there were no shoes to bother with. In the kitchen he waited until his mother got from in front of the sink and went back to the stove. Then he washed himself and brushed back his wet hair with his fingers. His mother turned sharply on him as he left the sink. Jody looked shyly away.

"I've got to cut your hair before long," his mother said. "Breakfast's on the table. Go on in, so Billy can come."

Jody sat at the long table, which was covered with white oilcloth washed through to the fabric in some places. The fried eggs lay in rows on their platter. Jody took three eggs on his plate and followed with three thick slices of crisp bacon. He carefully scraped a spot of blood from one of the egg yolks.

Billy Buck clumped in. "That won't hurt you," Billy explained. "That's only a sign the rooster leaves."

Jody's tall stern father came in then and Jody knew from the noise on the floor that he was wearing boots, but he looked under the table anyway, to make sure. His father turned off the oil lamp over the table, for plenty of morning light now came through the windows.

Jody did not ask where his father and Billy Buck were riding that day, but he wished he might go along. His father was a disciplinarian. Jody obeyed him in everything without questions of any kind. Now, Carl Tiflin sat down and reached for the egg platter.

"Got the cows ready to go, Billy?" he asked.

"In the lower corral," Billy said. "I could just as well take them in alone."

"Sure you could. But a man needs company. Besides your throat gets pretty dry." Carl Tiflin was jovial this morning.

Jody's mother put her head in the door. "What time do you think to be back, Carl?"

"I can't tell. I've got to see some men in Salinas. Might be gone till dark."

The eggs and coffee and big biscuits disappeared rapidly. Jody followed the two men out of the house. He watched them mount their horses and drive six old milk cows out of the corral and start over the hill toward Salinas. They were going to sell the old cows to the butcher.

When they had disappeared over the crown of the ridge Jody walked up the hill in back of the house. The dogs trotted around the house corner hunching their shoulders and grinning horribly with pleasure. Jody patted their heads—Doubletree Mutt with the big thick tail and yellow eyes, and Smasher, the shepherd, who had killed a coyote and lost an ear in doing it. Smasher's one good ear stood up higher than a collie's ear should. Billy Buck said that always happened. After the frenzied greeting the dogs lowered their noses to the ground in a businesslike way and went ahead, looking back now and then to make sure that the boy was coming. They walked up through the chicken yard and saw the quail eating with the chickens. Smasher chased the chickens a little to keep in practice in case there should ever be sheep to herd. Jody continued on through the large vegetable patch where the green corn was higher than his head. The cowpumpkins were green and small yet. He went on to the sagebrush line where the cold spring ran out of its pipe and fell into a round wooden tub. He leaned over and drank close to the green mossy wood where the water, tasted best. Then he turned and looked back on the ranch, on the low, whitewashed house girded with red geraniums, and on the long bunkhouse by the cypress tree where Billy Buck lived alone. Jody could see the great black kettle under the cypress tree. That was where the pigs were scalded. The sun was coming over the ridge now, glaring on the whitewash of the houses and barns, making the wet grass blaze softly. Behind him, in the tall sagebrush, the birds were scampering on the ground, making a great noise among the dry leaves; the squirrels piped shrilly on the side-hills. Jody looked along at the farm buildings. He felt an uncertainty in the air, a feeling of change and of loss and of the gain of new and unfamiliar things. Over the hillside two big black buzzards sailed low to the ground and their shadows slipped smoothly and quickly ahead of them. Some animal had died in the vicinity. Jody knew it. It might be a cow or it might be the remains of a rabbit. The buzzards overlooked nothing. Jody hated them as all decent things hate them, but they could not be hurt because they made away with carrion.

After a while the boy sauntered down hill again. The dogs had long ago given him up and gone into the brush to do things in their own way. Back through the vegetable garden he went, and he paused for a moment to smash a green muskmelon with his heel, but he was not happy about it. It was a bad thing to do, he knew perfectly well. He kicked dirt over the ruined melon to conceal it.

Back at the house his mother bent over his rough hands, inspecting his fingers and nails. It did little good to start him clean to school for too many things could happen on the way. She sighed over the black cracks on his fingers, and then gave him his books and his lunch and started him on the mile walk to school. She noticed that his mouth was working a good deal this morning.

Jody started his journey. He filled his pockets with little pieces of white quartz that lay in the road, and every so often he took a shot at a bird or at some rabbit that had stayed sunning itself in the road too long. At the crossroads over the bridge he met two friends and the three of them walked to school together, making ridiculous strides and being rather silly. School had just opened two weeks before. There was still a spirit of revolt among the pupils.

It was four o'clock in the afternoon when Jody topped the hill and looked down on the ranch again. He looked for the saddle horses, but the corral was empty. His father was not back yet. He went slowly, then, toward the afternoon chores. At the ranch house, he found his mother sitting on the porch, mending socks.

"There's two doughnuts in the kitchen for you," she said. Jody slid to the kitchen, and returned with half of one of the doughnuts already eaten and his mouth full. His mother asked him what he had learned in school that day, but she didn't listen to his doughnut-muffled answer. She interrupted, "Jody, tonight see you fill the woodbox clear full. Last night you crossed the sticks and it wasn't only about half full. Lay the sticks flat tonight. And Jody, some of the hens are hiding eggs, or else the dogs are eating them. Look about in the grass and see if you can find any nests."

Jody, still eating, went out and did his chores. He saw the quail come down to eat with the chickens when he threw out the grain. For some reason his father was proud to have them come. He never allowed any shooting near the house for fear the quail might go away.

When the woodbox was full, Jody took his twenty-two rifle up to the cold spring at the brush line. He drank again and then aimed the gun at all manner of things, at rocks, at birds on the wing, at the big black pig kettle under the cypress tree, but he didn't shoot for he had no cartridges and wouldn't have until he was twelve. If his father had seen him aim the rifle in the direction of the house he would have put the cartridges off another year. Jody remembered this and did not point the rifle down the hill again. Two years was enough to wait for cartridges. Nearly all of his father's presents were given with reservations which hampered their value somewhat. It was good discipline.

The supper waited until dark for his father to return. When at last he came in with Billy Buck, Jody could smell the delicious brandy on their breaths. Inwardly he rejoiced, for his father sometimes talked to him when he smelled of brandy, sometimes even told things he had done in the wild days when he was a boy.

After supper, Jody sat by the fireplace and his shy polite eyes sought the room corners, and he waited for his father to tell what it was he contained, for Jody knew he had news of some sort. But he was disappointed. His father pointed a stern finger at him.

"You'd better go to bed, Jody. I'm going to need you in the morning."

That wasn't so bad. Jody liked to do the things he had to do as long as they weren't routine things. He looked at the floor and his mouth worked out a question before he spoke it. "What are we going to do in the morning, kill a pig?" he asked softly.

"Never you mind. You better get to bed."

When the door was closed behind him, Jody heard his father and Billy Buck chuckling and he knew it was a joke of some kind. And later, when he lay in bed, trying to make words out of the murmurs in the other room, he heard his father protest, "But, Ruth, I didn't give much for him."

Jody heard the hoot owls hunting mice down by the barn, and he heard a fruit tree limb tap-tapping against the house. A cow was lowing when he went to sleep.

When the triangle sounded in the morning, Jody dressed more quickly even than usual. In the kitchen, while he washed his face and combed back his hair, his mother addressed him irritably. "Don't you go out until you get a good breakfast in you."

He went into the dining-room and sat at the long white table. He took a steaming hotcake from the platter, arranged two fried eggs on it, covered them with another hotcake and squashed the whole thing with his fork.

His father and Billy Buck came in. Jody knew from the sound of the floor that both of them were wearing flat-heeled shoes, but he peered under the table to make sure. His father turned off the oil lamp, for the day had arrived, and he looked stern and disciplinary, but Billy Buck didn't look at Jody at all. He avoided the shy questioning eyes of the boy and soaked a whole piece of toast in his coffee.

Carl Tiflin said crossly, "You come with us after breakfast!"

Jody had trouble with his food then, for he felt a kind of doom in the air. After Billy had tilted his saucer and drained the coffee which had slopped into it, and had wiped his hands on his jeans, the two men stood up from the table and went out into the morning light together, and Jody respectfully followed a little behind them. He tried to keep his mind from running ahead, tried to keep it absolutely motionless.

His mother called, "Carl! Don't you let it keep him from school."

They marched past the cypress, where a singletree hung from a limb to butcher the pigs on, and past the black iron kettle, so it was not a pig killing. The sun shone over the hill and threw long, dark shadows of the trees and buildings. They crossed a stubble-field to shortcut to the barn. Jody's father unhooked the door and they went in. They had been walking toward the sun on the way down. The barn was black as night in contrast and warm from the hay and from the beasts. Jody's father moved over toward the one box stall. "Come here!" he ordered. Jody could begin to see things now. He looked into the box stall and then stepped back quickly.

A red pony colt was looking at him out of the stall. Its tense ears were forward and a light of disobedience was in its eyes. Its coat was rough and thick as an airedale's fur and its mane was long and tangled. Jody's throat collapsed in on itself and cut his breath short.

"He needs a good currying," his father said, "and if I ever hear of you not feeding him or leaving his stall dirty, I'll sell him off in a minute."

Jody couldn't bear to look at the pony's eyes any more. He gazed down at his hands for a moment, and he asked very shyly, "Mine?" No one answered him. He put his hand out toward the pony. Its gray nose came close, sniffing loudly, and then the lips drew back and the strong teeth closed on Jody's fingers. The pony shook its head up and down and seemed to laugh with amusement. Jody regarded his bruised fingers. "Well," he said with pride— "Well, I guess he can bite all right." The two men laughed, somewhat in relief. Carl Tiflin went out of the barn and walked up a sidehill to be by himself, for he was embarrassed, but Billy Buck stayed. It was easier to talk to Billy Buck. Jody asked again—"Mine?"

Billy became professional in tone. "Sure! That is, if you look out for him and break him right. I'll show you how. He's just a colt. You can't ride him for some time."

Jody put out his bruised hand again, and this time the red pony let his nose be rubbed. "I ought to have a carrot," Jody said. "Where'd we get him, Billy?"

"Bought him at a sheriff's auction," Billy explained. "A show went broke in Salinas and had debts. The sheriff was selling off their stuff."

The pony stretched out his nose and shook the forelock from his wild eyes. Jody stroked the nose a little. He said softly, "There isn't a—saddle?"

Billy Buck laughed. "I'd forgot. Come along."

In the harness room he lifted down a little saddle of red morocco leather. "It's just a show saddle," Billy Buck said disparagingly. "It isn't practical for the brush, but it was cheap at the sale."

Jody couldn't trust himself to look at the saddle either, and he couldn't speak at all. He brushed the shining red leather with his fingertips, and after a long time he said, "It'll look pretty on him though." He thought of the grandest and prettiest things he knew. "If he hasn't a name already, I think I'll call him Gabilan Mountains," he said.

Billy Buck knew how he felt. "It's a pretty long name. Why don't you just call him Gabilan? That means hawk. That would be a fine name for him." Billy felt glad. "If you will collect tail hair, I might be able to make a hair rope for you sometime. You could use it for a hackamore."

Jody wanted to go back to the box stall. "Could I lead him to school, do you think—to show the kids?"

But Billy shook his head. "He's not even halter-broke yet. We had a time getting him here. Had to almost drag him. You better be starting for school though."

"I'll bring the kids to see him here this afternoon," Jody said.

Six boys came over the hill half an hour early that afternoon, running hard, their heads down, their forearms working, their breath whistling. They swept by the house and cut across the stubble-field to the barn. And then they stood self-consciously before the pony, and then they looked at Jody with eyes in which there was a new admiration and a new respect. Before today Jody had been a boy, dressed in overalls and a blue shirt— quieter than most, even suspected of being a little cowardly. And now he was different. Out of a thousand centuries they drew the ancient admiration of the footman for the horseman. They knew instinctively that a man on a horse is spiritually as well as physically bigger than a man on foot. They knew that Jody had been miraculously lifted out of equality with them, and had been placed over them. Gabilan put his head out of the stall and sniffed them.

"Why'n't you ride him?" the boys cried. "Why'n't you braid his tail with ribbons like in the fair?" "When you going to ride him?"

Jody's courage was up. He too felt the superiority of the horseman. "He's not old enough. Nobody can ride him for a long time. I'm going to train him on the long halter. Billy Buck is going to show me how."

"Well, can't we even lead him around a little?"

"He isn't even halter-broke," Jody said. He wanted to be completely alone when he took the pony out the first time. "Come and see the saddle."

They were speechless at the red morocco saddle, completely shocked out of comment. "It isn't much use in the brush," Jody explained. "It'll look pretty on him though. Maybe I'll ride bareback when I go into the brush."

"How you going to rope a cow without a saddle horn?"

"Maybe I'll get another saddle for every day. My father might want me to help him with the stock." He let them feel the red saddle, and showed them the brass chain throat-latch on the bridle and the big brass buttons at each temple where the head-stall and brow band crossed. The whole thing was too wonderful. They had to go away after a little while, and each boy, in his mind, searched among his possessions for a bribe worthy of offering in return for a ride on the red pony when the time should come.

Jody was glad when they had gone. He took brush and currycomb from the wall, took down the barrier of the box stall and stepped cautiously in. The pony's eyes glittered, and he edged around into kicking position. But Jody touched him on the shoulder and rubbed his high arched neck as he had always seen Billy Buck do, and he crooned, "So-o-o, Boy," in a deep voice. The pony gradually relaxed his tenseness. Jody curried and brushed until a pile of dead hair lay in the stall and until the pony's coat had taken on a deep red shine. Each time he finished he thought it might have been done better. He braided the mane into a dozen little pigtails, and he braided the forelock, and then he undid them and brushed the hair out straight again.

Jody did not hear his mother enter the barn. She was angry when she came, but when she looked in at the pony and at Jody working over him, she felt a curious pride rise up in her. "Have you forgot the woodbox?" she asked gently. "It's not far off from dark and there's not a stick of wood in the house, and the chickens aren't fed."

Jody quickly put up his tools. "I forgot, ma'am."

"Well, after this do your chores first. Then you won't forget. I expect you'll forget lots of things now if I don't keep an eye on you."

"Can I have carrots from the garden for him, ma'am?"

She had to think about that. "Oh—I guess so, if you only take the big tough ones."

"Carrots keep the coat good," he said, and again she felt the curious rush of pride.

Jody never waited for the triangle to get him out of bed after the coming of the pony. It became his habit to creep out of bed even before his mother was awake, to slip into his clothes and to go quietly down to the barn to see Gabilan. In the gray quiet mornings when the land and the brush and the houses and the trees were silver-gray and black like a photograph negative, he stole toward the barn, past the sleeping stones and the sleeping cypress tree. The turkeys, roosting in the tree out of coyotes' reach, clicked drowsily. The fields glowed with a gray frostlike light and in the dew the tracks of rabbits and of field mice stood out sharply. The good dogs came stiffly out of their little houses, hackles up and deep growls in their throats. Then they caught Jody's scent, and their stiff tails rose up and waved a greeting—Doubletree Mutt with the big thick tail, and Smasher, the incipient shepherd—then went lazily back to their warm beds.

It was a strange time and a mysterious journey, to Jody—an extension of a dream. When he first had the pony he liked to torture himself during the trip by thinking Gabilan would not be in his stall, and worse, would never have been there. And he had other delicious little self-induced pains. He thought how the rats had gnawed ragged holes in the red saddle, and how the mice had nibbled Gabilan's tail until it was stringy and thin. He usually ran the last little way to the barn. He unlatched the rusty hasp of the barn door and stepped in, and no matter how quietly he opened the door, Gabilan was always looking at him over the barrier of the box stall and Gabilan whinnied softly and stamped his front foot, and his eyes had big sparks of red fire in them like oakwood embers.

Sometimes, if the work horses were to be used that day, Jody found Billy Buck in the barn harnessing and currying. Billy stood with him and looked long at Gabilan and he told Jody a great many things about horses. He explained that they were terribly afraid for their feet, so that one must make a practice of lifting the legs and patting the hoofs and ankles to remove their terror.

He told Jody how horses love conversation. He must talk to the pony all the time, and tell him the reasons for everything. Billy wasn't sure a horse could understand everything that was said to him, but it was impossible to say how much was understood. A horse never kicked up a fuss if some one he liked explained things to him. Billy could give examples, too. He had known, for instance, a horse nearly dead beat with fatigue to perk up when told it was only a little farther to his destination. And he had known a horse paralyzed with fright to come out of it when his rider told him what it was that was frightening him. While he talked in the mornings, Billy Buck cut twenty or thirty straws into neat three-inch lengths and stuck them into his hatband. Then during the whole day, if he wanted to pick his teeth or merely to chew on something, he had only to reach up for one of them.

Jody listened carefully, for he knew and the whole country knew that Billy Buck was a fine hand with horses. Billy's own horse was a stringy cayuse with a hammer head, but he nearly always won the first prizes at the stock trials. Billy could rope a steer, take a double half-hitch about the horn with his riata, and dismount, and his horse would play the steer as an angler plays a fish, keeping a tight rope until the steer was down or beaten.

Every morning, after Jody had curried and brushed the pony, he let down the barrier of the stall, and Gabilan thrust past him and raced down the barn and into the corral. Around and around he galloped, and sometimes he jumped forward and landed on stiff legs. He stood quivering, stiff ears forward, eyes rolling so that the whites showed, pretending to be frightened. At last he walked snorting to the water-trough and buried his nose in the water up to the nostrils. Jody was proud then, for he knew that was the way to judge a horse. Poor horses only touched their lips to the water, but a fine spirited beast put his whole nose and mouth under, and only left room to breathe.

Then Jody stood and watched the pony, and he saw things he had never noticed about any other horse, the sleek, sliding flank muscles and the cords of the buttocks, which flexed like a closing fist, and the shine the sun put on the red coat. Having seen horses all his life, Jody had never looked at them very closely before. But now he noticed the moving ears which gave expres-

sion and even inflection of expression to the face. The pony talked
with his ears. You could tell exactly how he felt about everything
by the way his ears pointed. Sometimes they were stiff and upright and sometimes lax and sagging. They went back when he
was angry or fearful, and forward when he was anxious and
curious and pleased; and their exact position indicated which
emotion he had.

Billy Buck kept his word. In the early fall the training began.
First there was the halter-breaking, and that was the hardest
because it was the first thing. Jody held a carrot and coaxed and
promised and pulled on the rope. The pony set his feet like
a burro when he felt the strain. But before long he learned. Jody
walked all over the ranch leading him. Gradually he took to
dropping the rope until the pony followed him unled wherever
he went.

And then came the training on the long halter. That was
slower work. Jody stood in the middle of a circle, holding the
long halter. He clucked with his tongue and the pony started to
walk in a big circle, held in by the long rope. He clucked again to
make the pony trot, and again to make him gallop. Around and
around Gabilan went thundering and enjoying it immensely.
Then he called, "Whoa," and the pony stopped. It was not long
until Gabilan was perfect at it. But in many ways he was a bad
pony. He bit Jody in the pants and stomped on Jody's feet. Now
and then his ears went back and he aimed a tremendous kick at
the boy. Every time he did one of these bad things, Gabilan settled back and seemed to laugh to himself.

Billy Buck worked at the hair rope in the evenings before
the fireplace. Jody collected tail hair in a bag, and he sat and
watched Billy slowly constructing the rope, twisting a few hairs
to make a string and rolling two strings together for a cord, and
then braiding a number of cords to make the rope. Billy rolled
the finished rope on the floor under his foot to make it round and
hard.

The long halter work rapidly approached perfection. Jody's
father, watching the pony stop and start and trot and gallop,
was a little bothered by it.

"He's getting to be almost a trick pony," he complained. "I
don't like trick horses. It takes all the—dignity out of a horse to
make him do tricks. Why, a trick horse is kind of like an actor—

no dignity, no character of his own." And his father said, "I guess you better be getting him used to the saddle pretty soon."

Jody rushed for the harness room. For some time he had been riding the saddle on a sawhorse. He changed the stirrup length over and over, and could never get it just right. Sometimes, mounted on the sawhorse in the harness room, with collars and hames and tugs hung all about him, Jody rode out beyond the room. He carried his rifle across the pommel. He saw the fields go flying by, and he heard the beat of the galloping hoofs.

It was a ticklish job, saddling the pony the first time. Gabilan hunched and reared and threw the saddle off before the cinch could be tightened. It had to be replaced again and again until at last the pony let it stay. And the cinching was difficult, too. Day by day Jody tightened the girth a little more until at last the pony didn't mind the saddle at all.

Then there was the bridle. Billy explained how to use a stick of licorice for a bit until Gabilan was used to having something in his mouth. Billy explained, "Of course we could force-break him to everything, but he wouldn't be as good a horse if we did. He'd always be a little bit afraid, and he wouldn't mind because he wanted to."

The first time the pony wore the bridle he whipped his head about and worked his tongue against the bit until the blood oozed from the corners of his mouth. He tried to rub the headstall off on the manger. His ears pivoted about and his eyes turned red with fear and with general rambunctiousness. Jody rejoiced, for he knew that only a mean-souled horse does not resent training.

And Jody trembled when he thought of the time when he would first sit in the saddle. The pony would probably throw him off. There was no disgrace in that. The disgrace would come if he did not get right up and mount again. Sometimes he dreamed that he lay in the dirt and cried and couldn't make himself mount again. The shame of the dream lasted until the middle of the day.

Gabilan was growing fast. Already he had lost the long-leggedness of the colt; his mane was getting longer and blacker. Under the constant currying and brushing his coat lay as smooth and gleaming as orange-red lacquer. Jody oiled the hoofs and kept them carefully trimmed so they would not crack.

The hair rope was nearly finished. Jody's father gave him an old pair of spurs and bent in the side bars and cut down the strap and took up the chainlets until they fitted. And then one day Carl Tiflin said:

"The pony's growing faster than I thought. I guess you can ride him by Thanksgiving. Think you can stick on?"

"I don't know," Jody said shyly. Thanksgiving was only three weeks off. He hoped it wouldn't rain, for rain would spot the red saddle.

Gabilan knew and liked Jody by now. He nickered when Jody came across the stubble field, and in the pasture he came running when his master whistled for him. There was always a carrot for him every time.

Billy Buck gave him riding instructions over and over. "Now when you get up there, just grab tight with your knees and keep your hands away from the saddle, and if you get throwed, don't let that stop you. No matter how good a man is, there's always some horse can pitch him. You just climb up again before he gets to feeling smart about it. Pretty soon, he won't throw you no more, and pretty soon he *can't* throw you no more. That's the way to do it."

"I hope it don't rain before," Jody said.

"Why not? Don't want to get throwed in the mud?"

That was partly it, and also he was afraid that in the flurry of bucking Gabilan might slip and fall on him and break his leg or his hip. He had seen that happen to men before, had seen how they writhed on the ground like squashed bugs, and he was afraid of it.

He practiced on the sawhorse how he would hold the reins in his left hand and a hat in his right hand. If he kept his hands thus busy, he couldn't grab the horn if he felt himself going off. He didn't like to think of what would happen if he did grab the horn. Perhaps his father and Billy Buck would never speak to him again, they would be so ashamed. The news would get about and his mother would be ashamed too. And in the schoolyard— it was too awful to contemplate.

He began putting his weight in a stirrup when Gabilan was saddled, but he didn't throw his leg over the pony's back. That was forbidden until Thanksgiving.

Every afternoon he put the red saddle on the pony and

cinched it tight. The pony was learning already to fill his stomach out unnaturally large while the cinching was going on, and then to let it down when the straps were fixed. Sometimes Jody led him up to the brush line and let him drink from the round green tub, and sometimes he led him up through the stubble field to the hilltop from which it was possible to see the white town of Salinas and the geometric fields of the great valley, and the oak trees clipped by the sheep. Now and then they broke through the brush and came to little cleared circles so hedged in that the world was gone and only the sky and the circle of brush were left from the old life. Gabilan liked these trips and showed it by keeping his head very high and by quivering his nostrils with interest. When the two came back from an expedition they smelled of the sweet sage they had forced through.

Time dragged on toward Thanksgiving, but winter came fast. The clouds swept down and hung all day over the land and brushed the hilltops, and the winds blew shrilly at night. All day the dry oak leaves drifted down from the trees until they covered the ground, and yet the trees were unchanged.

Jody had wished it might not rain before Thanksgiving, but it did. The brown earth turned dark and the trees glistened. The cut ends of the stubble turned black with mildew; the haystacks grayed from exposure to the damp, and on the roofs the moss, which had been all summer as gray as lizards, turned a brilliant yellow-green. During the week of rain, Jody kept the pony in the box stall out of the dampness, except for a little time after school when he took him out for exercise and to drink at the water-trough in the upper corral. Not once did Gabilan get wet.

The wet weather continued until little new grass appeared. Jody walked to school dressed in a slicker and short rubber boots. At length one morning the sun came out brightly. Jody, at his work in the box stall, said to Billy Buck, "Maybe I'll leave Gabilan in the corral when I go to school today."

"Be good for him to be out in the sun," Billy assured him. "No animal likes to be cooped up too long. Your father and me are going back on the hill to clean the leaves out of the spring." Billy nodded and picked his teeth with one of his little straws.

"If the rain comes, though—" Jody suggested.

"Not likely to rain today. She's rained herself out." Billy pulled up his sleeves and snapped his arm bands. "If it comes on to rain—why a little rain don't hurt a horse."

"Well, if it comes on to rain, you put him in, will you, Billy? I'm scared he might get cold so I couldn't ride him when the time comes."

"Oh sure! I'll watch out for him if we get back in time. But it won't rain today."

And so Jody, when he went to school, left Gabilan standing out in the corral.

Billy Buck wasn't wrong about many things. He couldn't be. But he was wrong about the weather that day, for a little after noon the clouds pushed over the hills and the rain began to pour down. Jody heard it start on the schoolhouse roof. He considered holding up one finger for permission to go to the outhouse and, once outside, running for home to put the pony in. Punishment would be prompt both at school and at home. He gave it up and took ease from Billy's assurance that rain couldn't hurt a horse. When school was finally out, he hurried home through the dark rain. The banks at the sides of the road spouted little jets of muddy water. The rain slanted and swirled under a cold and gusty wind. Jody dog-trotted home, slopping through the gravelly mud of the road.

From the top of the ridge he could see Gabilan standing miserably in the corral. The red coat was almost black, and streaked with water. He stood head down with his rump to the rain and wind. Jody arrived running and threw open the barn door and led the wet pony in by his forelock. Then he found a gunny sack and rubbed the soaked hair and rubbed the legs and ankles. Gabilan stood patiently, but he trembled in gusts like the wind.

When he had dried the pony as well as he could, Jody went up to the house and brought hot water down to the barn and soaked the grain in it. Gabilan was not very hungry. He nibbled at the hot mash, but he was not very much interested in it, and he still shivered now and then. A little steam rose from his damp back.

It was almost dark when Billy Buck and Carl Tiflin came home. "When the rain started we put up at Ben Herche's place, and the rain never let up all afternoon," Carl Tiflin explained.

Jody looked reproachfully at Billy Buck and Billy felt guilty.

"You said it wouldn't rain," Jody accused him.

Billy looked away. "It's hard to tell, this time of year," he said, but his excuse was lame. He had no right to be fallible, and he knew it.

"The pony got wet, got soaked through."

"Did you dry him off?"

"I rubbed him with a sack and I gave him hot grain."

Billy nodded in agreement.

"Do you think he'll take cold, Billy?"

"A little rain never hurt anything," Billy assured him.

Jody's father joined the conversation then and lectured the boy a little. "A horse," he said, "isn't any lap-dog kind of thing." Carl Tiflin hated weakness and sickness, and he held a violent contempt for helplessness.

Jody's mother put a platter of steaks on the table and boiled potatoes and boiled squash, which clouded the room with their steam. They sat down to eat. Carl Tiflin still grumbled about weakness put into animals and men by too much coddling.

Billy Buck felt bad about his mistake. "Did you blanket him?" he asked.

"No. I couldn't find any blanket. I laid some sacks over his back."

"We'll go down and cover him up after we eat, then." Billy felt better about it then. When Jody's father had gone in to the fire and his mother was washing dishes, Billy found and lighted a lantern. He and Jody walked through the mud to the barn. The barn was dark and warm and sweet. The horses still munched their evening hay. "You hold the lantern!" Billy ordered. And he felt the pony's legs and tested the heat of the flanks. He put his cheek against the pony's gray muzzle and then he rolled up the eyelids to look at the eyeballs and he lifted the lips to see the gums, and he put his fingers inside the ears. "He don't seem so chipper," Billy said. "I'll give him a rub-down."

Then Billy found a sack and rubbed the pony's legs violently and he rubbed the chest and the withers. Gabilan was strangely spiritless. He submitted patiently to the rubbing. At last Billy brought an old cotton comforter from the saddle room, and threw it over the pony's back and tied it at neck and chest with string.

"Now he'll be all right in the morning," Billy said.

Jody's mother looked up when he got back to the house. "You're late up from bed," she said. She held his chin in her hard hand and brushed the tangled hair out of his eyes and she said, "Don't worry about the pony. He'll be all right. Billy's as good as any horse doctor in the country."

Jody hadn't known she could see his worry. He pulled gently away from her and knelt down in front of the fireplace until it burned his stomach. He scorched himself through and then went in to bed, but it was a hard thing to go to sleep. He awakened after what seemed a long time. The room was dark but there was a grayness in the window like that which precedes the dawn. He got up and found his overalls and searched for the legs, and then the clock in the other room struck two. He laid his clothes down and got back into bed. It was broad daylight when he awakened again. For the first time he had slept through the ringing of the triangle. He leaped up, flung on his clothes and went out of the door still buttoning his shirt. His mother looked after him for a moment and then went quietly back to her work. Her eyes were brooding and kind. Now and then her mouth smiled a little but without changing her eyes at all.

Jody ran on toward the barn. Halfway there he heard the sound he dreaded, the hollow rasping cough of a horse. He broke into a sprint then. In the barn he found Billy Buck with the pony. Billy was rubbing his legs with his strong thick hands. He looked up and smiled gaily. "He just took a little cold," Billy said. "We'll have him out of it in a couple of days."

Jody looked at the pony's face. The eyes were half closed and the lids thick and dry. In the eye corners a crust of hard mucus stuck. Gabilan's ears hung loosely sideways and his head was low. Jody put out his hand, but the pony did not move close to it. He coughed again and his whole body constricted with the effort. A little stream of thin fluid ran from his nostrils.

Jody looked back at Billy Buck. "He's awful sick, Billy."

"Just a little cold, like I said," Billy insisted. "You go get some breakfast and then go back to school. I'll take care of him."

"But you might have to do something else. You might leave him."

"No, I won't. I won't leave him at all. Tomorrow's Saturday.

Then you can stay with him all day." Billy had failed again, and he felt badly about it. He had to cure the pony now.

Jody walked up to the house and took his place listlessly at the table. The eggs and bacon were cold and greasy, but he didn't notice it. He ate his usual amount. He didn't even ask to stay home from school. His mother pushed his hair back when she took his plate. "Billy'll take care of the pony," she assured him.

He moped through the whole day at school. He couldn't answer any questions nor read any words. He couldn't even tell anyone the pony was sick, for that might make him sicker. And when school was finally out he started home in dread. He walked slowly and let the other boys leave him. He wished he might continue walking and never arrive at the ranch.

Billy was in the barn, as he had promised, and the pony was worse. His eyes were almost closed now, and his breath whistled shrilly past an obstruction in his nose. A film covered that part of the eyes that was visible at all. It was doubtful whether the pony could see any more. Now and then he snorted, to clear his nose, and by the action seemed to plug it tighter. Jody looked dispiritedly at the pony's coat. The hair lay rough and unkempt and seemed to have lost all of its old luster. Billy stood quietly beside the stall. Jody hated to ask, but he had to know.

"Billy, is he—is he going to get well?"

Billy put his fingers between the bars under the pony's jaw and felt about. "Feel here," he said and he guided Jody's fingers to a large lump under the jaw. "When that gets bigger, I'll open it up and then he'll get better."

Jody looked quickly away, for he had heard about that lump. "What is the matter with him?"

Billy didn't want to answer, but he had to. He couldn't be wrong three times. "Strangles," he said shortly, "but don't you worry about that. I'll pull him out of it. I've seen them get well when they were worse than Gabilan is. I'm going to steam him now. You can help."

"Yes," Jody said miserably. He followed Billy into the grain room and watched him make the steaming bag ready. It was a long canvas nose bag with straps to go over a horse's ears. Billy filled it one-third full of bran and then he added a couple of handfuls of dried hops. On the top of the dry substance he poured a little carbolic acid and a little turpentine. "I'll be mixing it all up while you run to the house for a kettle of boiling water," Billy said.

When Jody came back with the steaming kettle, Billy buckled the straps over Gabilan's head and fitted the bag tightly around his nose. Then through a little hole in the side of the bag he poured the boiling water on the mixture. The pony started away as a cloud of strong steam rose up, but then the soothing fumes crept through his nose and into his lungs, and the sharp steam began to clear out the nasal passages. He breathed loudly. His legs trembled in an ague, and his eyes closed against the biting cloud. Billy poured in more water and kept the steam rising for fifteen minutes. At last he set down the kettle and took the bag from Gabilan's nose. The pony looked better. He breathed freely, and his eyes were open wider than they had been.

"See how good it makes him feel," Billy said. "Now we'll wrap him up in the blanket again. Maybe he'll be nearly well by morning.

"I'll stay with him tonight," Jody suggested.

"No. Don't you do it. I'll bring my blankets down here and put them in the hay. You can stay tomorrow and steam him if he needs it."

The evening was falling when they went to the house for their supper. Jody didn't even realize that someone else had fed the chickens and filled the woodbox. He walked up past the house to the dark brush line and took a drink of water from the tub. The spring water was so cold that it stung his mouth and drove a shiver through him. The sky above the hills was still light. He saw a hawk flying so high that it caught the sun on its breast and shone like a spark. Two blackbirds were driving him down the sky, glittering as they attacked their enemy. In the west, the clouds were moving in to rain again.

Jody's father didn't speak at all while the family ate supper, but after Billy Buck had taken his blankets and gone to sleep in the barn, Carl Tiflin built a high fire in the fireplace and told stories. He told about the wild man who ran naked through the country and had a tail and ears like a horse, and he told about the rabbit-cats of Moro Cojo that hopped into the trees for birds. He revived the famous Maxwell brothers who found a vein of gold and hid the traces of it so carefully that they could never find it again.

Jody sat with his chin in his hands; his mouth worked nervously, and his father gradually became aware that he wasn't listening very carefully. "Isn't that funny?" he asked.

Jody laughed politely and said, "Yes, sir." His father was angry and hurt, then. He didn't tell any more stories. After a while, Jody took a lantern and went down to the barn. Billy Buck was asleep in the hay, and, except that his breath rasped a little in his lungs, the pony seemed to be much better. Jody stayed a little while, running his fingers over the red rough coat, and then he took up the lantern and went back to the house. When he was in bed, his mother came into the room.

"Have you enough covers on? It's getting winter."

"Yes, ma'am."

"Well, get some rest tonight." She hesitated to go out, stood uncertainly. "The pony will be all right," she said.

Jody was tired. He went to sleep quickly and didn't awaken until dawn. The triangle sounded, and Billy Buck came up from the barn before Jody could get out of the house.

"How is he?" Jody demanded.

Billy always wolfed his breakfast. "Pretty good. I'm going to open that lump this morning. Then he'll be better maybe."

After breakfast, Billy got out his best knife, one with a needle point. He whetted the shining blade a long time on a little carborundum stone. He tried the point and the blade again and again on his callused thumb-ball, and at last he tried it on his upper lip.

On the way to the barn, Jody noticed how the young grass was up and how the stubble was melting day by day into the new green crop of volunteer. It was a cold sunny morning.

As soon as he saw the pony, Jody knew he was worse. His eyes were closed and sealed shut with dried mucus. His head hung so low that his nose almost touched the straw of his bed. There was a little groan in each breath, a deep-seated, patient groan.

Billy lifted the weak head and made a quick slash with the knife. Jody saw the yellow pus run out. He held up the head while Billy swabbed out the wound with weak carbolic acid salve.

"Now he'll feel better," Billy assured him. "That yellow poison is what makes him sick."

Jody looked unbelieving at Billy Buck. "He's awful sick."

Billy thought a long time what to say. He nearly tossed off a careless assurance, but he saved himself in time. "Yes, he's pretty sick," he said at last. "I've seen worse ones get well. If he doesn't get pneumonia, we'll pull him through. You stay with him. If he gets worse, you can come and get me."

For a long time after Billy went away, Jody stood beside the pony, stroking him behind the ears. The pony didn't flip his head the way he had done when he was well. The groaning in his breathing was becoming more hollow.

Doubletree Mutt looked into the barn, his big tail waving provocatively, and Jody was so incensed at his health that he found a hard black clod on the floor and deliberately threw it. Doubletree Mutt went yelping away to nurse a bruised paw.

In the middle of the morning, Billy Buck came back and made another steam bag. Jody watched to see whether the pony improved this time as he had before. His breathing eased a little, but he did not raise his head.

The Saturday dragged on. Late in the afternoon Jody went to the house and brought his bedding down and made up a place to sleep in the hay. He didn't ask permission. He knew from the way his mother looked at him that she would let him do almost anything. That night he left a lantern burning on a wire over the box stall. Billy had told him to rub the pony's legs every little while.

At nine o'clock the wind sprang up and howled around the barn. And in spite of his worry, Jody grew sleepy. He got into his blankets and went to sleep, but the breathy groans of the pony sounded in his dreams. And in his sleep he heard a crashing noise which went on and on until it awakened him. The wind was rushing through the barn. He sprang up and looked down the lane of stalls. The barn door had blown open, and the pony was gone.

He caught the lantern and ran outside into the gale, and he saw Gabilan weakly shambling away into the darkness, head down, legs working slowly and mechanically. When Jody ran up and caught him by the forelock, he allowed himself to be led back and put into his stall. His groans were louder, and a fierce whistling came from his nose. Jody didn't sleep any more then. The hissing of the pony's breath grew louder and sharper.

He was glad when Billy Buck came in at dawn. Billy looked for a time at the pony as though he had never seen him before. He felt the ears and flanks. "Jody," he said, "I've got to do something you won't want to see. You run up to the house for a while."

Jody grabbed him fiercely by the forearm. "You're not going to shoot him?"

Billy patted his hand. "No. I'm going to open a little hole in his windpipe so he can breathe. His nose is filled up. When he gets well, we'll put a little brass button in the hole for him to breathe through."

Jody couldn't have gone away if he had wanted to. It was awful to see the red hide cut, but infinitely more terrible to know it was being cut and not to see it. "I'll stay right here," he said bitterly. "You sure you got to?"

"Yes. I'm sure. If you stay, you can hold his head. If it doesn't make you sick, that is."

The knife came out again and was whetted again just as carefully as it had been the first time. Jody held the pony's head up and the throat taut, while Billy felt up and down for the right place. Jody sobbed once as the bright knife point disappeared into the throat. The pony plunged weakly away and then stood still, trembling violently. The blood ran thickly out and up the knife and across Billy's hand and into his shirtsleeve. The sure square hand sawed out a round hole in the flesh, and the breath came bursting out of the hole, throwing a fine spray of blood. With the rush of oxygen, the pony took a sudden strength. He lashed out with his hind feet and tried to rear, but Jody held his head down while Billy mopped the new wound with carbolic salve. It was a good job. The blood stopped flowing and the air puffed out of the hole and sucked it in regularly with a little bubbling noise.

The rain brought in by the night wind began to fall on the barn roof. Then the triangle rang for breakfast. "You go up and eat while I wait," Billy said. "We've got to keep this hole from plugging up."

Jody walked slowly out of the barn. He was too dispirited to tell Billy how the barn door had blown open and let the pony out. He emerged into the wet gray morning and sloshed up to the house, taking a perverse pleasure in splashing through all the puddles. His mother fed him and put dry clothes on. She didn't question him. She seemed to know he couldn't answer questions. But when he was ready to go back to the barn she brought him a pan of steaming meal. "Give him this," she said.

But Jody did not take the pan. He said, "He won't eat anything," and ran out of the house. At the barn, Billy showed him how to fix a ball of cotton on a stick, with which to swab out the breathing hole when it became clogged with mucus.

Jody's father walked into the barn and stood with them in front of the stall. At length he turned to the boy. "Hadn't you better come with me? I'm going to drive over the hill." Jody shook his head. "You better come on, out of this," his father insisted.

Billy turned on him angrily. "Let him alone. It's his pony, isn't it?"

Carl Tiflin walked away without saying another word. His feelings were badly hurt.

All morning Jody kept the wound open and the air passing in and out freely. At noon the pony lay wearily down on his side and stretched his nose out.

Billy came back. "If you're going to stay with him tonight, you better take a little nap," he said. Jody went absently out of the barn. The sky had cleared to a hard thin blue. Everywhere the birds were busy with worms that had come to the damp surface of the ground.

Jody walked to the brush line and sat on the edge of the mossy tub. He looked down at the house and at the old bunkhouse and at the dark cypress tree. The place was familiar, but curiously changed. It wasn't itself any more, but a frame for things that were happening. A cold wind blew out of the east now, signifying that the rain was over for a little while. At his feet Jody could see the little arms of new weeds spreading out over the ground. In the mud about the spring were thousands of quail tracks.

Doubletree Mutt came sideways and embarrassed up through the vegetable patch, and Jody, remembering how he had thrown the clod, put his arm about the dog's neck and kissed him on his wide black nose. Doubletree Mutt sat still, as though he knew some solemn thing was happening. His big tail slapped the ground gravely. Jody pulled a swollen tick out of Mutt's neck and popped it dead between his thumbnails. It was a nasty thing. He washed his hands in the cold spring water.

Except for the steady swish of the wind, the farm was very quiet. Jody knew his mother wouldn't mind if he didn't go in to eat his lunch. After a little while he went slowly back to the barn. Mutt crept into his own little house and whined softly to himself for a long time.

Billy Buck stood up from the box and surrendered the cotton swab. The pony still lay on his side and the wound in his throat bellowed in and out. When Jody saw how dry and dead the hair looked, he knew at last that there was no hope for the pony. He had seen the dead hair before on dogs and on cows, and it was a sure sign. He sat heavily on the box and let down the barrier of the box stall. For a long time he kept his eyes on the moving wound, and at last he dozed, and the afternoon passed quickly. Just before dark his mother brought a deep dish of stew and left it for him and went away. Jody ate a little of it, and, when it was dark, he set the lantern on the floor by the pony's head so he could watch the wound and keep it open. And he dozed again until the night chill awakened him. The wind was blowing fiercely, bringing the north cold with it. Jody brought a blanket from his bed in the hay and wrapped himself in it. Gabilan's breathing was quiet at last; the hole in his throat moved gently. The owls flew through the hayloft, shrieking and looking for mice. Jody put his hands down on his head and slept. In his sleep he was aware that the wind had increased. He heard it slamming about the barn.

It was daylight when he awakened. The barn door had swung open. The pony was gone. He sprang up and ran out into the morning light.

The pony's tracks were plain enough, dragging through the frostlike dew on the young grass, tired tracks with little lines between them where the hoofs had dragged. They headed for the brush line halfway up the ridge. Jody broke into a run and followed them. The sun shone on the sharp white quartz that stuck through the ground here and there. As he followed the plain trail, a shadow cut across in front of him. He looked up and saw a high circle of black buzzards, and the slowly revolving circle dropped lower and lower. The solemn birds soon disappeared over the ridge. Jody ran faster then, forced on by panic and rage.

The trail entered the brush at last and followed a winding route among the tall sagebrushes.

At the top of the ridge Jody was winded. He paused, puffing noisily. The blood pounded in his ears. Then he saw what he was looking for. Below, in one of the little clearings in the brush, lay the red pony. In the distance, Jody could see the legs moving slowly and convulsively. And in a circle around him stood the buzzards, waiting for the moment of death they know so well.

Jody leaped forward and plunged down the hill. The wet ground muffled his steps and the brush hid him. When he arrived, it was all over. The first buzzard sat on the pony's head and its beak had just risen dripping with dark eye fluid. Jody plunged into the circle like a cat. The black brotherhood arose in a cloud, but the big one on the pony's head was too late. As it hopped along to take off, Jody caught its wing tip and pulled it down. It was nearly as big as he was. The free wing crashed into his face with the force of a club, but he hung on. The claws fastened on his leg and the wing elbows battered his head on either side. Jody groped blindly with his free hand. His fingers found the neck of the struggling bird. The red eyes looked into his face, calm and fearless and fierce; the naked head turned from side to side. Then the beak opened and vomited a stream of putrefied fluid. Jody brought up his knee and fell on the great bird. He held the neck to the ground with one hand while his other found a piece of sharp white quartz. The first blow broke the beak sideways and black blood spurted from the twisted, leathery mouth corners. He struck again and missed. The red fearless eyes still looked at him, impersonal and unafraid and detached. He struck again and again, until the buzzard lay dead, until its head was a red pulp. He was still beating the dead bird when Billy Buck pulled him off, and held him tightly to calm his shaking.

Carl Tiflin wiped the blood from the boy's face with a red bandanna. Jody was limp and quiet now. His father moved the buzzard with his toe. "Jody," he explained, "the buzzard didn't kill the pony. Don't you know that?"

"I know it," Jody said wearily.

It was Billy Buck who was angry. He had lifted Jody in his arms, and had turned to carry him home. But he turned back on Carl Tiflin. " 'Course he knows it," Billy said furiously, "Jesus Christ! man, can't you see how he'd feel about it?"

THE SELF-SACRIFICING HORSE

MY BONNY BLACK BESS
Anonymous

Dick Turpin bold! Dick, hie away,
Was the cry of my pals, who were startled, I guess,
For the pistols were leveled, the bullets whizzed by,
As I leapt on the back of Black Bess.
Three Officers mounted, led forward the chase,
Resolv'd in the capture to share;
But I smil'd on their efforts, tho' swift was their pace,
As I urg'd on my bonny Black Mare.
So when I've a bumper, what can I do less,
    Than the memory drink of my bonny Black Bess?

Hark away, hark away! still onward they press,
As we saw by the glimmer of morn,
Tho' many a mile on the back Black Bess,
That night I was gallantly borne;
Hie over, my pet, the fatigue I must bear
Well clear'd! never falter for breath,
Hark forward, my girl, my bonny Black Mare,
We speed it for life or for death.
But when I've a bumper, what can I do less,
    Than the memory drink of my bonny Black Bess?

The spires of York now burst on my view,
But the chimes, they were ringing her knell,
Halt! Halt! my brave mare, they no longer pursue,
She halted, she staggered, she fell!
Her breathing was o'er, all was hushed as the grave,
Alas! poor Black Bess, once my pride,
Her heart she had burst, her rider to save,
For Dick Turpin, she lived, and she died.
Then the memory drink of my bonny Black Bess,
Hurrah for poor bonny Black Bess!

THE ALMOST-INDESTRUCTIBLE HORSE

THE SCARECROW
by Vardis Fisher

We were threshing on the ranch of Jon Weeg and when we went to the machine one morning we discovered that a stray animal had been to the piled sacks of grain and had ripped several of them wide open. Around the pile were the hoofprints of a horse. We searched the yard and the outlying land, expecting to find the beast foundered; but there was no trace of it. Around the stacks of wheat and the piled sacks we built a fence of barbed wire. That would hold him, we said.

But the next morning we found another half dozen bags torn open. The prowler had returned during the night, had leapt our three-wire fence, had eaten and gone. This evening we added two wires to the fence. It was now chin high, and we didn't think that even an elk would jump it. Our astonishment the third morning left us speechless. The beast had come again, had vaulted our five-wire fence, and had plundered another half dozen sacks. On the top wire was some of his hair, but that was all. At this point the matter began to be a little unreal for all of us. For Joe Burt, a big, rather dimwitted lubber, it was nothing less than miraculous. Because ordinarily, as in turn we said to one another, a horse doesn't eat its fill of grain without foundering; doesn't come slyly under cover of darkness and vanish before daylight; and doesn't leap a five-wire fence.

Maybe it was a mule, Curt Obbing said. We searched and found tracks, but they were not the tracks of a mule.

"I'm going to sleep out here," I said. "I'll find out."

And so the third night I laid my bed in the grain yard and waited for the thief. I fell asleep. I was awakened by a terrific screeching of wire, and on looking up saw a very tall and fantastically gaunt horse caught on the fence. In the moonlight it seemed to be nothing but hide and bones and eyes. It had

THE HORSE. Alexander Calder. *Courtesy, The Museum of Modern Art, New York: Acquired through the Lillie P. Bliss Bequest.*

jumped, and now stood with its front legs over the wire and with the taut wires under its belly; and a more woebegone and helpless creature I had never seen.

I rose and went over to it, intending to flog the ungainly creature off the place. Something in its eyes made me pause. It was a kind of sad resignation, a hopeless surrender, all mixed up with shame for having got into such a predicament. Instead of flogging the old thief I patted its gaunt fleshless skull and looked at the eyes. "You damned old fool," I said. "Haven't you enough brains to keep off barbed wire?" All but a few horses have. I went over and stirred the torn bags of wheat and watched the beast's eyes, but it gave no sign. It did not even put an ear forward or turn its head to watch me. I put a halter on it, cut the wires to get it off the fence, and tied it to a post.

The next morning the men walked round and round the drooping skeleton, wondering what should be done with it. There was no agreement among us. Joe Burt wanted to tie tin cans to its tail and set the dogs on it; Curt, to turpentine it; and Jack Brody wanted to put a girth around it, with sharp nails set to the flesh, give it a big dose of something to bloat it up, and then turn it loose. As they spoke, the men kicked the beast or smote its ears, but it did not flinch. It was like a dead horse, tied to a post. I persuaded the men to let me take it two or three miles down the road and give it a big shove toward the valley. I said it was a good Christian practice to give all pests to your neighbors.

So I took it down the road, turned it loose, and hurled stones at it; and as far as I could see that scarecrow it was heading toward the valley and out of sight. But the next morning, so help me, God, there it was, standing before our bags of grain, stuffed and contented.

Curt said to me, "I suppose you'd like to play with it some more."

"Let me fix him," Jack said. "Put a spiked cinch tight around him, fill him up with ginger and soda fizz and watch him travel."

"No," I said, "we'd better kill him."

We talked about the matter and decided that it would be best to kill the old fool; and so this night, which was moonless and dark, we took Jon Weeg's double-barrel shotgun and led the horse away to a patch of timber. All of us, I observed, were quiet and acted mysterious, like people who plotted a crime. Joe Burt cackled in a foolish way a time or two, but none of us said a word. Curt led the horse and we followed in single file. The old beast led easily, never drawing back or turning aside, as if he had spent all his years on the end of a rope. Possibly it was his dumb surrender to our wills, almost the eager way with which he went with us, that explains, in part at least, what happened later.

After Curt stopped in a dark recess of the woods none of us wanted to be the executioner. At the time I thought this unusual, for we had all slain animals, and none of us thought anything of twisting the head off a rooster, or putting pups in a sack with stones and throwing them into water. This execution was different somehow. I don't know why we all hesitated, as if there would be guilt on our souls. We seemed to have developed a friendliness for this old vagabond-thief who had broken our fence and destroyed half a ton of Weeg's wheat. Or was it because Joe put his hands to his ears and began to whimper?

Whatever the reason, I suspect now that none of us would have shot the old crowbait if any one of us had raised a protest. If Curt had led him back to the yard, I think we would have given him food and drink and a pat on his rump. But we had come out to murder the creature, and none of us could afford to show weakness or change of heart. When Curt said, "Who's got the gun?" we all stepped forward, as though eager to seize it and fire.

One of the men held the shotgun aloft, and there was a pause. Who was to do it?

"Who'll blow his head off?" Curt asked.

"It don't make no difference," Jack said. "Shoot him behind his ear."

I saw that Joe Burt was still trembling and clasping his skull.

Curt swore a great oath now and said we were a hell of a bunch of men! Where was the gun? "Give it here," he said.

The gun was handed to him, and we all stepped back. We could hear Curt loading both barrels. Dimly in the dark we could see him take the halter off. We felt it when he hurled it at our feet. We could see him biting off a huge quid of tobacco as he looked speculatively at the skull. We saw him raise the gun to his shoulder.

"Just behind his ear," Jack said.

"I can't see the damn sights," Curt said. "Someone light a match."

"You don't have to see," Jack said. "Stick it behind his ear."

"Light a match."

I struck a match, and in its feeble light the horse looked monstrously huge and gaunt. Its head was drooping. The match sputtered and went out. I struck another. In that moment we could see the gleaming barrels of the gun, and Curt squinting along the sights. Then there was a thunderous roar, the match went out, and we stood in overwhelming darkness. I struck another match. We saw the beast, standing as if propped, blood pouring down over its face. I struck still another, held it high, and Curt fired the other barrel. The horse squealed and dropped to the earth.

On our way back we said nothing. Curt went ahead, the smoking gun on his shoulder, and we followed him in single file. I stopped once to listen but could hear no sound. We took our separate ways to bed and for a while I lay sleepless, thinking of the dead beast out in the night.

What happened next is strange, and as incredible for me as I am sure it will be for you. The next morning when we went to the yard the horse was there. He was there, standing bloody and forlorn before the piles of grain. Still, that's not exactly the way it happened. Joe saw him first. Joe had gone out, and had come running to the house, his voice squealing. He was in such a frenzy that he had difficulty telling us what he had seen. He had had a nightmare, we said. We laughed at him and did not believe him at all.

Joe kept babbling and chattering at us, and when at last we went out, still unconvinced, we saw the horse that had been shot twice with a 12-gauge gun. We just stopped and looked at him and then looked at one another. He hadn't torn any sacks this time, so far as we could tell, or eaten any wheat. So much blood had run from his skull down to the bags and was now so clotted and dried that we supposed the beast had stood here most of the night. We now looked at him more sharply and saw that one eye had been blown out, an ear and the whole side of his skull blown off.

It's what happened next that I am reluctant to tell, for it seemed strange and unreal to me then, and seems so still. None of us ate much breakfast. None of us spoke a word after our first amazement. I went to the woods to be sure this was the horse we had shot. I found there signs of a terrific struggle, as if it had taken the beast a long while to get back on his legs. I followed his bloody trail back to the yard.

This day we didn't work, and for hours, as I recall it, we didn't speak. We sat for a while in the yard, smoking cigarettes one after another and staring with astonishment at the horse. We turned now and then to look at the world around us. It was not the same world we had known. And all the while the beast stood there, without moving, apparently without pain, like a horrible apparition from the dead, with flies buzzing around its open skull. More than his return, I think, was the way he stood that filled us with strange emotion. In spite of all our opposition, he now possessed the yard and the piles of grain. He seemed to possess the sky and the earth, for he had all around him a quiet deeper than life. He looked as if he might stand there forever, having by some privilege unknown to us claimed his inheritance and his rights.

I remember that after a while one of the men sat on the doorstep with his chin in his hands and that when I passed him

he never looked at me. Neither did the others. Curt pretended
to be busy tinkering with a piece of machinery; Jack lay out in
the sun with hands under his head, a dead cigarette hanging
from his lips. Joe Burt, of course, acted more queerly than any
other, and made us all feel a little queer. During the whole forenoon he hid behind bags of wheat and peered at that horse, his
round face above the sacks looking like a moon against the sky.
I've wondered since if what took place next would have happened if Joe had not been out there like a gibbering moon. I'll
never know. I do know that an inexplicable thing was busy in
our minds and souls; a notion of great power which slowly took
hold of all of us but Joe.

When at last I said, "Well, fellows, let's get busy," all but
Joe seemed to know exactly what I had in mind. They followed
me to the stackyard, as if we had discussed the matter and
planned what to do. We all went up to the horse and looked at it.
Not a one of us said a word, but I knew that we were all thinking
the same thing. It's this part of the experience that still baffles
me most.

For why should we have wanted to save that creature's
life?—of a worthless and homeless thing that was a nuisance to
everybody, and more than half dead from loss of blood? Well,
there we were, men who had suggested one kind of torture after
another—who had tried to blow the beast's head off—all now
resolved to save its life! Did our experience—our attempt to kill
it and then bring it back to health—become in a deeper way than
human knowing a symbolic thing for all of us?—a struggle between ourselves and all the dark blind forces set against us? This
is idle speculation, I know; but Death was our enemy too, and we
brought to bear against it all the knowledge and skill we had.
The fight we made here, I have sometimes thought, was more
than a fight that six men made on the Antelope hills that September day in 1928. At least it was more than that for us.

For three days and nights we labored to save that horse's
life. Not one of us ever suggested that we should call a veterinarian: this was our fight, our small saga of skill and devotion.
We wanted no professional aid. If a doctor had come the matter
would not have been the same at all. There would not have been
those immense implications that sank us deep in silence, and
chastened our souls and hands. We so devoted ourselves to this

struggle that everything else in our lives stood aside and waited.

With a pile of empty sacks we made a bed and forced the horse to lie; and we put liniment and salves on the wounds and bandaged them; and hunted in the coves for tender grass. We took turns sitting up with the creature, quite as if it were a human being—as if our whole life and happiness depended on it. In everything that we did we moved and felt in common, and were driven by the same desire. During those three days we achieved the deepest kinship that I have ever known to exist among men.

On my night with the horse I didn't sleep at all. I sat by it a while, looking at the lonely sick eye, wondering what I could do to relieve the pain or bring healing blood to the wound. A horse in pain is such a mute and pathetic thing. I was so foolish as to offer it grass, ground oats, water, knowing that it would not eat and would never eat again.

A little after daylight Jack called to me from the bunkhouse where the men slept.

"How is he?"

"Better, I think."

"Is he—is he in as much pain?"

"He's resting easy, I guess."

Curt appeared. "You say he's better?"

"He seems to be—a little."

They all left the bunkhouse and came to the yard. They looked at the horse, patted his lean hide, stared at the lone eye. Jack went away and returned with grass that had dew on it and forced some into the beast's mouth. But it would not eat. It did drink a little water for the first time, and we looked at one another and said it was getting well. At breakfast we ate with a little of our former appetite.

But in spite of all we could do, the horse died on the fourth day. Joe wept. I thought I saw mist in some of the other eyes, for I felt it in my own. We ate no breakfast that morning. Upon all of us there had fallen a depressing sadness—a loneliness that ached in our throats, as though something good and beautiful had been taken from life. Out in the woods we searched for a good spot for a grave. At last Curt said, "Here," and we dug a hole where the horse had stood when it was shot. We didn't drag it to the grave, as is the custom, with a log chain around its neck. We rolled it onto some planks and hauled it to the grave; and after it was in the hole, we placed an inverted box over the unsightly skull so that earth would not strike into the open wound. Upon the carcass we let the earth fall gently. . . .

Then as one man we returned to the yard and tore the fence down.

THE FREEDOM-LOVING HORSE

THE MUSTANG BAY
by S. Omar Barker

His mane and tail flowed long and black, his coat was blood-red bay.
Freeborn, he roamed the Texas range in a long-gone, lusty day.
Untamed prince of the wild horse breed, proud in his stallion stride,
Never a rope had touched his neck and never an iron his hide.
But men believed, who lived by spur, by rope, by horse and saddle,
That even the mustang breed must serve, born for a man to straddle.

Herding his mares the mustang bay sped for the open plain,
The day wind hot on his lathered flanks, the night wind cool in his mane.
But ever and ever as back he turned to circle for home once more,
Like silent wolves upon his trail, men followed as before.
By day, by night, from hill to plain, from burning plain to hill,
The mustang fled, nor ate nor drank, his snort defiant still.
But men who live by horse and rope know patience, too. Their snares
Entrapped the worn-out mustang band, the stallion and his mares.
Upon the wild king's blood-red neck their hempen loops drew tight.
From saddle and from hackamore he shrank but did not fight.

"His spirit's busted, Jim," said one. "He won't be worth a dime."
"He's thirsty-weak," said Jim, "and smart enough to bide his
  time."
Jim mounted him. He did not pitch. They hazed him to the creek.
The stallion's head swung high to gaze at far Tecumseh Peak.
Thus had they seen him, wild and free, on many a dawn-lit crest,
His mane tossed black upon the wind in challenge to their quest.
A moment thus the proud horse stood, son of the windy skies,
Then into the stream his muzzle thrust, deep to his dauntless eyes.
But not to drink! "Quick! Loose the girth!" (The bay had laid
  him down).
"Grab holt and help me raise his head! Don't let the booger
  drown!"
"Don't let him drown!" they cried in vain, and strove to give him
  breath,
But mustang freedom, lost awhile, was found again in death.

Herding his phantom mares again, look! To the hills he flees!
Sunset prince son of the blood-bay skies, son of the black-maned
  breeze!

THE REJUVENATED HORSE

HOW THE OLD HORSE WON THE BET
by Oliver Wendell Holmes

DEDICATED BY A CONTRIBUTOR TO THE
COLLEGIAN, 1830, TO THE EDITORS OF
THE HARVARD ADVOCATE, 1876.

'Twas on the famous trotting-ground,
The betting men were gathered round
From far and near; the "cracks" were there
Whose deeds the sporting prints declare:
The swift g. m., Old Hiram's nag,
The fleet s. h., Dan Pfeiffer's brag,
With these a third—and who is he
That stands beside his fast b. g.?
Budd Doble, whose catarrhal name
So fills the nasal trump of fame.
There too stood many a noted steed
Of Messenger and Morgan breed;
Green horses also, not a few;
Unknown as yet what they could do;
And all the hacks that know so well
The scourgings of the Sunday swell.

Blue are the skies of opening day;
The bordering turf is green with May;
The sunshine's golden gleam is thrown
On sorrel, chestnut, bay, and roan;
The horses paw and prance and neigh,
Fillies and colts like kittens play,
And dance and toss their rippled manes
Shining and soft as silken skeins;
Wagons and gigs are ranged about,

And fashion flaunts her gay turn-out;
Here stands—each youthful Jehu's dream—
The jointed tandem, ticklish team!
And there in ampler breadth expand
The splendors of the four-in-hand;
On faultless ties and glossy tiles
The lovely bonnets beam their smiles;
(The style's the man, so books avow;
The style's the woman, anyhow);
From flounces frothed with creamy lace
Peeps out the pug-dog's smutty face,
Or spaniel rolls his liquid eye,
Or stares the wiry pet of Skye—
O woman, in your hours of ease
So shy with us, so free with these!

"Come on! I'll bet you two to one
I'll make him do it!" "Will you? Done!"

What was it who was bound to do?
I did not hear and can't tell you—
Pray listen till my story's through.

Scarce noticed, back behind the rest,
By cart and wagon rudely prest,
The parson's lean and bony bay
Stood harnessed in his one-horse shay—
Lent to his sexton for the day;
(A funeral—so the sexton said;
His mother's uncle's wife was dead.)

Like Lazarus bid to Dives' feast,
So looked the poor forlorn old beast;
His coat was rough, his tail was bare,
The gray was sprinkled in his hair;
Sportsmen and jockeys knew him not,
And yet they say he once could trot
Among the fleetest of the town,
Till something cracked and broke him down—
The steed's, the statesman's, common lot!

"And are we then so soon forgot?"
Ah me! I doubt if one of you
Has ever heard the name "Old Blue,"
Whose fame through all this region rung
In those old days when I was young!

"Bring forth the horse!" Alas! he showed
Not like the one Mazeppa rode;
Scant-maned, sharp-backed, and shaky-kneed,
The wreck of what was once a steed,
Lips thin, eyes hollow, stiff in joints;
Yet not without his knowing points.
The sexton laughing in his sleeve,
As if 't were all a make-believe,
Led forth the horse, and as he laughed
Unhitched the breeching from a shaft,
Unclasped the rusty belt beneath,
Drew forth the snaffle from his teeth,
Slipped off his head-stall, set him free
From strap and rein—a sight to see!

So worn, so lean in every limb,
It can't be they are saddling him!
It is! his back the pigskin strides
And flaps his lank, rheumatic sides;
With look of mingled scorn and mirth
They buckle round the saddle-girth;
With horsy wink and saucy toss
A youngster throws his leg across,
And so, his rider on his back,
They lead him, limping, to the track,
Far up behind the starting point,
To limber out each stiffened joint.

As through the jeering crowd he past,
One pitying look Old Hiram cast;
"Go it, ye cripple, while you can!"
Cried out unsentimental Dan;
"A Fast-Day dinner for the crows!"
Budd Doble's scoffing shout arose.

Slowly, as when the walking beam
First feels the gathering head of steam,
With warning cough and threatening wheeze
The stiff old charger crooks his knees;
At first with cautious step sedate,
As if he dragged a coach of state;
He's not a colt; he knows full well
That time is weight and sure to tell;
No horse so sturdy but he fears
The handicap of twenty years;
As through the throng on either hand
The old horse nears the judges' stand,
Beneath his jockey's featherweight
He warms a little to his gait,
And now and then a step is tried
That hints of something like a stride.

"Go!"—Through his ear the summons stung
As if a battle trump had rung;
The slumbering instincts long unstirred
Start at the old familiar word;
It thrills like flame through every limb—
What mean his twenty years to him?
The savage blow his rider dealt
Fell on his hollow flanks unfelt;
The spur that pricked his staring hide
Unheeded tore his bleeding side;
Alike to him are spur and rein—
He steps a five-year-old again!

Before the quarter pole was past,
Old Hiram said, "He's going fast."
Long ere the quarter was a half,
The chuckling crowd had ceased to laugh;
Tighter his frightened jockey clung
As in a mighty stride he swung,
The gravel flying in his track,
His neck stretched out, his ears laid back,
His tail extended all the while
Behind him like a rat-tail file!

Off went a shoe—away it spun,
Shot like a bullet from a gun;
The quaking jockey shapes a prayer
From scraps of oaths he used to swear;
He drops his whip, he drops his rein,
He clutches fiercely for a mane;
He'll lose his hold—he sways and reels—
He'll slide beneath those trampling heels!
The knees of many a horseman quake,
The flowers on many a bonnet shake,
And shouts arise from left and right,
"Stick on! Stick on!" "Hould tight! Hould tight!"
"Cling round his neck and don't let go—
"That pace can't hold—there! steady! whoa!"
But like the sable steed that bore
The spectral lover of Lenore,
His nostrils snorting foam and fire,
No stretch his bony limbs can tire;
And now the stand he rushes by,
And "Stop him!—stop him!" is the cry.
Stand back! he's only just begun—
He's having out three heats in one!

"Don't rush in front! he'll smash your brains;
But follow up and grab the reins!"
Old Hiram spoke. Dan Pfeiffer heard,
And sprang impatient at the word;
Budd Doble started on his bay,
Old Hiram followed on his gray,
And off they spring, and round they go,
The fast ones doing "all they know."
Look! twice they follow at his heels,
As round the circling course he wheels,
And whirls with him that clinging boy
Like Hector round the walls of Troy;
Still on, and on, the third time round!
They're tailing off! they're losing ground!
Budd Doble's nag begins to fail!
Dan Pfeiffer's sorrel whisks his tail!
And see! in spite of whip and shout,

Old Hiram's mare is giving out!
Now for the finish! at the turn,
The old horse—all the rest astern—
Comes swinging in, with easy trot;
By Jove! he's distanced all the lot!

That trot no mortal could explain;
Some said, "Old Dutchman come again!"
Some took his time—at least they tried,
But what it was could none decide;
One said he couldn't understand
What happened to his second hand;
One said 2.10; *that* couldn't be—
More like two twenty-two or three;
Old Hiram settled it at last:
"The time was two—too dee-vel-ish fast!"

The parson's horse had won the bet;
It cost him something of a sweat;
Back in the one-horse shay he went;
The parson wondered what it meant,
And murmured, with a mild surprise
And pleasant twinkle of the eyes,
"That funeral must have been a trick,
Or corpses drive at double-quick;
I shouldn't wonder, I declare,
If brother—Jehu—made the prayer!"

And this is all I have to say
About that tough old trotting bay,
Huddup! Huddup! G'lang! Good day!

Moral for which this tale is told:
A horse *can* trot, for all he's old.

THE COMPASSIONATE HORSE

THE FAITHFUL BRADY
by Larrey Bowman

A few springs ago a man in Arizona named Chapin became infatuated with a certain Miss Dasher, and shot a rival for the lady's favor; whereupon he was tried and condemned, and sent off to the territorial prison. But that is not the end of Chapin's story, for he left a friend behind him.

It was only a saddle horse, a little white-faced buckskin, with pretty kittenish tricks and a kind disposition, and it had no finer name than Brady.

Chapin broke the horse early in the spring, and won Brady's confidence then, for he was kind to animals. For all his overmastering temper and strange primitive ideas of justice, Chapin's ways were almost always gentle; and a horse is quick to notice that.

Brady helped his master with the luckless courting of Miss Dasher. That is, he carried Chapin into town, always prancing when the house came in sight, and swinging about so, as the lover dismounted, that you might have exclaimed, "Here's a fearless rider on a desperate steed!" But that sidling, those prances, and all, were part of an amiable game between the two. Chapin, dismounted at his divinity's door, would turn his back on the untethered Brady; and Brady, the lines pulled over his head till they rested on the ground, would roll the bit in his mouth, and stand there till he was wanted.

There are gossips in Arizona, and the Dasher girl was on their lips—before Chapin began to see her, and after. But however that may be, Chapin went about his business, which was getting good yields off a ranch; and about his pleasure—his honest devotion—which centered around Sophy Dasher.

And, one fine day in early April, it seemed he had won the girl. Chapin came riding back to his ranch and loosed Brady; but the little pony stopped and whinnied. All about was the knee-deep alfalfa—ambrosial beds for a horse to roll in—and, back of him, from where a big mesquite in yellow blossom spread an odor like honeysuckle, you caught the tinkle of fresh, running water. Yet the friendly Brady hesitated, for all the world as if he asked a question.

"Oh, it's all right with me, little horse," said Chapin, patting a sturdy brown shoulder. "She's said yes, and we're going to be married."

The bronco snuffed his master over, horse fashion, and laid his head on Chapin's shoulder. He was not much to look at, was Brady, but his heart was right, as they say. He had never known unkind treatment, and he thought all men were his friends—but especially Chapin, big and strong and honest, who was the bravest man he knew.

"It's a grand world to live in, pony," cried Chapin, as he played with Brady's mane. Up above in the clean-swept Arizona sky there was not the trace of a cloud; and the world, as the two looked at it, was a wonderful stretch of green—trees in blossom, oleanders flaming red, and larks and blackbirds everywhere. Brady must have seen these things very dimly; and if they struck through the man's perception it was only in a nameless way. Yet they both, simple creatures, exulted to feel the warm sun on their backs; and the air was sweet to their nostrils and they felt it was good to be alive.

So much for Chapin's dream of love. Two days later there came a cousin of his, who had ridden hard to bring bad news.

The talebearer burst in breathless. "Oh, you fool," he cried. "Didn't I tell you from the first? The girl has played with you. She's a— Take your hands off my throat. She's a— Let me loose, Ed Chapin. You don't believe me? Go and learn for yourself." The cousin laughed. "It's no secret now."

And then, as Chapin turned white and caught his breath, the other told the sordid story, and there was no doubting him: what the gossips had whispered was all true. It was not a worthy woman whose fine eyes had made a slave of Chapin. She stood openly dishonored now, through her favors to another man.

"But never mind *him*," the cousin said. "Leave him and leave her to each other. Forget you ever knew the girl—" He stopped, seeing a strange look in Chapin's face. "Ed," he urged, "you ain't thinking of *that?*" They seemed to read each other's thoughts. "What good would it do you, Ed? It wouldn't help you to kill anyone."

Chapin looked his cousin between the eyes. "No," said he, "you're right, it wouldn't." He turned away, but he came back again. "I believe—what you've told me, Harry. Now go away; I want to be alone."

Chapin fought with himself all that day, to bring himself to accept what had happened. He beat back the passionate anger that kept rising to his head. A dozen times Chapin told himself, "I will let the fellow have her. The girl is nothing to me." At length it was night, and dark outside; and then it was that that which he fought against—the primal instinct—conquered. In a sort of daze, while the clock in the house ticked as from an immeasurable distance, and the breath caught in his throat and his ears sang, Chapin took down his revolver from the wall.

A minute later he was out in the corral, saddling Brady with trembling fingers. He set the little horse blindly at the point where the town lights made a blur against the sky; and up a dusty hill they galloped, and down the long, ill-graded slope beyond. It was the familiar way they took, but never before had Chapin used the quirt.

The man dismounted at a well-known hitching rack, and left Brady. The curious animal whinnied once or twice. He was thirsty after the rapid going, and being a rather spoiled bronco, he thought of hay in the boarding corral that Chapin patronized when in town. But Brady was obedient first of all; and he stood now, with the lines pulled over his head so that they rested on the ground, and rolled his bit and bode his time.

Pretty soon he heard a pistol shot, and was conscious of voices shouting. But the noise subsided in a little.

It was the pampered stomach in him that began to bother Brady. In his minute-long naps by the hitching rack, he dreamed of hay that was all blossom and no stalk at all; he rolled in shady places and rose to cool his hoofs in running water, where he drank till the joy of it woke him up. Waking, it vexed him that Chapin did not come—it was not like his master to forget him. After a while a real thirst came, his throat was coated and hot, and almost pained him. Towards morning the wind blew cold. Brady shifted his weight from foot to fòot, letting his head drop lower and lower.

Remember, he was not tied. The reins lay on the ground before him; and they were his written instructions to stand, that was all.

The sun came up after a while. Mexican loafers, fresh from their squalid breakfast, began to line the sunny side of the street. Each found the hitching-post or yard of wall that his special back had helped to wear smooth. As the day grew hot and breathless, conversation would languish among them. But now they spoke excitedly.

With the sun and the Mexicans came flies, seeming as if they would devour Brady. But at length two men approached. "Hello," said one, "ain't that Ed Chapin's horse?" Brady whinnied to let them know he wanted Ed. If they could, they did not produce the master. But they took Brady away with them, to the familiar boarding corral.

When a man kills another, and has been tried by his peers and sent away to some solemn keep like the Yuma penitentiary, a public auction disposes of his goods. Brady waited days in vain for Chapin; and then—Brady went under the hammer.

It was a man they called a Tenderfoot that bought him, and the first thing the Tenderfoot did was, to ride Brady forty miles through a blazing sun. Precisely, it was thirty-nine miles, for Brady dropped with the end in sight. As he lay he appeared to be dying, and quirt and spurs were useless to arouse him. So the Tenderfoot hailed a passing wagon, into which he threw his saddle and bridle: and, not without a sense of mystification (complicated by a chastened regret) he went on, leaving Brady to the buzzards.

But it happens that the buckskin color is the mark of a sturdy stock. Brady had his awful agony, but in the end—hours later— he found his feet. Misty-eyed and weak of knee, with fires blazing in his chest, he wandered till he found a canal. He was drinking there, painfully, when along came Toppy McGune.

Now, this McGune was a vagrant and a scamp. In a city he would have belonged to a gang, and perhaps drifted into petty thieving. But living in Arizona, where the social conditions are peculiar, he found "chuck-line riding" the thing. With a horse and a blanket roll he went from ranch to ranch (and the territory is a large one). He had a specious adaptable story of having just come from somewhere and being eager to get somewhere else. And because he seemed an honest wayfarer, the good folk were glad to give him food and shelter—not in charity, by any means; for it were an impious thing, most isolated ranchers think, to turn a traveler away at nightfall.

McGune, then, was a chuck-line rider. That is, he was a mounted tramp. And being such, he admired a good horse, knowing the prestige it gives a man. From the back of his own knee-sprung sorrel, he now observed Brady gulping water; and he recognized the Chapin brand on Brady's flank. He annexed Brady at once, leading him away with his lasso rope. As he did not care—quite apart from ethical reasons—to incur suspicion of horse stealing, he made some careful inquiries. And in the end he learned enough to make him think he could risk keeping Brady. The little buckskin was in a state of partial collapse. But McGune reflected, "You couldn't kill a buckskin off." Thereupon he disposed of the sorrel, and made Brady his particular steed.

And so, from being left for dead, Brady passed into the life of this vagrant. Brady had little kittenish tricks, a joy in prancing; and sometimes he liked to buck a little. McGune was not an eminently good rider, though he knew neither fear nor pity. He wanted his horse to rear and plunge while going down the street of a town, so that people would turn and look at him.

He bought a special bit for Brady that lay along Brady's tongue like a trowel and made a bone-breaking lever against the jaw. And, being long dissatisfied with his spurs, Toppy got a blacksmith to make him a pair; and the new spurs were long in the shank, with rowels that would tear the flesh.

Then McGune educated Brady in the school of fear. Mounting Brady he would draw him in till the scared little beast started back. Then, clap! and the spurs stabbed his flanks, and Brady's shoulders tingled from the flailing of the quirt.

You see, Brady was new to rough treatment. At first he thought the fault was in him. And then, driven to desperation, with bleeding mouth and his poor brains confounded, rebellion took him and he fought to shake his tyrant. He plunged and twisted while the rider yelled and beat him. But he never could quite get Toppy off.

To belong to a fellow like McGune is to work long hours and have broken rest; it is to end the day often with an empty stomach, and sometimes to begin it that way; it is to know thirst—not simple dryness, but the cruel, sharp, biting pain. And a horse's nature goes wrong, and in the end his spirit breaks.

Often Brady thought of a ranch where the sweetest alfalfa grew. Why had they taken him from it? Where was the master all this time? Of all the incomprehensible hurts he endured, this neglect of Chapin's was the hardest. And yet—Brady, on the hard road of life, was headed the way of forgetting.

McGune, as has been said, liked to clatter through a town for the edification of whoever would look. Was there a woman

HORSE AND RIDER. Marino Marini. *Courtesy, The Museum of Modern Art, New York: Acquired through the Lillie P. Bliss Bequest.*

this side the skyline, he would display his horsemanship. In a way, you might say, it was a woman that severed Brady and McGune forever.

Horse and master were traveling some dreary road, with a little white schoolhouse ahead. It was later than three in the afternoon, and the children were gone; but there at the door of the schoolhouse stood that hand of fate, the woman. She was merely a country schoolmistress, adjusting the bands of her neat white sunbonnet. The sound of Brady's hoofs caused her to look up at the approaching chuck-line rider.

In the buckram soul of McGune sprang a wish to attitudinize. He "thumbed" Brady, and covertly spurred. The show that followed took place before the schoolhouse.

"Oh, your cinch, your cinch!"—it was the voice of a young woman, calling.

Brady's girth had loosened and was weak; the strands had shown badly raveled that morning. But Toppy, though he noted it then, had forgotten—and now Brady was bucking.

Brady bucked with his body and his soul, as a drowning man fights for his life. He bucked in the memory of pain, and the presence of fear, and the rage of hate; feeling the frayed cinch loosen and give, and that incubus above him totter. Then—a great, supreme effort—he was free.

The lines, somehow, came over his head and touched the ground, and—strange fidelity to an older custom—he stood in his tracks as he had used to do for Chapin. Presently the unhorsed Toppy rose from the dust of the road and found his saddle which lay by itself to one side. He came over and kicked Brady in the side. Then, blinded with anger and shame, Toppy clubbed his quirt and struck out; he struck Brady on the neck and between the ears; he struck one of Brady's eyes and put it out.

For a moment, through the pain he endured, Brady staggered out against a wall of darkness. Filling the wronged, astounded soul of the horse was one desire—to regain the bright, sunshiny world. The light came back, in flaming points, in exquisite drenching showers. He saw the road, the few trees, and the sky above. But it was not the same world, somehow; nor would it ever be quite the same.

It was two years after this that a questionable company of men rode into the town of Globe. There were in the cavalcade perhaps a dozen lean men in leather trousers, booted and spurred, and sitting their mounts with ineffable swagger. A string of wicked-looking ponies, unsaddled, completed the procession.

It was Sappington's Bronco Congress, according to the premonitory handbill.

If you never heard of Sappington, know, then, that he conducts a sort of traveling circus. The members of his congress are, first, detestable, wrong-headed horses that Circe's swine would not associate with. Some graduate cowboys complete the outfit. It is for the cowboys to amuse, instruct, and elevate the daily audience by riding the horses: which, to their discredit as sane-minded gentlemen, they usually do.

And among the outlawed herd of horses was Brady, a strange fierceness in the eye which was left him. Where had Brady been these two years? It would be easier to account for Chapin that was strayed even farther from his home; and dwelt down beside the Colorado River, and was a "good man," according to his warden.

This much concerning Brady, at least. The whip and spur had done their work. He had become a "wicked" horse.

Some people, so they say, always play in hard luck. Brady, it seems, had cruel luck in his masters. And since the days of Toppy McGune he had not found a master like his present one, Pete Ovens, drunken, bragging, cowardly Ovens: Ovens whom Sappington employed but took, it must be said, little pride in.

As the bronco congress passed through Globe, a hint of rain was in the air; and later, that afternoon, the Globe audience which came together to see the show marked the gathering of a dust storm in the east. It was a weird, uncanny day—to Ovens purely notable for the fact that he was drunker than was his custom.

Of late it had been thrust upon him by his companions that he was a poltroon—had been suggested, even, that he, Ovens, rode indifferently. Today, as his turn to mount came, he swaggered into the arena, where the dust was swirling into spirals; and as the wind flattened out his leather trousers, and tore his hat awry—rushed through his unsavory teeth, even—Ovens swore he would show them all.

They fought with Brady to get the saddle on, and Brady lunged and squealed in his anger. It was delicate pleasure to the audience to see a horse nature so perverted. Ovens got a foot in the stirrup and lurched across the saddle. Then they loosed the little fighting bronco. A driving wind swept down on the flat. The shingled grandstand clattered and shook. Like a great yellow curtain, dust blotted out the arena.

When it cleared they saw a riderless horse, and Ovens lying on his face, stunned and disgraced.

Sappington discharged the man that evening. "You're no good," said the owner of the show. "Drunk or sober you're no good." Ovens muttered but made no reply: he had a score that he would settle later. The wretched Brady had shamed him, and he had a word to say to Brady.

Late that night he sneaked Brady out of the corral, and led him to a place he thought safe. Ovens had a rifle and a shovel with him, and with the latter he proceeded to dig a pit. The earth resisted him, the wind blew wildly; and as he worked he swore to himself.

At last the grave was dug, and Brady stood picketed beside it. The man stepped off a few paces and threw a cartridge into his rifle chamber.

He raised the rifle, then lowered it. Ovens was thirsty. He wrenched the cork from a flask he carried, and drank. He raised the rifle, aimed, and fired.

A startled cry from Brady as the bullet grooved along his flank. Brady plunged to escape this new terror. Into the fresh-made grave he fell, wrenching his shoulder, but he pulled his picket free. Ovens fired distractedly. The horse struggled up the embankment and cleared it.

Ovens never spoke of the affair. He was not prepared to explain it. For, though he fired shot after shot, the horse, dragging his picket-rope, got away.

It was what they call a good year in the hills, with grass in plenty, and the canyons running water. Brady, a refugee from men, ranged wild, in a sort of dull contentment.

When his belly was fairly filled, sometimes, a whiff of breeze or a trick of the sunshine sent a kind of tremor through him. All the memory he had would revert to preposterous kindness, to a world where one lived gently. So illogical is a horse that he had no bitterness for the man who broke him to the saddle, and had Chapin ever come to him he would have gone where the master led.

But another servitude awaited the horse. Through the Pinal Mountains where he was came a vagabondish trio of prospectors, who aimed to gain the level slope towards the Gila, and follow the Gila to the California line. Sighting Brady, they set after him with ropes, ran him into a blind canyon, and made him a prisoner; and they made a packhorse of him.

Maimed and broken as Brady was, he fought his captors, then and after. But, since Providence had seen fit to throw a beast of burden in their path, they did not propose to give the beast up; and they worked to slay the spirit in Brady, in ways calculated to have that effect. It naturally incensed them that a broken-down horse, a brute that no one claimed, should set himself against the primal law: which, applying to horses, seems to read—The horse is the slave of man.

But the prospectors were bungling fellows. Brady's back became raw; the burlap pad across the withers was merely salt to his wounds. With the constant pressure of a pain that every step seemed to aggravate, Brady's ribs began to show; he grew quite weak. The limp he got from the premature grave became a violent lurch. Sometimes he even fell down. This was considered in the light of an insult, for now the Gila grew wider every day; Yuma lay just beyond the horizon, and the prospectors were for straining every fiber, now the California line was so near.

For there was a Find beyond the Colorado. Other gold hunters passed them on the trail. It was: Hurry or be left, hurry or be too late, hurry or you'll curse yourselves! Yet even now the three cursed themselves; they cursed Brady, hobbling and slipping with his load.

At length it seemed they must leave the failing horse. They got them another somewhere, and they abandoned Brady in the desert. "You darned crowbait," were their parting words, "get out and rustle, and see how you like it." Brady did not attempt to follow, and the three prospectors faded in the dust that lay white along the Yuma trail.

Now, it happens that even with that trail run the tracks of a great Western railroad, and the dirt is packed hard between the rails. If you are a tramp set down in the desert and want to get to Yuma or beyond, the walking here is better than on the trail. Sometimes the time-expired felon, whom the Yuma penitentiary returns to the world with five dollars in the pocket of his prison-made denims, takes this footpath, going east; for it will bring him clear of the desert in the end, and back to the life he used to know.

Whether Brady, discarded in the desert, wandered there many days, no one can say. Simply, there in the desert one white-hot morning, he had a peculiar and strange adventure.

He felt the heat and was thirsty, and by a railroad water tank, where the maddening drip, drip from the unattainable water merely wetted the sand, Brady stood—setting his tongue to the moistened ground. A man's footsteps upon the interspace of the rails caused him to start and arch a gaunted neck. A man was approaching Brady upon Brady's blind side, and the horse shifted curiously to bring his good eye to bear on the stranger.

It was a man of some stature—strangely bent, and seemingly deteriorated before his time. The pallid skin of his face was not the skin of those who live in the sun. It was a piece with the man's uneasy carriage, which might have been lithe and graceful once, but lacked the assurance of the outdoor world. He wore a coarse blue suit of denim, the uniform of the time-expired convict.

He came nearer, till his features showed—clean-cut, honest features of their sort: you would have picked him for a man kind and brave, though the lines of strength and weakness mingled. He was just a man, no better than you and me, and Fate might have made a hero of him. But she had dealt far otherwise.

The man's mouth quivered a little from his unused exertion in the sun; and his brows were beaded with sweat.

Suddenly, when quite near, he stopped, staring oddly at the gaunted horse. To Brady, meeting the look with his mutilated stare, the wildest flashes of things past and things dead came back. Years had passed, time had used him harshly, and yet Brady had not forgotten. He whinnied, out of his parched, dry throat. The man with the white face was Chapin.

"Good God!" cried the man, and sat him down with his face in his hands. Then, "Brady," he called doubtfully, timidly. Brady, timid himself, limped closer.

OLD HORSE. Thomas Gainsborough. *Courtesy, The Trustees of the Tate Gallery, London.*

"What have they done to you, pony?" cried Chapin. "Lame, and blind, and starved, and— Good God, I won't strike you, Brady—for you're Brady, you remembered me. Don't flinch; w-won't you let me touch your mane?" His fingers closed on the yellow comb, and there, against Brady's neck, he laid his face. A rush of hot tears took him then, and he cried for the years that were past.

It was loneliness that gripped the master's heart. Well enough he knew, as the prison gates opened on his freedom, that it was not the same world he re-entered. That boyish zest in merely living was gone; he felt that nature was indifferent and cruel. The massive silence of the desert awed him. The sky looked old, and underfoot it seemed he trod on ancient ashes. Here and there a dust whirl formed and spent itself: through the power, as it seemed to him, of that iron-souled Will which creates that it may destroy.

He stood away from the horse. "Brady, Brady," he said, "don't you know what I am and where I've been? . . . I thought so much of a girl that I shot a man because he did her wrong; and I've served my time. I ain't got any ranch to go back to, and friends—why, friends forget—when you've been away."

Brady came and laid his head on Chapin's shoulder as if he, somehow, understood. Strange thing, a horse—so willing to work, satisfied with such simple pleasures, faithful, sometimes, with such a simple faith.

". . . And you've come back to me," Chapin said. "You ain't thinking—Oh, you aren't thinking, Brady, we can take up the life where we left it. Why, Brady, you're all broken, old pony; and I'm—I ain't the man I was."

The man looked out upon the old, gray desert, where nothing grew but twisted deformities, and nothing moved but the dancing sand whirls. The desolation had chilled him; and now, all at once, he knew he had read it wrong. For the voice of the Silence was not cruel. It was the voice of the unsubdued earth, saying: *I am as a woman. And who conquers me I shall reward.* The wind of the desert was sweet and clean, and breathed against his cheek like caresses.

"Brady," cried the man to the horse. "There's land that no man has taken, there's wealth that's never been gathered. Because a man is down he ain't beaten—while he has hands—while he has someone to work for. That's it—someone to work for. Brady, we'll begin again."

He set his back to the Yuma hills, and the horse followed after him. Chapin could not read the future to know that the ground would repay his honest efforts as the ground has done. Then, merely with "someone to work for," he was stiffened to face the world. And so he went back to the world, and the faithful Brady went with him.

THE RESTLESS HORSE

THE HORSES OF THE SEA
by Christina Rossetti

The horses of the sea
    Rear a foaming crest,
But the horses of the land
    Serve us the best.

The horses of the land
    Munch corn and clover,
While the foaming sea horses
    Toss and turn over.

THE DEVOTED HORSE

MISSION FOR BABY

by Ivey Noah Drinkard

Snorting for breath in the stifling noonday heat and dust, Bobby wasn't giving an inch in his straining gallop. His master above kept mumbling gentle but urgent words. And Bobby sensed something was wrong. Never before had his master taken him out of the plow and started running him in this burning sun.

In the field he had heard the mistress at the house begin yelling frantically to his master, and the master, wheeling, had started running too. Toward the mistress who was holding the baby and crying. Grasping the soundless baby from its mother's arm, the master turned its head down and began pounding it violently on the back. Still the baby didn't cry. And the master, suddenly shaking his head, handed the baby back to its mother and wheeled toward the house. When he ran back out of the house he had a revolver in his hand, and began racing across the plowed field toward Bobby, with the mistress starting with fresh frightened cries behind him. The master began yelling, "I'll have to try to get by the Strawbridge place, regardless. The five miles the other way might be too late. I'll stop long enough at Mama's to tell her to send Dickie around, just in case . . ."

Rounding the bend before a small white house, the master was straightening in the saddle and letting go a keen, warning yell: "Whoo-pee! Whoo-pee . . . !" Bobby wasn't letting up, although he sensed his master was going to stop at the house where he usually stopped when he came by.

The master was suddenly beginning to tighten the rein— "Ho! Ho, Bobby!" And there, running out of the house, was the master's mother and young brother. With all four feet clear of the ground, Bobby, at the master's next sharp "Ho!" stiffened. The hard road came straight up, with a terrific impact. Bobby's taut haunches gave slightly, then braced solidly as he whirled, pawing the air midst the swirling hot dust filling his nostrils. His master was yelling, "Send Dickie for Doc Bailey, Mamma—round the other way. The baby's choking—"

Bobby, never still, was lunging again at the shake of the rein, when the old woman gave a frightened cry, "Son! Oh, son, the Strawbridges . . . !"

Almost immediately came the master's voice again, strained with emotion, "Maybe they won't be out o' the fields, Mamma . . . !"

Still his mother cried, as Bobby galloped on.

Rounding the last bend, there gradually loomed ahead a familiar weathered farmhouse, half-concealed behind tasseling green corn and orchard. His master hadn't come this way in a long time.

Feeling his master's legs tightening against his sides, Bobby obediently strained a little harder. Drawing nearer and nearer the orchard alongside the road, he was aware of no sound or activity out there at the house and fields.

The first noise he caught was a sudden yell from the corn adjoining the orchard. A sharp, harsh yell, it immediately grew louder and confused, the person tearing through the corn, shouting, "Aaron! Aaron!" at each lunge.

The master was straight in the stirrups, his body twisted tensely. Bobby was edging past the orchard when the shouting broke out of the corn and a gun began cracking in the orchard. Startled, Bobby jerked tautly. As his master's gun exploded deafeningly with simultaneous whistlings close above, stark fear struck Bobby. A few lunges farther he caught a new sound of scrambling footsteps inside the house and someone was running out onto the porch, and suddenly there were noisier explosions and louder whistlings.

Almost past the house, Bobby barely heard the thud above. He felt his master's foot jerk from the right stirrup and was aware of trying to halt, when his master's body lunged down his side and instantly something sharp and hot plowed over Bobby's rump. Stricken by a fresh terror, with his master rolling over and over toward the ditch alongside, Bobby leaped again.

On the open road, he knew no distance nor slowing, until nearly a mile later, the fear began subsiding, the pain to grow less painful. Even then he knew not whether to stop, or where, until finally ahead there, at the three stores and other small buildings, he gradually grew aware of an old stopping place—the hitching post at the well. Already several men were running out of the stores, pointing toward Bobby and yelling. Two were at the hitching post almost by the time Bobby drew up, snorting and foamflecked. One, staring hard at Bobby, suddenly yelled, "Blood!" He pointed at the saddle blanket.

Half a dozen men were running from every direction, when the other man beside Bobby yelled, "Dave and the Strawbridges! Still fightin' over the horse."

A white-haired, bespectacled man, with a black grip in his hand, was running out of a small building toward one of the several cars in sight. Other men were running toward the cars, while still others were running in and out of the stores yelling, "Guns! Get the Strawbridges!"

In the startling confusion of the cars' roaring and the men's running and shouting, Bobby sensed a strange new fear. He whirled and started for home. One by one the cars sped noisily by, and each time Bobby sensed a new urgency to go still faster.

Even when the last car disappeared ahead, he kept galloping, going home. Only when he came in sight of the cars again, did he slow down some. The cars had stopped this side of the weather-beaten old farmhouse, and the men were darting around behind the cars, their guns exploding furiously. Several of the men ran out to wave him down and grasp the bridle rein. The white-haired man with the black grip was hurriedly legged up onto Bobby's back.

At the shake of the rein, Bobby started again, toward home. The guns were cracking all around, whistling sounds passing close by, but the white-haired man's long legs still hugged tightly to Bobby's sides and Bobby galloped hard again to get away.

He still wasn't out of the firing, however, when he felt a hot streak plow into his hip. In fresh fright, he gained speed somehow on the next jump or two and kept moving.

Still, the farther Bobby galloped, the worse the pain grew, the slower his legs moved. With all his straining, with all the noise behind him now, his legs grew heavier, and he had to wince and give to his right hip.

The white-haired man on his back shook the rein and Bobby strained still harder. But suddenly his right hip gave way altogether and he stumbled and almost fell. Within sight of home, he gained his footing and tried again. Still again he stumbled, almost to the ground.

The white-haired man, thrown over on Bobby's head, jerked Bobby to a halt then. The next moment he had jumped to the ground and was running as fast as his long legs would carry him toward the house. Bobby stumbled in quivering exhaustion and pain to the side of the road and lay down in the ditch.

After a while the white-haired man returned with Bobby's mistress and the baby. The baby smiled and put out its little hands to Bobby like it always did. But the mistress had tears in her eyes. Then while the doctor examined the painful place in Bobby's hip, the cars began to drive up, the men to get out and crowd around Bobby.

The master, with his shirt off and his shoulder bandaged tightly, was among the first out. He had tears in his eyes, too, as he hugged the baby and his mistress and then turned to Bobby.

The third car brought the three tall, rough-looking Strawbridge brothers. One of them leaned on the other two and held his limp, bleeding arm. Even they stopped and looked soberly at Bobby.

In the surprising quiet, the master turned to the tallest of the Strawbridge boys.

"Like I told you to start with, Aaron," he said, "I never would have taken Bobby from your uncle if he hadn't given him to the baby before he died."

Aaron Strawbridge hesitated a moment and then spoke without raising his eyes from Bobby.

"Yeah, I'm willin' to agree with you now, Dave," he said, "he belongs to the baby. We'll help you get him to the house an' put him in a sling."

THE OBEDIENT HORSE

THE HUCKSTER'S HORSE
by Julia Hurd Strong

His well-shaped ears were chestnut brown and they
Stuck up like beans run through the braided hat
That shaded him, as down the alleyway
He walked from gate to gate. The huckster sat
With broad patched breeches on the wagon seat
And hawked commercials, while the housewives ran
To stand bareheaded in the August heat
And measure snap beans in a granite pan.

The huckster's horse was neither dull nor slow
But patient, with his energy reined in
By strict obedience to the stop and go
Of his profession. But no discipline
Could check the tail, fly conscious and alert,
That switched his slim legs like a hula skirt.

THE UNTAMED HORSE

THE CORRALLING OF FLICKA
by Mary O'Hara

When Ken opened his eyes next morning and looked out he saw
that the house was wrapped in fog. There had been no rain at all
since the day a week ago when the wind had torn the "sprinkling
system" to pieces and blown all the tattered clouds away. That

THE HORSES. William Charles Palmer. *Courtesy, The Metropolitan Museum of Art: George T. Hearn Fund, 1941.*

was the day he had found Flicka. And it had been terribly hot since then. They had hardly been able to stand the sun out on the terrace. They had gone swimming in the pool every day. On the hills, the grass was turning to soft tan.

Now there were clouds and they had closed down. After a severe hot spell there often came a heavy fog, or hail, or even snow.

Standing at the window, Ken could hardly see the pines on the Hill opposite. He wondered if his father would go after the yearlings in such a fog as this—they wouldn't be able to see them; but at breakfast McLaughlin said there would be no change of plans. It was just a big cloud that had settled down over the ranch —it would lift and fall—perhaps up on Saddle Back it would be clear.

They mounted and rode out.

The fog lay in the folds of the hills. Here and there a bare summit was in sunshine, then a little farther on came a smother of cottony white that soaked the four riders to the skin and hung rows of moonstones on the whiskers of the horses.

It was hard to keep track of each other. Suddenly Ken was lost—the others had vanished. He reined in Shorty and sat listening. The clouds and mist rolled around him. He felt as if he were alone in the world.

A bluebird, color of the deep blue wild delphinium that dots the plains, became interested in him, and perched on a bush near by; and as he started Shorty forward again, the bluebird followed along, hopping from bush to bush.

The boy rode slowly, not knowing in which direction to go. Then, hearing shouts, he touched heels to Shorty and cantered, and suddenly came out of the fog and saw his father and Tim and Ross.

"There they are!" said McLaughlin, pointing down over the curve of the hill. They rode forward and Ken could see the yearlings standing bunched at the bottom, looking up, wondering who was coming. Then a huge coil of fog swirled over them and they were lost to sight again.

McLaughlin told them to circle around, spread out fanwise on the far side of the colts, and then gently bear down on them so they would start towards the ranch. If the colts once got running in this fog, he said, there'd be no chance of catching them.

The plan worked well; the yearlings were not so frisky as usual, and allowed themselves to be driven in the right direction. It was only when they were on the County Road, and near the gate where Howard was watching, that Ken, whose eyes had been scanning the bunch, as they appeared and disappeared in the fog, realized that Flicka was missing.

McLaughlin noticed it at the same moment, and as Ken rode toward his father, McLaughlin turned to him and said, "She's not in the bunch."

They sat in silence a few moments while McLaughlin planned the next step. The yearlings, dispirited by the fog, nibbled languidly at the grass by the roadside. McLaughlin looked at the Saddle Back and Ken looked too, the passionate desire in his heart reaching out to pierce the fog and the hillside and see where Flicka had hidden herself away. Had she been with the bunch when they first were found? Had she stolen away through the fog? Or hadn't she been there in the beginning? Had she run away from the ranch entirely, after her bad experience a week ago? Or—and this thought made his heart drop sickeningly —had she perhaps died of the hurts she had received when she broke out of the corral and was lying stark and riddled with ants and crawling things on the breast of one of those hills?

McLaughlin looked grim. "Lone wolf—like her mother," he said. "Never with the gang. I might have known it."

Ken remembered what the Colonel had said about the Lone Wolf type—it wasn't good to be that way.

"Well, we'll drive the yearlings back up," said Rob finally. "No chance of finding her alone. If they happen to pass anywhere near her, she's likely to join them."

They drove the yearlings back. Once over the first hill, the colts got running and soon were out of sight. The fog closed down again so that Ken pulled up, unable to see where he was going, unable to see his father, or Ross or Tim.

He sat listening, astonished that the sound of their hoofs had been wiped out so completely. Again he seemed alone in the world.

The fog lifted in front of him and showed him that he stood at the brink of a sharp drop, almost a precipice, though not very deep. It led down into a semicircular pocket on the hillside which was fed by a spring; there was a clump of young cottonwoods, and a great bank of clover dotted with small yellow blossoms.

In the midst of the clover stood Flicka, quietly feasting. She had seen him before he saw her and was watching him, her head up, clover sticking out of both sides of her mouth, her jaws going busily.

At sight of her, Ken was incapable of either thought or action.

Suddenly from behind him in the fog, he heard his father's low voice. "Don't move—"

"How'd she get in there?" said Tim.

"She scrambled down this bank. And she could scramble up again, if we weren't here. I think we've got her," said McLaughlin.

"Other side of that pocket the ground drops twenty feet sheer," said Tim. "She can't go down there."

Flicka had stopped chewing. There were still stalks of clover sticking out between her jaws, but her head was up and her ears pricked, listening, and there was a tautness and tension in her whole body.

Ken found himself trembling too.

"How're you going to catch her, Dad?" he asked in a low voice.

"I kin snag her from here," said Ross, and in the same breath McLaughlin answered, "Ross can rope her. Might as well rope her here as in the corral. We'll spread out in a semicircle above this bank. She can't get up past us, and she can't get down."

They took their postions and Ross lifted his rope off the horn of his saddle.

Ahead of them, far down below the pocket, the yearlings were running. A whinny or two drifted up, and the sound of their hoofs, muffled by the fog.

Flicka heard them too. Suddenly she was aware of danger. She leaped out of the clover to the edge of the precipice which fell away down the mountainside toward where the yearlings were running. But it was too steep and too high. She came straight up on her hind legs with a neigh of terror, and whirled back toward the bank down which she had slid to reach the pocket. But on the crest of it, looming uncannily in the fog, were four black figures—she screamed, and ran around the base of the bank.

Ken heard Ross's rope sing. It snaked out just as Flicka dove into the bank of clover. Stumbling, she went down and for a moment was lost to view.

"Goldarn—" said Ross, hauling in his rope, while Flicka floundered up and again circled her small prison, hurling herself at every point, only to realize that there was no way out.

She stood over the precipice, poised in despair and frantic longing. There drifted up the sound of the colts running below. Flicka trembled and strained over the brink—a perfect target for Ross, and he whirled his lariat again. It made a vicious whine.

Ken longed for the filly to escape the noose—yet he longed for her capture. Flicka reared up, her delicate forefeet beat the air, then she leaped out; and Ross's rope fell short again as McLaughlin said, "I expected that. She's like all the rest of them."

Flicka went down like a diver. She hit the ground, her legs folded under her, then rolled and bounced the rest of the way. It was exactly like the bronco that had climbed over the side of the truck and rolled down the forty-foot bank; and in silence the four watchers sat in their saddles waiting to see what would happen when she hit the bottom—Ken already thinking of the Winchester, and the way the crack of it had echoed back from the hills.

Flicka lit, it seemed, on four steel springs that tossed her up and sent her flying down the mountainside—perfection of speed and power and action. A hot sweat bathed Ken from head to foot, and he began to laugh, half choking—

The wind roared down and swept up the fog, and it went bounding away over the hills, leaving trailing streamers of white in the gullies, and coverlets of cotton around the bushes. Way below, they could see Flicka galloping toward the yearlings. In a moment she joined them, and then there was just a many colored blur of moving shapes, with a fierce sun blazing down, striking sparks of light off their glossy coats.

"Get going!" shouted McLaughlin. "Get around behind them. They're on the run now, and it's cleared—keep them running, and we may get them all in together, before they stop. Tim, you take the short way back to the gate and help Howard turn them and get them through."

Tim shot off toward the County Road and the other three riders galloped down and around the mountain until they were at the back of the band of yearlings. Shouting and yelling and spurring their mounts, they kept the colts running, circling them around toward the ranch until they had them on the County Road.

Way ahead, Ken could see Tim and Howard at the gate, blocking the road. The yearlings were bearing down on them. Now McLaughlin slowed up, and began to call, "Whoa, whoa—" and the pace decreased. Often enough the yearlings had swept down that road and through the gate and down to the corrals. It was the pathway to oats, and hay, and shelter from winter storms —would they take it now? Flicka was with them—right in the middle—if they went, would she go too?

It was all over almost before Ken could draw a breath. The yearlings turned at the gate, swept through, went down to the corrals on a dead run, and through the gates that Gus had opened.

Flicka was caught again.

Mindful that she had clawed her way out when she was corralled before, McLaughlin determined to keep her in the main corral into which the stable door opened. It had eight-foot walls of aspen poles. The rest of the yearlings must be maneuvered away from her.

Now that the fog had gone, the sun was scorching, and horses and men alike were soaked with sweat before the chasing was over and, one after the other, the yearlings had been driven into the other corral, and Flicka was alone.

She knew that her solitude meant danger, and that she was singled out for some special disaster. She ran frantically to the high fence through which she could see the other ponies standing, and reared and clawed at the poles; she screamed, whirled, circled the corral first in one direction, and then the other. And while McLaughlin and Ross were discussing the advisability of roping her, she suddenly espied the dark hole which was the open upper half of the stable door, and dove through it. McLaughlin rushed to close it, and she was caught—safely imprisoned in the stable.

The rest of the colts were driven away, and Ken stood outside the stable, listening to the wild hoofs beating, and the screams, the crashes. His Flicka within there—close at hand—imprisoned. He was shaking. He felt a desperate desire to quiet her somehow, to *tell her*. If she only knew how he loved her, that there was nothing to be afraid of, that they were going to be friends—

Ross shook his head with a one-sided grin. "Sure a wild one," he said, coiling his lariat.

"Plumb loco," said Tim briefly.

McLaughlin said, "We'll leave her to think it over. After dinner, we'll come up and feed and water her and do a little work with her."

But when they went up after dinner, there was no Flicka in the barn. One of the windows above the manger was broken, and the manger was full of pieces of glass.

Staring at it, McLaughlin gave a short laugh. He looked at Ken. "She climbed into the manger—see? Stood on the feed box, beat the glass out with her front hoofs and climbed through."

The window opened into the Six Foot Pasture. Near it was a wagonload of hay. When they went around the back of the stable to see where she had gone they found her between the stable and the hay wagon, eating.

At their approach, she leaped away, then headed east across the pasture.

"If she's like her mother," said Rob, "she'll go right through the wire."

"Ay bet she'll go over," said Gus. "She yumps like a deer."

"No horse can jump that," said McLaughlin.

Ken said nothing because he could not speak. It was the most terrible moment of his life. He watched Flicka racing toward the eastern wire.

A few yards from it, she swerved, turned and raced diagonally south.

"It turned her! it turned her!" cried Ken, almost sobbing. It was the first sign of hope for Flicka. "Oh, Dad, she has got sense, she has! She has!"

Flicka turned again as she met the southern boundary of the pasture, again at the northern; she avoided the barn. Without abating anything of her whirlwind speed, following a precise, accurate calculation, and turning each time on a dime, she investigated every possibility. Then, seeing that there was no hope, she raced south towards the range where she had spent her life, gathered herself, and rose to the impossible leap.

Each of the men watching had the impulse to cover his eyes, and Ken gave a howl of despair.

Twenty yards of fence came down with her as she hurled herself through. Caught on the upper strands, she turned a complete somersault, landing on her back, her four legs dragging the wires down on top of her, and tangling herself in them beyond hope of escape.

"Damn the wire!" cursed McLaughlin. "If I could afford decent fences—"

Ken followed the men miserably as they walked to the filly. They stood in a circle watching while she kicked and fought and thrashed until the wire was tightly wound and tangled about her, piercing and tearing her flesh and hide. At last she was unconscious, streams of blood running on her golden coat, and pools of crimson widening on the grass beneath her.

With the wire cutters which Gus always carried in the hip pocket of his overalls, he cut the wire away; and they drew her into the pasture, repaired the fence, placed hay, a box of oats, and a tub of water near her, and called it a day.

"I doubt if she pulls out of it," said McLaughlin briefly. "But it's just as well. If it hadn't been this way it would have been another. A loco horse isn't worth a damn."

THE HAPPY HORSE

LOREINE: A HORSE
by Arthur Davison Ficke

She lifted up her head
With the proud incredible poise
Of beauty recovered
From the Mycenaean tombs.

She opened her nostrils
With the wild arrogance
Of life that knows nothing
Except that it is life.

Her slender legs
Quivered above the soft grass.
Her hard hoofs
Danced among the dandelions.

Her great dark eyes
Saw all that could be seen.
Her large lips
Plucked at my coat sleeve.

All the wisdom of the prophets
Vanished into laughter
As Loreine lifted her small foot
And pawed the air.

All the learning of the sages
Turned to ribald rubrics
When that proud head
Looked at a passing cloud.

And so, amid this godless
God-hungry generation
Let us, my friends, take Loreine
And worship her.

She would demand nothing,
Nor would she utter thunders.
She is living, and real,
And she is beautiful.

THE HEROIC HORSE

THE HORSE WHO WOULD
NOT BE SCRATCHED
by James Holledge

The fisherman shivered in the winter's chill as he hurried along the lonely beach of Ireland's east coast in early 1904. Against the wild rocky shore mountainous green waves thundered ceaselessly. The fisherman could not recall a worse winter. For weeks on end he had not been able to get out in his boat. Almost daily, ships of every size were reported in trouble out there in the storm-whipped Irish Sea, separating England from Ireland.

Rounding a bend, the fisherman came upon a section of beach he rarely visited. At the water's edge he saw a strange object. From a distance it appeared to be a large barrel. Scenting a windfall, he broke into a run. His eyes opened wide when he got closer for the object was a horse, collapsed as though dead. Every line denoted a thoroughbred.

The fisherman bent close; a faint spark of life still remained. Immediately, he fetched feed and water. After much patient attention the cast-away horse finally rose shakily and permitted himself to be led to the fisherman's cottage and bedded down in an outbuilding. His rescuer kept him warm with blankets and a fire and the whole night through sat up tending him.

The fisherman had a theory. While he watched over the sleeping horse, he composed a letter to British turf authorities suggesting someone from the Jockey Club be sent to have a look. He had convinced himself (for the markings and color were the same) that he had rescued the great Australian steeplechaser, Moifaa.

In a newspaper he had received in the last mail, the fisherman had read that a steamer bound from an Australian port to Liverpool had run into a violent storm off the Irish coast a few days before. Moifaa, who had been traveling in a box on deck, had been washed overboard and drowned. An impossible rescue, the fisherman realized, for it would mean that Moifaa had not only managed to free himself from the box as it slammed about the raging Irish sea, but that he had then swum—or bent swept—the nearly 100 miles from the spot where he had been lost overboard to this beach.

Moifaa's owner, Australian sportsman Spencer Gollan, was notified by the English Jockey Club of the fisherman's letter. Gollan could not believe the rescued horse was his, but just the same, he set out for Ireland.

Nearly two weeks had passed, but the horse was still very weak and sick. He was hardly able to stand; yet when Gollan touched him, he whinnied a friendly little welcome. "Moifaa, it is," declared Gollan.

A veterinary was called. He said Moifaa would recover; but the feat of survival had taken a heavy toll. Neither Gollan nor vet even considered Moifaa could run in the coming Grand National Steeplechase, for which he had traveled 12,000 miles. Their only hope was that he could be saved for stud purposes. Accordingly, Moifaa was shipped to Spencer Gollan's stables at Aintree.

The English Grand National is conducted annually at Aintree Racecourse near Liverpool. It is a turf marathon of more than four miles, over 30 jumps. Since its inception in 1839, it has been acknowledged as the toughest test in the world for horses and riders.

In March of 1904, on the day of the race, A. Birch, the stable jockey, approached Spencer Gollan. Birch pointed to Moifaa who,

THE JOCKEY. Edgar Degas. *Courtesy, Philadelphia Museum of Art: The Wilstach Collection.*

in his stall, was bright-eyed and restless with prerace excitement. Racing blood was telling. Apparently Moifaa knew what was afoot and that he should soon be saddling up.

Birch reminded Gollan that through an oversight Moifaa had not been scratched from the Grand National. Then he blurted out: "Why not give Moifaa a run? It could do no harm, as he could be pulled up after a short distance."

Gollan's first reaction was ridicule. Racing a crock who had been nearly dead only weeks before! Moifaa's trainer, however, sided with Jockey Birch. He revealed that he'd given Moifaa a short trial that very morning and Moifaa had galloped smoothly enough.

So Spencer Gollan acquiesced, but more as a sporting gesture and to see his colors carried. At post time, Moifaa trotted to the start and as soon as the vast crowd caught a glimpse of him, a roar went up: tribute to his magnificent endurance and gallantry. No one imagined he could possibly figure in the finish.

The starter sent the field away. Moifaa, back with the tail-enders, went at little more than a canter. At the first fence, he appeared to falter, but Jockey Birch bent low with a reassuring whisper and pat. The leap was all blunder and scramble and Moifaa nearly toppled. On the other side, though, he stayed on his feet somehow and set off for the next obstacle, which, now that he was more certain, he cleared creditably. Birch (who later confessed he'd been on the verge of pulling up) decided to let Moifaa run his own pace for a few furlongs.

Almost immediately, Moifaa seemed to regain his old brilliance. He galloped in effortless style. Fences that stopped horses all around him he cleared now as if he were a sort of soaring machine.

They entered the straight. Moifaa took on the leaders. From the spectators came shouts of amazement as they recognized this dangerous challenger flashing up on the outside. Then, roars of admiration as Moifaa crept past the front runners, one by one; then he swept past the post, the winner of the 1904 Grand National and the object of an ovation seldom equalled on any racecourse.

No one was more impressed with Moifaa's fantastic performance than King Edward VII. He approached Spencer Gollan and offered to purchase Moifaa. Gollan was not eager to sell but a King is not be denied. So Moifaa changed hands for 2,000 guineas.

The next year, wearing the royal colors, Moifaa started favorite in the Grand National. The first time around he led the field but then crashed heavily at notorious Becher's Brook and was out of it.

Edward VII immediately retired Moifaa and, thereafter, used him as his own personal mount at ceremonial parades.

When Edward died in 1910, Moifaa, with empty saddle, was in the funeral procession, immediately behind the gun carriage upon which rested the body of his last master.

THE DESERTED HORSE

CHAMPIONS OF THE PEAKS
by Paul Annixter

Slipstream, he was called—Slippy for short—and he'd been named for his speed. He was only a two-year-old, but already the pride of High Ranch. Someday, Jesse Hunnicutt believed, Slippy would be as good as any of the champion polo ponies he had raised.

There was nothing really bad about Slippy. He was just too full of ideas and pranks which walled him off from serious training. Let a day dawn when a visiting buyer was to appear and Slippy would disappear up the mountain.

It was old Sounder, the ranch dog, who had really gotten Slippy into the habit of these disappearances. He was the special property of young Jesse, who was fifteen, and old Jesse's only son. Sounder had a seamed and melancholy face, big bones, great lubberly paws, and the heart of a lion. Sounder spent a great share of his days on the heights, tracking rabbit, fox, or wildcat.

Slippy had met Sounder one day in spring far up among the piñon pines. They had smelled noses and each had belonged specially to the other from there on in. They had met often after that, up there in the peaks, far from the sounds and scents of the ranch. Sometimes, the pair would remain away for two days and two nights; Slippy feeding and rolling in some cup between the peaks where the grass grew lush all summer, Sounder digging for marmots on a nearby slope or tracking rabbits in the brush, till darkness brought them close together. Great days for them both.

With Sounder to lead the way, the long wanderings among the crags were an endless adventure. At such times, not even young Jesse or old Jesse himself could get near the two when they happened to sight them among the peaks.

So it was on the November day in question. For some time knife-edged blasts of wind had warned of bad weather close at hand. But Jesse Hunnicutt had decided to stay at High Ranch till snow actually fell. Then one morning the ranch hands awoke at dawn with a norther sobbing through the cracks and chinks of the bunkhouse and a sting of sleet in the air. Dark clouds hung low over the peaks and the valleys were lost in a smudgy haze. There was not an hour to spare if they expected to get stock and equipment to the lowlands in time to escape the oncoming blizzard.

Slippy and Sounder were missing again. Both had been away overnight. Within an hour gear and stock were ready to move, and still no sign of the runaways. Grudgingly Jesse gave the order to leave, but he rode up-trail for one last look for Slipstream. Young Jesse followed.

For nearly an hour the two searched and called into the teeth of the wind, but to no avail. Slippy and Sounder were far up the mountain at the time. Old Jesse hated to abandon the search. When he turned his mount down-trail that day he never expected to see Slipstream alive again, though he hid the fact from his son.

"We'll come back when the weather breaks and look for them again, Son," he said. "Old Sounder'll come through, never fear. But we've got to go now, or we'll never get down the mountain."

When the storm broke shortly before dawn, Slipstream was sheltered in a high spruce grove where he had spent a chilly and restless night. Sounder was afar, engaged in his endless game of digging out mountain marmots, and now and then chasing after snowshoe rabbits. Slippy could hear him from time to time, sounding his hoarse bell-like hunting cry.

By the time the sleet had turned to driving snow, Sounder gave up his splendid game and sought his friend among the trees. When morning came with the storm increasing, uneasiness began to ride the pair. What feeding there was had already been covered with snow. Slippy's thoughts turned to the warmth and security of the great barns at High Ranch. He had had enough for a time of this fodderless freedom. So, too, had Sounder. But when their steps turned down-trail and they emerged from the shelter of the spruce, they were almost swept from their feet by the gale. In places the snow was already belly-deep on Sounder.

Sounder and Slipstream pressed on, heads bent to the blast. Trails were gone. Only their sure feet and their wild instincts kept them to the right way. On the steep slopes they slipped and scrambled, then picked a slow course along a mile of rock ledges that pinched off into space. Later it was an even greater battle bucking through the drifts of the sheltered places.

It was far past midday when they sighted the ranch buildings and Sounder experienced one of his first great shocks. The ranch was deserted. Not a trace of smoke rose from the ranchhouse chimneys. There were not even any fresh tracks to show which way the men had gone.

Behind the summer lean-to the two took refuge. There Slippy found a few wisps of hay and straw in the long feed trough. Still others he uncovered by pawing the snowy ground underneath. Somewhat heartened by these signs of man he settled down, eyes half closed, sensitive ears atwitch, to await the ranchers' return. But Sounder had no such illusions. He prowled forlornly, whining with a growing unrest.

All that day the storm continued. Slippy finished every last sprig of hay in the lean-to. As the darkness of another night descended on the mountain wilderness, he lifted his voice in sharp neighs. But no one came.

Through the dark hours the two runaways huddled together for warmth. When another day dawned with no lessening of the storm, loneliness and growing fear gripped Slippy. All that day the two waited and shivered in a world filled with storm, cold, and misery. But no one came. Through a second stormy night they pressed together for very life's sake, their coats covered with a thickening layer of frost and snow.

By noon of the third day the storm had died down. Sounder set off down the mountain, where he knew the ranch hands had gone. Slippy fell in behind him. The snow by now had piled belly-high on the horse and in two hours the pair progressed scarcely a mile, with the going harder every yard. Twice Slippy almost pitched over the sheer cliffs; at last he turned back up the trail. Sounder followed him.

When hunger drove them forth from the lean-to again, it was up the mountain instead of down, for on the heights the snow was far less deep. In places the ridges were swept almost bare by the force of the wind. Up along the sparse spruce valleys they plodded, Slippy finding here and there some uncovered forage,

and chewing many evergreen twigs for good measure. Sounder
ran rabbits through the thickets.

Later that afternoon Slippy came upon a small herd of deer
banded together in a winter "yard." Moved by an urge for companionship, he moved forward eagerly to join them. But the two
leading bucks of the herd shook menacing heads.

Slippy was too forlorn and miserable to care what the deer
thought of him. Even ill feeling was better than the empty loneliness of the peaks. He waited meekly, some fifty paces away, to
see what would happen.

The snow roundabout was too deep for the deer to flee their
yard. So the bucks contented themselves with stampings and repeated challenges. But Slippy had a disarming way of his own.
He ruckled softly in his chest, and after an hour or so his quiet
presence broke down resistance. The deer resumed their sketchy
feeding, nibbling at the hanging branches of the trees and pawing down to the sparse feeding beneath the snow.

Later, when Sounder came in from a successful hunt, the
deer were thrown into fresh panic. In fall or summer the deer
would have fled like shadows and Sounder would have given
chase. Now he came up meek and silent as Slippy himself and
dropped panting beside his friend. Before long even his presence
was accepted by the deer, for a magic truce had descended upon
all.

By the time darkness came, horse and dog were learning that
shelter and warmth lies in snow when one is wise enough to
burrow into it.

Each of the next four days they visited the ranch house, returning to the heights in the afternoon. Then on the fourth day
they returned to find their wild friends had moved. The feeding
had given out in the vicinity of the yard, and the deer had left.

Slippy followed along their trail, laboring slowly through
the deep snow. He came upon the herd again a half-mile away,
tramping out a new yard which was to become a tragic prison
for all of them. A thaw the next day was followed by another
snowstorm. The high walls of the deer yard froze to the hardness
of concrete, forming a prison from which there was no escape
until another thaw.

Only Slippy's restlessness, and his urge to find his human friends saved him from sharing the fate of the deer. He was keeping watch again at the ranch house when the freeze came. When he labored back to the deer yard he was unable to join his friends as usual. An iron crust had formed over the snow, and the pony stood nearly seven feet above the yard, looking dejectedly down on his imprisoned friends.

After four days, the feeding in the yard was consumed and the deer grew leaner and leaner, until the does and younglings were so weak they could hardly stand. Still no thaw came to free them.

The slow drama ended in tragedy one night when a mountain lion discovered the starving herd.

What followed was swifter and more merciful than starvation. Death came to them all, in their prison of ice.

Slippy, growing woodswise and wary, was warned of the menace that threatened. A faint rank smell had come creeping into his consciousness, the musty reek of mountain lion. He knew it though he had never scented it before. That smell meant death. It sent him scrambling wildly out of the woods and onto a cleared slope just above.

Two days later Slippy and Sounder returned to find what was left of their friends, the deer. They did not wait for any chance encounter with the cougar. Keeping close together, they left that part of the mountain far behind and climbed toward the frozen peaks of the Divide. Now, because of the cougar, they avoided the dense timber for the rest of that day and therefore went hungry. And to add to their misery, another snowstorm started toward nightfall.

It was morning of the third day, with Sounder hunting far below, when Slippy rounded an outcrop of rock high above timber line and had the surprise of his life. A dozen or more fleecy hummocks of snow suddenly came to life about a hundred feet ahead of him.

Slippy was staring at his first band of mountain goats. One of them, the biggest, with pale fierce eyes, had a long, frosted white beard and black horns curling above his head. He snoofed explosively in challenge while the others melted away behind him.

The goats, fifteen of them, fled up over the rims as Slippy

moved forward, but they could not go far because of the drifted snow. Slippy pressed on, disregarding the loud snoofing challenges of the old leader, who sought to engage Slippy in combat. But it takes two to make any sort of battle. Finally the old billy subsided into an occasional angry snorting and stamping.

When Sounder approached in search of his friend, the whole goat band disappeared like magic beyond a peak. Slippy thought he had lost them for good. But next morning he found them again.

When the band moved, Slippy followed silently, edging closer by degrees. When they uncovered the short cured grass of the heights and ate, he also ate and found it good. The goats began to look upon him as a friendly, harmless creature. By the third day Slippy was suffered to feed and bed at will on the edge of the band during the daytime hours when Sounder was hunting afar. But the dog they would not accept.

At night cold Sounder always found Slippy, and the two slept together out of the wind. But by day Slippy continued to follow the goats. He found their feeding lean, but it kept life in his body.

In the second week the goat leader led the band along a series of narrow ledges to the distant peaks. Slippy's small, trim hoofs were becoming almost as sure as those of the goats themselves. Acrobatic feats, however, were beyond him. The narrow ledge the band had been following pinched sharply off into space. But ten feet below it a two-foot chunk of rock protruded from the face of the cliff. The old goat leaped for it, balanced a moment, then dropped to another still farther on, and thence to another narrow ledge beyond. One by one the rest of the goats followed.

Slippy stood at the end of the ledge looking miserably after them. He could not follow, or even turn around. Misery seized upon him and he lifted his voice in a protesting neigh. The goats paid no heed. Already they were out of sight.

There was but one thing to do. Cautiously, feeling for each foothold, Slippy began backing along the ledge down which he had come. There were four hundred yards of that before he reached a spot where he could turn. Up over the rims he went by a roundabout way, but the goats were nowhere in sight.

For ten days thereafter Slippy wandered the heights, miserably searching for his friends along all the streets and avenues of the high goat cities. And each day two bald eagles sailed close, waiting for some mischance to strike him down. But Slippy was doing the unbelievable—meeting and beating the winter wild.

A fighting spirit had awakened in him. His clever brain, that had formerly made up small tricks of mischief, now worked for self-protection. He had profited by all the object lessons of the deer and goats, and added observations of his own. The fierce winds of the heights, he knew, would uncover enough feeding to keep life in his body. At night he kept from freezing to death by huddling close to Sounder on the sheltered side of the peaks.

Sounder, too, was doing the unbelievable. Wolfish instincts told him how to consume snow for water, how to tell from afar when a deep snowbank held sleeping partridge, and how to dig out wood mice when all other food failed. He grew lean and gaunt, but he survived.

A third week went by and January came, bringing with it a cold unlike anything Slippy had yet known. He still searched the heights for his friends, and one afternoon he sighted a number of white specks against a far-off cliff. A valley lay between, but Slippy descended clear to timber line, bucked the deep drifts, and labored grimly up. Before nightfall he had come up with the goat band.

January was a terrible month. Storm after storm swept the heights. From the forested valleys below the hunger call of wolves and coyotes sounded nightly. Sometimes the whining scream of a cougar split the breeze. Even the wild goats began to feel the pinch of hunger, for the snows were such that the highest peaks became mantled with white.

Now came the time of greatest peril. Hunting in the valleys grew lean and the mountain lions sought the peaks for meat. The broad pads of these killers held them up on the deep snow where the sharp hoofs of the goats cut through. The cougars would prowl until they found some point where the goats would have to pass. Lying in wait until the band approached, a lion would drop like a bolt from some overhanging rock, and one of the band would pay with its life.

After each attack by a lion the goats would take refuge for days among the rim rocks. But when hunger drove them down again the killers would again hang to their trail. By the end of January, five of the original fifteen goats had been killed.

Slippy came through that grim month partly because he was

always at the tail end of the file of goats, and partly because the lions were suspicious of him. They associated him and his scent with man, their greatest enemy. The old leader of the goats also escaped attack. He would have welcomed facing a lion in fair combat. But the killers were cowards at heart, and had no stomach for tackling a four-hundred-pound fighting machine.

February came. The deep snows still made hunting in the lower forests impossible for the cougars and the contest between the goats and the great cats came to a dramatic head. For weeks the goats had been growing warier and warier. For a fortnight they had lived on the leanest fare in order to avoid every possible ambush.

At last, the lions, driven by unbearable hunger, brought the battle to the old goat leader.

Slippy and Sounder were some five hundred feet below the band this night. All were bedded near the brink of a broad, open ledge, where no enemy could possibly approach without first appearing boldly in the open. It was that hour before the dawn when night hunters that have found no kill turn desperate.

A breeze carried the scent of lion to the old leading goat. He had the band on their feet in an instant. Then, after long minutes, a mountain lion showed among the rocks of the distant cliff, another close behind. This was the pair that had ravaged the peaks all winter. Beyond all caution now, they advanced, green-eyed with hunger.

The goats backed to the brink of the ledge. Minutes of waiting passed. The lions flattened themselves to the snow, advancing but a few inches at a time. Never before had they carried the war into the open like this. The big muscles of their shoulders bulged above their gaunt, crouched bodies.

Slippy, standing five hundred feet downslope, was trembling faintly. Weakened by cold and hunger, he wanted only to sink down in the snow; wanted only to creep away and sleep. But the lions came on—so steadily that they seemed not to move at all, save for their long tails that twitched like snakes.

Even old Sounder seemed to have no battle challenge in him this night. For once he made no sound, but merely got to his feet.

The foremost lion launched himself forward in an attempt to pass the old leader's guard. But the bulky goat, agile as any kid, reared and whirled on his hind legs with a bawl of defiance.

CHEVAL SAUVAGE TERRASSÉ PAR UN TIGRE. Eugène Delacroix. *Courtesy, The Metropolitan Museum of Art: Rogers Fund, 1922.*

A lightning thrust of his crinkly black horns caught the killer in midair. The lion was jerked to one side as if by invisible wires. Almost in the instant he alighted he returned to the attack. The *wheep-wheep* of his great mailed paws tore patches from the old goat's white coat but, wheeling and pivoting with flashing horns, the leader still managed to block the lion at every turn.

Back to the very brink of the ledge they moved, till another step would have pitched them both over. Still the cougar was unable to break through to the huddled kids and nannies behind.

Then, help came flying in a shaggy wolfish form. Old Sounder, who might have crept away unnoticed, had hesitated but a brief minute. Straight into the face of the cougar he launched his hundred fighting pounds. What followed was a storm of tawny arms and legs and flying snow, amid screams and growls and the white flash of fang and claw.

The lion's mate, meanwhile, had been circling the rocks to come in from the opposite side and make a swift kill while the old goat was engaged. But no opening offered. Instead, there stood Slippy in her way, a chunky, sorrel-colored horse trembling to every limb but with white teeth bared, hoofs dancing, nostrils ruckling in a frenzy of fear. Even as Sounder attacked, the lioness sprang from haunches like coiled springs. Slippy moved in the same instant. He pivoted and powerful hind legs shot out, catching the lioness a glancing blow on the shoulder.

With a fiendish squall the big cat struck the snow, then bounded to the pony's back, her four sets of claws sinking deep. Slippy staggered, pitched to his nose but struggled up again.

The mailed paw of the lioness crooked beneath Slippy's neck and wrenched cunningly. Her custom was to kill by dislocation. Slippy bucked like a demon. His blunt teeth caught one silky ear of the attacker and ground it into a bleeding rag. The lioness screamed with rage and sprang free—unable, like all cats, to stand pain. She crouched for another spring, close to the lip of the ledge, as Slippy wheeled with a desperate whinny. In that instant old Sounder was beside him. Somehow the dog had broken free of the lion and come to the aid of his friend.

Sounder sprang in with a roar; the lioness struck and sprang aside. Once more, terrible and avenging, Slippy swung around to deliver a broadside kick with his powerful hind legs. It landed squarely against the big cat's ribs, flinging her back. She teetered a moment on the very brink, her claws rasping on the ice and snow, and Slippy kicked again. The tawny body slipped and pitched downward.

The male lion, circling the old goat, turned his head at the death cry of his mate. It was only an instant, but for the goat it was enough. He drove in with a mighty thrust of lowered horns that rolled the killer over. Before he found his feet, the old goat hit him again, while from the opposite side old Sounder was closing in.

It was too much for the lion. Before either opponent could reach him again, the killer of the peaks was streaking, belly down, for the shelter of the cliffs.

Old Sounder was wounded far more seriously than he knew. Torn and red and hardly recognizable, he collapsed presently on his side, his blood staining the snow. He gave but a few feeble thumps of his tail when Slippy came and stood above him.

It was two hours before his fevered wounds stopped bleeding. All that day Slippy stayed close to his friend.

That victory over the cougars seemed a winning over famine

and the winter hardships as well, for at nightfall there came an abrupt break in the weather.

Before morning the snowy slopes were melting in a thousand tiny rivulets and through the silence sounded the occasional long, sucking *chug* of sinking snow. Mountain and forest seemed to relax and breathe again. There might come other freezes, but the worst of the winter was now over.

Meanwhile Sounder was fighting with the last supreme Enemy, and barely holding his own. Somehow Slippy seemed to know. By gentle nudges of his warm, inquiring nose, he kept rousing the old dog from his coma of pain and fever, urging him to follow down the mountain to the ranch house. Again and again through that long day the dog would rise on shaky legs and follow Slippy for a hundred and fifty yards, only to sink down again and rest until strength was renewed.

Night had fallen when they reached the ranch. All was deserted still, but the corrals and pastures were almost free of snow and the breeze was warm. Stretched out on the ranch porch, Sounder let the old familiar scents and sounds slide through his ears and nose. His heart took strength and the shadowy Enemy faded away, defeated.

It was about noon next day, as the goat band fed slowly along the snowline above the ranch, that something startled them into sudden flight. Slippy saw them go and flung up his head, then wheeled at the old familiar sound of human voices.

Jesse Hunnicut, with Jake Marden and young Jesse behind him, had just rounded a bend in the valley trail. At sight of Slippy, all three spurred forward with whoops and yells.

And Slippy? Flinging up his head with a wild whinny, he sprang from complete rest to full speed in a single shutter-click of time. Down the length of the great pasture he thundered to meet his friends, running with all that was in him. To the watching men his flying hoofs seemed never to strike the ground.

The riders reined in to gape, sitting their horses as though struck in stone. On he came, until he was eight feet in front of the horsemen. In the final instant before head-on collision, Slippy jerked aside with no slackening of speed, then swept round and round them in great wild circles, whinnying again and again with happiness.

Jesse Hunnicutt was muttering as he watched. "Look at

him, just look at him!" he cried. "There's an antelope and a grey-hound rolled up in him—to say nothin' of a cannon ball! And that legwork! And to think I left him for dead!"

They waited until Slippy had worked off some of his steam and joy and come to a stand. Then Jesse Hunnicutt dismounted, while young Jesse spurred toward the ranch house to look for his dog. The rancher was aware of a vague but definite shame as he approached the game little horse. He was guilty, as he saw it now, of desertion, Slippy's mane was a gnarled and matted mass from the winter winds; his lean sides were no longer sleek, but woolly as a range horse's—nature's desperate effort to help ward off the cold. The man's eye picked out the wounds along his back.

"Cougars, Boss!" cried Jake Marden. "The pore little cuss! I reckon he saw a thing or two besides cold and hunger up there among the peaks!"

Jesse put a hand on Slippy's sturdy neck, then bent to run exploring, unbelieving fingers over the solid chest and hocks and pasterns. Never had he dreamed of seeing a two-year-old in such superb condition. In spite of cougars and cold, winter and hunger, or perhaps because of them, he was looking at a champion.

For a space, man and horse stood gazing at each other across the great gulf of silence that hangs forever between the human and animal world. Had Slippy been human the gulf might never have been spanned after what had happened in the fall. But being animal, he bent his head to rub it lovingly against the man's sleeve. It was enough for him that the voices of his human friends once more fell blessedly on his ears.

Up at the ranch house old Sounder, too, had rubbed away that gulf as if it had never been, and young Jesse was kneeling on the porch steps, his arms full of his old dog.

THE INVINCIBLE HORSE

THE BLOOD HORSE
by Bryan Waller Procter

Gamarra is a dainty steed,
Strong, black, and of a noble breed,
Full of fire, and full of bone,
With all his line of fathers known;
Fine his nose, his nostrils thin,
But blown abroad by the pride within!
His mane is like a river flowing,
And his eyes like embers glowing
In the darkness of the night,
And his pace as swift as light.

Look—how 'round his straining throat
Grace and shifting beauty float!
Sinewy strength is on his reins,
And the red blood gallops through his veins;
Richer, redder, never ran
Through the boasting heart of man.
He can trace his lineage higher
Than the Bourbon dare aspire—
Douglas, Guzman, or the Guelph,
Or O'Brien's blood itself!

He, who hath no peer, was born
Here, upon a red March morn:
But his famous fathers dead
Were Arabs all, and Arab bred,
And the last of that great line
Trod like one of a race divine!

And yet—he was but friend to one
Who fed him at the set of sun,
By some lone fountain fringed with green:
With him, a roving Bedouin,
He liv'd—(none else would he obey
Through all the hot Arabian day)—
And died untam'd upon the sands
Where Balkh amidst the desert stands!

THE UNLOVING HORSE

CHU CHU
by Bret Harte

I do not believe that the most enthusiastic lover of that "useful and noble animal," the horse, will claim for him the charm of geniality, humor, or expansive confidence. Any creature who will not look you squarely in the eye—whose only oblique glances are inspired by fear, distrust, or a view to attack; who has no way of returning caresses, and whose favorite expression is one of head-lifting disdain, may be "noble" or "useful," but can be hardly said to add to the gaiety of nations. Indeed it may be broadly stated that, with the single exception of goldfish, of all animals kept for the recreation of mankind the horse is alone capable of exciting a passion that shall be absolutely hopeless. I deem these general remarks necessary to prove that my unreciprocated affection for Chu Chu was not purely individual or singular. And I may add that to these general characteristics she brought the waywardness of her capricious sex.

She came to me out of the rolling dust of an emigrant wagon, behind whose tailboard she was gravely trotting. She was a half-broken colt—in which character she had at different times unseated everybody in the train—and, although covered with dust, she had a beautiful coat, and the most lambent gazelle-like eyes I had ever seen. I think she kept these latter organs purely for ornament—apparently looking at things with her nose, her sensitive ears, and, sometimes, even a slight lifting of her slim near foreleg. On our first interview I thought she favored me with a coy glance, but as it was accompanied by an irrelevant "Look out!" from her owner, the teamster, I was not certain. I only know that after some conversation, a good deal of mental reservation, and the disbursement of considerable coin, I found myself standing in the dust of the departing emigrant wagon with one end of a forty-foot riata in my hand, and Chu Chu at the other.

I pulled invitingly at my own end, and even advanced a step or two toward her. She then broke into a long disdainful pace, and began to circle round me at the extreme limit of her tether. I stood admiring her free action for some moments—not always turning with her, which was tiring—until I found that she was gradually winding herself up *on me!* Her frantic astonishment when she suddenly found herself thus brought up against me was one of the most remarkable things I ever saw, and nearly took me off my legs. Then, when she had pulled against the riata until her narrow head and prettily arched neck were on a perfectly straight line with it, she as suddenly slackened the tension and condescended to follow me, at an angle of her own choosing. Sometimes it was on one side of me, sometimes on the other. Even then the sense of my dreadful contiguity apparently would come upon her like a fresh discovery, and she would become hysterical. But I do not think that she really *saw* me. She looked at the riata and sniffed it disparagingly; she pawed some pebbles that were near me tentatively with her small hoof; she started back with a Robinson Crusoe-like horror of my footprints in the wet gully, but my actual personal presence she ignored. She would sometimes pause, with her head thoughtfully between her forelegs, and apparently say: "There is some extraordinary presence here: animal, vegetable, or mineral—I can't make out which—but it's not good to eat, and I loathe and detest it."

When I reached my house in the suburbs, before entering the "fifty vara" lot enclosure, I deemed it prudent to leave her outside while I informed the household of my purchase; and with this object I tethered her by the long riata to a solitary sycamore which stood in the center of the road, the crossing of two fre-

quented thoroughfares. It was not long, however, before I was
interrupted by shouts and screams from that vicinity, and on
returning thither I found that Chu Chu, with the assistance of
her riata, had securely wound up two of my neighbors to the
tree, where they presented the appearance of early Christian
martyrs. When I released them it appeared that they had been
attracted by Chu Chu's graces, and had offered her overtures of
affection, to which she had characteristically rotated with this
miserable result. I led her, with some difficulty, warily keeping
clear of the riata, to the enclosure, from whose fence I had previously removed several bars. Although the space was wide
enough to have admitted a troop of cavalry she affected not to
notice it, and managed to kick away part of another section on
entering. She resisted the stable for some time, but after carefully examining it with her hoofs, and an affectedly meek out-
stretching of her nose, she consented to recognize some oats in
the feedbox—without looking at them—and was formally installed. All this while she had resolutely ignored my presence. As
I stood watching her she suddenly stopped eating; the same reflective look came over her. "Surely I am not mistaken, but that
same obnoxious creature is somewhere about here!" she seemed to
say, and shivered at the possibility.

It was probably this which made me confide my unreciprocated affection to one of my neighbors—a man supposed to be
an authority on horses, and particularly of that wild species to
which Chu Chu belonged. It was he who, leaning over the edge
of the stall where she was complacently and, as usual, obliviously
munching, absolutely dared to toy with a pet lock of hair which
she wore over the pretty star on her forehead.

"Ye see, captain," he said, with jaunty easiness, "hosses is
like wimmen; ye don't want ter use any standoffishness or shyness
with *them;* a stiddy but keerless sort o' familiarity, a kind o' free
but firm handlin', jess like this, to let her see who's master—"

We never clearly knew *how* it happened; but when I picked
up my neighbor from the doorway, amid the broken splinters of
the stall rail, and a quantity of oats that mysteriously filled his
hair and pockets, Chu Chu was found to have faced around the
other way, and was contemplating her forelegs, with her hind
ones in the other stall. My neighbor spoke of damages while he
was in the stall, and of physical coercion when he was out of it

again. But here Chu Chu, in some marvelous way, righted herself, and my neighbor departed hurriedly with a brimless hat and an unfinished sentence.

My next intermediary was Enriquez Saltello—a youth of my own age, and the brother of Consuelo Saltello, whom I adored. As a Spanish Californian he was presumed, on account of Chu Chu's half-Spanish origin, to have superior knowledge of her character, and I even vaguely believed that his language and accent would fall familiarly on her ear. There was the drawback, however, that he always preferred to talk in a marvelous English, combining Castilian precision with what he fondly believed to be Californian slang.

"To confer then as to thees horse, which is not—observe me —a Mexican plug! Ah, no! you can your boots bet on that. She is of Castilian stock—believe me and strike me dead! I will myself at different times overlook and affront her in the stable, examine her as to the assault, and why she should do thees thing. When she is of the exercise I will also accost and restrain her. Remain tranquil, my friend! When a few days shall pass much shall be changed, and she will be as another. Trust your oncle to do thees thing! Comprehend me? Everything shall be lovely, and the goose hang high!"

Conformably with this he "overlooked" her the next day, with a cigarette between his yellow-stained fingertips, which made her sneeze in a silent pantomimic way, and certain Spanish blandishments of speech which she received with more complacency. But I don't think she even looked at him. In vain he protested that she was the "dearest" and "littlest" of his "little loves"—in vain he asserted that she was his patron saint, and that it was his soul's delight to pray to her; she accepted the compliment with her eyes fixed upon the manger. When he had exhausted his whole stock of endearing diminutives, adding a few playful and more audacious sallies, she remained with her head down, as if inclined to meditate upon them. This he declared was at least an improvement on her former performances. It may have been my own jealousy, but I fancied she was only saying to herself, "Gracious! can there be *two* of them?"

"Courage and patience, my friend," he said, as we were slowly quitting the stable. "Thees horse is yonge, and has not yet the habitude of the person. Tomorrow, at another season, I shall give to her a foundling" ("fondling," I have reason to believe, was the word intended by Enriquez)—"and we shall see. It shall be as easy as to fall away from a log. A leetle more of this chin music which your friend Enriquez possesses, and some tapping of the head and neck, and you are there. You are ever the right side up. Houp la! But let us not precipitate this thing. The more haste, we do not so much accelerate ourselves."

He appeared to be suiting the action to the word as he lingered in the doorway of the stable. "Come on," I said.

"Pardon," he returned, with a bow that was both elaborate and evasive, "but you shall yourself precede me—the stable is *yours*."

"Oh, come along!" I continued impatiently. To my surprise he seemed to dodge back into the stable again. After an instant he reappeared.

"Pardon! but I am restrain! Of a truth, in this instant I am grasp by the mouth of thees horse in the coattail of my dress! She will that I should remain. It would seem"—he disappeared again—"that"—he was out once more—"the experiment is a sooccess! She reciprocate! She is, of a truth, gone on me. It is lofe!" —a stronger pull from Chu Chu here sent him in again—"but"— he was out now triumphantly with half his garment torn away —"I shall coquet."

Nothing daunted, however, the gallant fellow was back next day with a Mexican saddle, and attired in the complete outfit of a vaquero. Overcome though *he* was by heavy deerskin trousers, open at the side from the knees down, and fringed with bullion buttons, an enormous flat sombrero, and a stiff, short embroidered velvet jacket, I was more concerned at the ponderous saddle and equipments intended for the slim Chu Chu. That these would hide and conceal her beautiful curves and contour, as well as overweight her, seemed certain; that she would resist them all to the last seemed equally clear. Nevertheless, to my surprise, when she was led out, and the saddle thrown deftly across her back, she was passive. Was it possible that some drop of her old Spanish blood responded to its clinging embrace? She did not either look at it or smell it. But when Enriquez began to tighten the cinch or girth a more singular thing occurred. Chu Chu visibly distended her slender barrel to twice its dimensions; the more he pulled the more she swelled, until I was actually ashamed of her. Not so Enriquez. He smiled at us, and complacently stroked his thin mustache.

"Eet is ever so! She is the child of her grandmother! Even when you shall make saddle thees old Castilian stock, it will make large—it will become a balloon! Eet is a trick—eet is a leetle game—believe me. For why?"

I had not listened, as I was at that moment astonished to see the saddle slowly slide under Chu Chu's belly, and her figure resume, as if by magic, its former slim proportions. Enriquez followed my eyes, lifted his shoulders, shrugged them, and said smilingly, "Ah, you see!"

When the girths were drawn in again with an extra pull or two from the indefatigable Enriquez, I fancied that Chu Chu nevertheless secretly enjoyed it, as her sex is said to appreciate tight lacing. She drew a deep sigh, possibly of satisfaction, turned her neck, and apparently tried to glance at her own figure—Enriquez promptly withdrawing to enable her to do so easily. Then the dread moment arrived. Enriquez, with his hand on her mane, suddenly paused and, with exaggerated courtesy, lifted his hat and made an inviting gesture.

"You will honor me to precede."

I shook my head laughingly.

"I see," responded Enriquez gravely. "You have to attend the obsequies of your aunt who is dèad, at two of the clock. You have to meet your broker who has bought you feefty share of the Comstock lode—at thees moment—or you are loss! You are excuse! Attend! Gentlemen, make your bets! The band has arrived to play! 'Ere we are!"

With a quick movement the alert young fellow had vaulted into the saddle. But, to the astonishment of both of us, the mare remained perfectly still. There was Enriquez bolt upright in the stirrups, completely overshadowing by his saddle-flaps, leggings, and gigantic spurs the fine proportions of Chu Chu, until she might have been a placid Rosinante, bestridden by some youthful Quixote. She closed her eyes, she was going to sleep! We were dreadfully disappointed. This clearly would not do. Enriquez lifted the reins cautiously! Chu Chu moved forward slowly—then stopped, apparently lost in reflection.

"Affront her on thees side."

I approached her gently. She shot suddenly into the air, coming down again on perfectly stiff legs with a springless jolt. This she instantly followed by a succession of other rocket-like propulsions, utterly unlike a leap, all over the enclosure. The movements of the unfortunate Enriquez were equally unlike any equitation I ever saw. He appeared occasionally over Chu Chu's head, astride of her neck and tail, or in the free air, but never *in* the saddle. His rigid legs, however, never lost the stirrups, but came down regularly, accentuating her springless hops. More than that, the disproportionate excess of rider, saddle, and accoutrements was so great that he had, at times, the appearance of lifting Chu Chu forcibly from the ground by superior strength, and of actually contributing to her exercise! As they came toward me, a wild tossing and flying mass of hoofs and spurs, it was not only difficult to distinguish them apart, but to ascertain how much of the jumping was done by Enriquez separately. At last Chu Chu brought matters to a close by making for the low-stretching branches of an oak tree which stood at the corner of the lot. In a few moments she emerged from it—but without Enriquez.

I found the gallant fellow disengaging himself from the fork of a branch in which he had been firmly wedged, but still smiling and confident, and his cigarette between his teeth. Then for the first time he removed it, and seating himself easily on the branch with his legs dangling down, he blandly waved aside my anxious queries with a gentle reassuring gesture.

"Remain tranquil, my friend. Thees does not count! I have conquer—you observe—for why? I have *never* for once *arrive at the ground!* Consequent she is disappoint! She will ever that I *should!* But I have got her when the hair is not long! Your oncle Henry"—with an angelic wink—"is fly! He is ever a bully boy, with the eye of glass! Believe me. Behold! I am here! Big Injun! Whoop!"

He leaped lightly to the ground. Chu Chu, standing watchfully at a little distance, was evidently astonished at his appearance. She threw out her hind hoofs violently, shot up into the air until the stirrups crossed each other high above the saddle, and made for the stable in a succession of rabbit-like bounds—taking the precaution to remove the saddle, on entering, by striking it against the lintel of the door.

"You observe," said Enriquez blandly, "she would make that thing of *me*. Not having the good occasion, she ees dissatisfied. Where are you now?"

Two or three days afterwards he rode her again with the same result—accepted by him with the same heroic complacency. As we did not, for certain reasons, care to use the open road for this exercise, and as it was impossible to remove the tree, we were obliged to submit to the inevitable. On the following day I mounted her—undergoing the same experience as Enriquez, with the individual sensation of falling from a third-story window on top of a counting-house stool, and the variation of being projected over the fence. When I found that Chu Chu had not accompanied me, I saw Enriquez at my side.

"More than ever it is become necessary that we should do thees things again," he said gravely, as he assisted me to my feet. "Courage, my noble General! God and Liberty! Once more on to the breach! Charge, Chestare, charge! Come on, Don Stanley! 'Ere we are!"

He helped me none too quickly to catch my seat again, for it apparently had the effect of the turned peg on the enchanted horse in the Arabian Nights, and Chu Chu instantly rose into the air. But she came down this time before the open window of the kitchen, and I alighted easily on the dresser. The indefatigable Enriquez followed me.

"Won't this do?" I asked meekly.

"It ees *better*—for you arrive *not* on the ground," he said cheerfully; "but you should not once but a thousand times make trial! Ha! Go and win! Nevare die and say so! 'Eave ahead! 'Eave! There you are!"

Luckily, this time I managed to lock the rowels of my long spurs under her girth, and she could not unseat me. She seemed to recognize the fact after one or two plunges, when, to my great surprise, she suddenly sank to the ground and quietly rolled over me. The action disengaged my spurs, but, righting herself without getting up, she turned her beautiful head and absolutely *looked* at me!—still in the saddle. I felt myself blushing! But the voice of Enriquez was at my side.

"Errise, my friend; you have conquer! It is *she* who has arrive at the ground! *You* are all right. It is done; believe me, it is feenish! No more shall she make thees thing. From thees instant you shall ride her as the cow—as the rail of thees fence—and remain tranquil. For she is a-broke! Ta-ta! Regain your hats, gentlemen! Pass in your checks! It is ovar! How are you now?" He lit a fresh cigarette, put his hands in his pockets, and smiled at me blandly.

For all that, I ventured to point out that the habit of alighting in the fork of a tree, or the disengaging of one's self from the saddle on the ground, was attended with inconvenience, and even ostentatious display. But Enriquez swept the objections away with a single gesture. "It is the *preencipal*—the bottom fact—at which you arrive. The next come of himself! Many horse have achieve to mount the rider by the knees, and relinquish after thees same fashion. My grandfather had a barb of thees kind—but she has gone dead, and so have my grandfather. Which is sad and strange! Otherwise I shall make of them both an instant example!"

I ought to have said that although these performances were never actually witnessed by Enriquez's sister—for reasons which he and I thought sufficient—the dear girl displayed the greatest interest in them, and, perhaps aided by our mutually complimentary accounts of each other, looked upon us both as invincible heroes. It is possible also that she overestimated our success, for she suddenly demanded that I should *ride* Chu Chu to her house, that she might see her. It was not far; by going through a back lane I could avoid the trees which exercised such a fatal fascination for Chu Chu. There was a pleading, childlike entreaty in Consuelo's voice that I could not resist, with a slight flash from her lustrous dark eyes that I did not care to encourage. So I resolved to try it at all hazards.

My equipment for the performance was modeled after Enriquez's previous costume, with the addition of a few fripperies of silver and stamped leather out of compliment to Consuelo, and even with a faint hope that it might appease Chu Chu. *She* certainly looked beautiful in her glittering accouterments, set off by her jet-black shining coat. With an air of demure abstraction she permitted me to mount her, and even for a hundred yards or so indulged in a mincing maidenly amble that was not without a touch of coquetry. Encouraged by this, I addressed a few terms of endearment to her, and in the exuberance of my youthful enthusiasm I even confided to her my love for Consuelo, and begged her to be "good" and not disgrace herself and me before my

Dulcinea. In my foolish trustfulness I was rash enough to add a caress, and to pat her soft neck. She stopped instantly with an hysteric shudder. I knew what was passing through her mind: she had suddenly become aware of my baleful existence.

The saddle and bridle Chu Chu was becoming accustomed to, but who was this living, breathing object that had actually touched her? Presently her oblique vision was attracted by the fluttering movement of a fallen oak leaf in the road before her. She had probably seen many oak leaves many times before; her ancestors had no doubt been familiar with them on the trackless hills and in field and paddock, but this did not alter her profound conviction that I and the leaf were identical, that our baleful touch was something indissolubly connected. She reared before that innocent leaf, she revolved round it, and then fled from it at the top of her speed.

The lane passed before the rear wall of Saltello's garden. Unfortunately, at the angle of the fence stood a beautiful madroño tree, brilliant with its scarlet berries, and endeared to me as Consuelo's favorite haunt, under whose protecting shade I had more than once avowed my youthful passion. By the irony of fate Chu Chu caught sight of it, and with a succession of spirited bounds instantly made for it. In another moment I was beneath it, and Chu Chu shot like a rocket into the air. I had barely time to withdraw my feet from the stirrups, to throw up one arm to protect my glazed sombrero and grasp an overhanging branch with the other, before Chu Chu darted off. But to my consternation, as I gained a secure perch on the tree, and looked about me, I saw her—instead of running away—quietly trot through the open gate into Saltello's garden.

Need I say that it was to the beneficent Enriquez that I again owed my salvation? Scarely a moment elapsed before his bland voice rose in a concentrated whisper from the corner of the garden below me. He had divined the dreadful truth!

"For the love of God, collect to yourself many kinds of thees berry! All you can! Your full arms round! Rest tranquil. Leave to your ole oncle to make for you a delicate exposure. At the instant!"

He was gone again. I gathered, wonderingly, a few of the larger clusters of parti-colored fruit, and patiently waited. Pres-

ently he reappeared, and with him the lovely Consuelo—her dear
eyes filled with an adorable anxiety.

"Yes," continued Enriquez to his sister, with a confidential
lowering of tone but great distinctness of utterance, "it is ever so
with the American! He will ever make *first* the salutation of the
flower or the fruit, picked to himself by his own hand, to the lady
where he call. It is the custom of the American hidalgo! My God
—what will you? I make it not—it is so! Without doubt he is in
this instant doing thees thing. That is why he have let go his horse
to precede him here; it is always the etiquette to offer these things
on the feet. Ah! behold! it is he!—Don Francisco! Even now he
will descend from thees tree! Ah! You make the blush, little sister
(archly)! I will retire! I am discreet; two is not company for the
one! I make tracks! I am gone!"

How far Consuelo entirely believed and trusted her ingenious brother I do not know, nor even then cared to inquire. For
there was a pretty mantling of her olive cheek, as I came forward
with my offering, and a certain significant shyness in her manner
that were enough to throw me into a state of hopeless imbecility.
And I was always miserably conscious that Consuelo possessed
an exalted sentimentality, and a predilection for the highest
medieval romance, in which I knew I was lamentably deficient.
Even in our most confidential moments I was always aware that
I weakly lagged behind this daughter of a gloomily distinguished
ancestry, in her frequent incursions into a vague but poetic past.
There was something of the dignity of the Spanish châtelaine in
the sweetly grave little figure that advanced to accept my specious
offering. I think I should have fallen on my knees to present it,
but for the presence of the all-seeing Enriquez. But why did I
even at that moment remember that he had early bestowed upon
her the nickname of "Pomposa"? This, as Enriquez himself might
have observed, was "sad and strange."

I managed to stammer out something about the madroño
berries being at her "disposicion" (the tree was in her own
garden!), and she took the branches in her little brown hand with
a soft response to my unutterable glances.

But here Chu Chu, momentarily forgotten, executed a happy
diversion. To our astonishment she gravely walked up to Consuelo
and, stretching out her long slim neck, not only sniffed curiously

at the berries, but even protruded a black underlip towards the young girl herself. In another instant Consuelo's dignity melted. Throwing her arms around Chu Chu's neck she embraced and kissed her. Young as I was, I understood the divine significance of a girl's vicarious effusiveness at such a moment, and felt delighted. But I was the more astonished that the usually sensitive horse not only submitted to these caresses, but actually responded to the extent of affecting to nip my mistress's little right ear.

This was enough for the impulsive Consuelo. She ran hastily into the house, and in a few moments reappeared in a bewitching riding skirt gathered round her jimp waist. In vain Enriquez and myself joined in earnest entreaty: the horse was hardly broken for even a man's riding yet; the saints alone could tell what the nervous creature might do with a woman's skirt flapping at her side! We begged for delay, for reflection, for at least time to change the saddle—but with no avail! Consuelo was determined, indignant, distressingly reproachful! Ah, well! if Don Pancho (an ingenious diminutive of my Christian name) valued his horse so highly—if he were jealous of the evident devotion of the animal to herself, he would—But here I succumbed! And then I had the felicity of holding that little foot for one brief moment in the hollow of my hand, of readjusting the skirt as she threw her knee over the saddle-horn, of clasping her tightly—only half in fear —as I surrendered the reins to her grasp. And to tell the truth, as Enriquez and I fell back, although I had insisted upon still keeping hold of the end of the riata, it was a picture to admire. The petite figure of the young girl, and the graceful folds of her skirt, admirably harmonized with Chu Chu's lithe contour, and as the mare arched her slim neck and raised her slender head under the pressure of the reins, it was so like the lifted velvet-capped toreador crest of Consuelo herself, that they seemed of one race.

"I would not that you should hold the riata," said Consuelo petulantly.

I hesitated—Chu Chu looked certainly very amiable—I let go. She began to amble towards the gate, not mincingly as before, but with a freer and fuller stride. In spite of the incongruous saddle the young girl's seat was admirable. As they neared the gate she cast a single mischievous glance at me, jerked at the rein, and Chu Chu sprang into the road at a rapid canter. I watched them fearfully and breathlessly, until at the end of the lane I saw

AT THE CIRCUS. Pablo Picasso. *Courtesy, The Museum of Modern Art, New York: Gift of Mrs. John D. Rockefeller, Jr.*

Consuelo rein in slightly, wheel easily, and come flying back. There was no doubt about it; the horse was under perfect control. Her second subjugation was complete and final!

Overjoyed and bewildered, I overwhelmed them with congratulations; Enriquez alone retaining the usual brotherly attitude of criticism, and a superior toleration of a lover's enthusiasm. I ventured to hint to Consuelo (in what I believed was a safe whisper) that Chu Chu only showed my own feelings towards her.

"Without doubt," responded Enriquez gravely. "She have of herself assist you to climb to the tree to pull to yourself the berry for my sister."

But I felt Consuelo's little hand return my pressure, and I forgave and even pitied him.

From that day forward, Chu Chu and Consuelo were not only firm friends but daily companions. In my devotion I would have presented the horse to the young girl, but with flattering delicacy she preferred to call it mine.

"I shall erride it for you, Pancho," she said. "I shall feel," she continued, with exalted although somewhat vague poetry, "that it is of *you!* You lofe the beast—it is therefore of a necessity *you,* my Pancho! It is *your* soul I shall erride like the wings of the wind—your lofe in this beast shall be my only cavalier forever."

I would have preferred something whose vicarious qualities were less uncertain than I still felt Chu Chu's to be, but I kissed the girl's hand submissively. It was only when I attempted to accompany her in the flesh, on another horse, that I felt the full truth of my instinctive fears. Chu Chu would not permit any one to approach her mistress's side. My mounted presence revived in her all her old blind astonishment and disbelief in my existence; she would start suddenly, face about, and back away from me in utter amazement as if I had been only recently created, or with an affected modesty as if I had been just guilty of some grave indecorum towards her sex which she really could not stand. The frequency of these exhibitions in the public highway were not only distressing to me as a simple escort, but as it had the effect on the casual spectators of making Consuelo seem to participate in Chu Chu's objections, I felt that, as a lover, it could not be borne. Any attempt to coerce Chu Chu ended in her run-

ning away. And my frantic pursuit of her was open to equal
misconstruction.

"Go it, miss, the little dude is gainin' on you!" shouted by a
drunken teamster to the frightened Consuelo, once checked me
in mid-career.

Even the dear girl herself saw the uselessness of my real
presence, and after a while was content to ride with "my soul."

Notwithstanding this, I am not ashamed to say that it was
my custom, whenever she rode out, to keep a slinking and distant
surveillance of Chu Chu on another horse, until she had fairly
settled down to her pace. A little nod of Consuelo's round black-
and-red toreador hat, or a kiss tossed from her riding whip, was
reward enough!

I remember a pleasant afternoon when I was thus awaiting
her in the outskirts of the village. The eternal smile of the Californian summer had begun to waver and grow less fixed; dust lay
thick on leaf and blade; the dry hills were clothed in russet
leather; the trade winds were shifting to the south with an
ominous warm humidity; a few days longer and the rains would
be here. It so chanced that this afternoon my seclusion on the
roadside was accidentally invaded by a village belle—a Western
young lady somewhat older than myself, and of flirtatious reputation. As she persistently and—as I now have reason to believe—
mischievously lingered, I had only a passing glimpse of Consuelo
riding past at an unaccustomed speed which surprised me at the
moment. But as I reasoned later that she was only trying to
avoid a merely formal meeting, I thought no more about it. It
was not until I called at the house to fetch Chu Chu at the
usual hour, and found that Consuelo had not yet returned, that a
recollection of Chu Chu's furious pace again troubled me. An
hour passed—it was getting towards sunset, but there were no
signs of Chu Chu or her mistress. I became seriously alarmed. I
did not care to reveal my fears to the family, for I felt myself
responsible for Chu Chu. At last I desperately saddled my horse,
and galloped off in the direction she had taken. It was the road to
Rosario and the hacienda of one of her relations, where she sometimes halted.

The road was a very unfrequented one, twisting like a mountain
river; indeed, it was the bed of an old water-course, between

brown hills of wild oats, and debouching at last into a broad blue lakelike expanse of alfalfa meadows. In vain I strained my eyes over the monotonous level; nothing appeared to rise above or move across it. In the faint hope that she might have lingered at the hacienda, I was spurring on again when I heard a slight splashing on my left. I looked around. A broad patch of fresher-colored herbage and a cluster of dwarfed alders indicated a hidden spring. I cautiously approached its quaggy edges, when I was shocked by what appeared to be a sudden vision! Mid-leg deep in the centre of a greenish pool stood Chu Chu! But without a strap or buckle of harness upon her—as naked as when she was foaled!

For a moment I could only stare at her in bewildered terror. Far from recognizing me, she seemed to be absorbed in a nymph-like contemplation of her own graces in the pool. Then I called "Consuelo!" and galloped frantically around the spring. But there was no response, nor was there anything to be seen but the all-unconscious Chu Chu. The pool, thank Heaven! was not deep enough to have drowned anyone; there were no signs of a struggle on its quaggy edges. The horse might have come from a distance! I galloped on, still calling. A few hundred yards further I detected the vivid glow of Chu Chu's scarlet saddle blanket, in the brush near the trail. My heart leaped—I was on the track. I called again; this time a faint reply, in accents I knew too well, came from the field beside me!

Consuelo was there! reclining beside a manzanita bush which screened her from the road, in what struck me, even at that supreme moment, as a judicious and picturesquely selected couch of scented Indian grass and dry tussocks. The velvet hat with its balls of scarlet plush was laid carefully aside; her lovely blue-black hair retained its tight coils undisheveled, her eyes were luminous and tender. Shocked as I was at her apparent helplessness, I remember being impressed with the fact that it gave so little indication of violent usage or disaster.

I threw myself frantically on the ground beside her.

"You are hurt, Consita! For Heaven's sake, what has happened?"

She pushed my hat back with her little hand, and tumbled my hair gently.

"Nothing. *You* are here, Pancho—eet is enofe! What shall

come after thees—when I am perhaps gone among the grave—make nothing! *You* are here—I am happy. For a little, perhaps—not mooch."

"But," I went on desperately, "was it an accident? Were you thrown? Was it Chu Chu?"—for somehow, in spite of her languid posture and voice, I could not, even in my fears, believe her seriously hurt.

"Beat not the poor beast, Pancho. It is not from *her* comes thees thing. She have make nothing—believe me! I have come upon your assignation with Miss Essmith! I make but to pass you—to fly—to never come back! I have say to Chu Chu, 'Fly!' We fly many miles. Sometimes together, sometimes not so mooch! Sometimes in the saddle, sometimes on the neck! Many things remain in the road; at the end, I myself remain! I have say, 'Courage, Pancho will come!' Then I say, 'No, he is talk with Miss Essmith!' I remember not more. I have creep here on the hands. Eet is feenish!"

I looked at her distractedly. She smiled tenderly, and slightly smoothed down and rearranged a fold of her dress to cover her delicate little boot.

"But," I protested, "you are not much hurt, dearest. You have broken no bones. Perhaps," I added, looking at the boot, "only a slight sprain. Let me carry you to my horse; I will walk beside you, home. Do, dearest Consita!"

She turned her lovely eyes towards me sadly.

"You comprehend not, my poor Pancho! It is not of the foot, the ankle, the arm, or the head that I can say, 'She is broke!' I would it were even so. But"—she lifted her sweet lashes slowly—"I have derrange my inside. It is an affair of my family. My grandfather have once toomble over the bull at a rodeo. He speak no more; he is dead. For why? He has derrange his inside. Believe me, it is of the family. You comprehend? The Saltellos are not as the other peoples for this. When I am gone, you will bring to me the berry to grow upon my tomb, Pancho; the berry you have picked for me. The little flower will come too, the little star will arrive, but Consuelo, who lofe you, she will come not more! When you are happy and talk in the road to the Essmith, you will not think of me. You will not see my eyes, Pancho; thees little grass"—she ran her plump little fingers through a tussock—"will hide them; and the small animals in the black coats that lif here will have much sorrow—but you will not. It ees better so! My father will not that I, a Catholique, should marry into a camp meeting, and lif in a tent, and make howl like the coyote." (It was one of Consuelo's bewildering beliefs that there was only one form of dissent—Methodism!) "He will not that I should marry a man who possess not the many horses, ox, and cow, like him. But *I* care not. *You* are my only religion, Pancho! I have enofe of the horse, and ox, and cow when *you* are with me! Kiss me, Pancho. Perhaps it is for the last time—the feenish! Who knows?"

There were tears in her lovely eyes; I felt that my own were growing dim; the sun was sinking over the dreary plain to the slow rising of the wind; an infinite loneliness had fallen upon us, and yet I was miserably conscious of some dreadful unreality in it all. A desire to laugh, which I felt must be hysterical, was creeping over me; I dared not speak. But her dear head was on my shoulder, and the situation was not unpleasant.

Nevertheless, something must be done! This was the more difficult as it was by no means clear what had already been done. Even while I supported her drooping figure I was straining my eyes across her shoulder for succor of some kind. Suddenly the figure of a rapid rider appeared upon the road. It seemed familiar. I looked again—it was the blessed Enriquez! A sense of deep relief came over me. I loved Consuelo; but never before had lover ever hailed the irruption of one of his beloved's family with such complacency.

"You are safe, dearest; it is Enriquez!"

I thought she received the information coldly. Suddenly she turned upon me her eyes, now bright and glittering.

"Swear to me at the instant, Pancho, that you will not again look upon Miss Essmith, even for once."

I was simple and literal. Miss Smith was my nearest neighbor, and, unless I was stricken with blindness, compliance was impossible. I hesitated—but swore.

"Enofe—you have hesitate—I will no more."

She rose to her feet with grave deliberation. For an instant, with the recollection of the delicate internal organization of the Saltellos on my mind, I was in agony lest she should totter and fall, even then, yielding up her gentle spirit on the spot. But when I looked again she had a hairpin between her white teeth,

and was carefully adjusting her toreador hat. And beside us was
Enriquez—cheerful, alert, voluble, and undaunted.

"Eureka! I have found! We are all here! Eet is a leetle public
—eh? a leetle to much of a front seat for a tête-à-tête, my yonge
friends," he said, glancing at the remains of Consuelo's bower,
"but for the accounting of taste there is none. What will you?
The meat of the one man shall envenom the meat of the other.
But" (in a whisper to me) "as to thees horse—thees Chu Chu,
which I have just pass—why is she undress? Surely you would
not make an exposition of her to the traveler to suspect! And
if not, why so?"

I tried to explain, looking at Consuelo, that Chu Chu had
run away, that Consuelo had met with a terrible accident, had
been thrown, and I feared had suffered serious internal injury.
But to my embarrassment Consuelo maintained a half-scornful
silence, and an inconsistent freshness of healthful indifference,
as Enriquez approached her with an engaging smile.

"Ah, yes, she have the headache, and the molligrubs. She
will sit on the damp stone when the gentle dew is falling. I comprehend. Meet me in the lane when the clock strike nine! But,"
in a lower voice, "of thees undress horse I comprehend nothing!
Look you—it is sad and strange."

He went off to fetch Chu Chu, leaving me and Consuelo
alone. I do not think I ever felt so utterly abject and bewildered
before in my life. Without knowing why, I was miserably conscious of having in some way offended the girl for whom I
believed I would have given my life, and I had made her and
myself ridiculous in the eyes of her brother. I had again failed
in my slower Western nature to understand her high romantic
Spanish soul! Meantime she was smoothing out her riding habit,
and looking as fresh and pretty as when she first left her house.

"Consita," I said hesitatingly, "you are not angry with me?"

"Angry?" she repeated haughtily, without looking at me.
"Oh no! Of a possibility eet is Mees Essmith who is angry that I
have interroopt her tête-à-tête with you, and have send here my
brother to make the same with me."

"But," I said eagerly, "Miss Smith does not even know
Enriquez!"

Consuelo turned on me a glance of unutterable significance.

"Ah!" she said darkly, "you *tink!*"

Indeed I *knew*. But here I believed I understood Consuelo, and was relieved. I even ventured to say gently, "And you are better?"

She drew herself up to her full height, which was not much.

"Of my health, what is it? A nothing. Yes! Of my soul let us not speak."

Nevertheless, when Enriquez appeared with Chu Chu she ran towards her with outstretched arms. Chu Chu protruded about six inches of upper lip in response—apparently under the impression, which I could quite understand, that her mistress was edible. And, I may have been mistaken, but their beautiful eyes met in an absolute and distinct glance of intelligence!

During the home journey Consuelo recovered her spirits, and parted from me with a magnanimous and forgiving pressure of the hand. I do not know what explanation of Chu Chu's original escapade was given to Enriquez and the rest of the family; the inscrutable forgiveness extended to me by Consuelo precluded any further inquiry on my part. I was willing to leave it a secret between her and Chu Chu. But, strange to say, it seemed to complete our own understanding, and precipitated, not only our love-making, but the final catastrophe which culminated that romance. For we had resolved to elope. I do not know that this heroic remedy was absolutely necessary from the attitude of either Consuelo's family or my own; I am inclined to think we preferred it, because it involved no previous explanation or advice. Need I say that our confidant and firm ally was Consuelo's brother—the alert, the linguistic, the ever happy, ever ready Enriquez! It was understood that his presence would not only give a certain mature respectability to our performance—but I do not think we would have contemplated this step without it. During one of our riding excursions we were to secure the services of a Methodist minister in the adjoining county, and later, that of the mission padre—when the secret was out.

"I will gif her away," said Enriquez confidently; "it will on the instant propitiate the old shadbelly who shall perform the affair, and withhold his jaw. A little chin music from your oncle 'Arry shall finish it! Remain tranquil and forget not a ring! One does not always, in the agony and dissatisfaction of the moment, a ring remember. I shall bring two in the pocket of my dress."

If I did not entirely participate in this roseate view it may have been because Enriquez, although a few years my senior, was much younger looking, and with his demure deviltry of eye, and his upper lip close shaven for this occasion, he suggested a depraved acolyte rather than a responsible member of a family. Consuelo had also confided to me that her father—possibly owing to some rumors of our previous escapade—had forbidden any further excursions with me alone. The innocent man did not know that Chu Chu had forbidden it also, and that even on this momentous occasion both Enriquez and myself were obliged to ride in opposite fields like outflankers. But we nevertheless felt the full guilt of disobedience added to our desperate enterprise. Meanwhile, although pressed for time, and subject to discovery at any moment, I managed at certain points of the road to dismount and walk beside Chu Chu (who did not seem to recognize me on foot), holding Consuelo's hand in my own, with the discreet Enriquez leading my horse in the distant field. I retain a very vivid picture of that walk—the ascent of a gentle slope towards a prospect as yet unknown, but full of glorious possibilities; the tender dropping light of an autumn sky, slightly filmed with the promise of the future rains, like foreshadowed tears, and the half-frightened, half-serious talk into which Consuelo and I had insensibly fallen. And then, I don't know how it happened, but as we reached the summit Chu Chu suddenly reared, wheeled, and the next moment was flying back along the road we had just traveled, at the top of her speed! It might have been that, after her abstracted fashion, she only at that moment detected my presence; but so sudden and complete was her evolution that before I could regain my horse from the astonished Enriquez she was already a quarter of a mile on the homeward stretch, with the frantic Consuelo pulling hopelessly at the bridle. We started in pursuit. But a horrible despair seized us. To attempt to overtake her, to even follow at the same rate of speed, would only excite Chu Chu and endanger Consuelo's life. There was absolutely no help for it, nothing could be done; the mare had taken her determined long, continuous stride; the road was a straight, steady descent all the way back to the village; Chu Chu had the bit between her teeth, and there was no prospect of swerving her. We could only follow hopelessly, idiotically, furiously, until Chu Chu dashed triumphantly into the Saltellos' courtyard, carrying the half-fainting Consuelo back to the arms of her assembled and astonished family.

It was our last ride together. It was the last I ever saw of Consuelo before her transfer to the safe seclusion of a convent in Southern California. It was the last I ever saw of Chu Chu, who in the confusion of that rencontre was overlooked in her half-loosed harness, and allowed to escape through the back gate to the fields. Months afterwards it was said that she had been identified among a band of wild horses in the Coast Range, as a strange and beautiful creature who had escaped the brand of the rodeo and had become a myth. There was another legend that she had been seen, sleek, fat, and gorgeously caparisoned, issuing from the gateway of the Rosario patio, before a lumbering Spanish cabriolet in which a short, stout matron was seated—but I will have none of it. For there are days when she still lives, and I can see her plainly still climbing the gentle slope towards the summit, with Consuelo on her back, and myself at her side, pressing eagerly forward towards the illimitable prospect that opens in the distance.

THE DREAMING HORSE

HORSES
by Dorothy Wellesley

Who, in the garden-pony carrying skeps
Of grass or fallen leaves, his knees gone slack,
Round belly, hollow back,
Sees the Mongolian Tarpan of the Steppes?
Or, in the Shire with plaits and feathered feet,
The war horse like the wind the Tartar knew?
Or, in the Suffolk Punch, spells out anew
The wild grey asses fleet

With stripe from head to tail, and moderate ears?
In cross sea-donkeys, sheltering as storm gathers,
The mountain zebras maned upon the withers,
With round enormous ears?

And who in thoroughbreds in stable garb
Of blazoned rug, ranged orderly, will mark
The wistful eyelashes so long and dark,
And call to mind the old blood of the Barb?
And that slim island on whose bare campaigns
Galloped with flying manes
For a King's pleasure, churning surf and scud,
A white Arabian stud?

That stallion, teazer to Hobgoblin, free
And foaled upon a plain of Barbary:
Godolphin Barb, who dragged a cart for hire
In Paris, but became a famous sire,
Covering all lovely mares, and she who threw
Rataplan to the Baron, loveliest shrew;
King Charles's royal mares; the Dodsworth Dam;
And the descendants: Yellow Turk, King Tom;
And Lath out of Roxana, famous foal;
Careless; Eclipse, unbeaten in the race,
With white blaze on his face;
Prunella who was dam to Parasol.

Blood Arab, pony, pedigree, no name,
All horses are the same:
The Shetland stallion stunted by the damp,
Yet filled with self-importance, stout and small;
The Cleveland slow and tall;
New Forests that may ramp
Their lives out, being branded, breeding free
When bluebells turn out the forest to a sea,
When mares with foal at foot flee down the glades,
Sheltering in bramble coverts
From mobs of corn-fed lovers;
Or, at the acorn harvest, in stockades
A roundup being afoot, will stand at bay,

Or, making for the heather clearings, splay
Wide-spread towards the bogs by gorse and whin,
Roped as they flounder in
By foresters.

        But hunters as day fails
Will take the short cut home across the fields;
With slackening rein will stoop through darkening wealds;
With creaking leathers skirt the swedes and kales;
Patient, adventurous still,
A horse's ears bob on the distant hill;
He starts to hear
A pheasant chuck or whirr, having the fear
In him of ages filled with war and raid,
Night gallop, ambuscade;
Remembering adventures of his kin
With giant winged worms that coiled round mountain bases,
And Nordic tales of young gods riding races
Up courses of the rainbow; here, within
The depth of Hampshire hedges, does he dream
How Athens woke, to hear above her roofs
The welkin flash and thunder to the hoofs
Of Dawn's tremendous team?

THE HUNGRY HORSE

ON A CLERGYMAN'S HORSE
BITING HIM
Anonymous

The steed bit his master;
    How came this to pass?
He heard the good pastor
    Cry, "All flesh is grass."

THE DUN HORSE
by George Grinnell

1/

Many years ago, there lived in the Pawnee tribe an old woman and her grandson, a boy about sixteen years old. These people had no relations and were very poor. They were so poor that they were despised by the rest of the tribe. They had nothing of their own; and always, after the village started to move the camp from one place to another, these two would stay behind the rest, to look over the old camp, and pick up anything that the other Indians had thrown away, as worn out or useless. In this way they would sometimes get pieces of robes, worn-out moccasins with holes in them, and bits of meat.

Now, it happened one day, after the tribe had moved away from the camp, that this old woman and her boy were following along the trail behind the rest, when they came to a miserable old worn-out dun horse, which they supposed had been abandoned by some Indians. He was thin and exhausted, was blind of one eye, had a bad sore back, and one of his forelegs was very much swollen. In fact, he was so worthless that none of the Pawness had been willing to take the trouble to try to drive him along with them. But when the old woman and her boy came along, the boy said, "Come now, we will take this old horse, for we can make him carry our pack." So the old woman put her pack on the horse, and drove him along, but he limped and could only go very slowly.

2/

The tribe moved up on the North Platte, until they came to Court House Rock. The two poor Indians followed them, and camped

HORSES. Jean Géricault. *Courtesy, Philadelphia Museum of Art: The Wilstach Collection.*

with the others. One day while they were here, the young men who had been sent out to look for buffalo came hurrying into camp and told the chiefs that a large herd of buffalo were near, and that among them was a spotted calf.

The Head Chief of the Pawnees had a very beautiful daughter, and when he heard about the spotted calf, he ordered his old crier to go about through the village, and call out that the man who killed the spotted calf should have his daughter for his wife. For a spotted robe is *ti-war'-uks-ti*—big medicine.

The buffalo were feeding about four miles from the village, and the chiefs decided that the charge should be made from there. In this way, the man who had the fastest horse would be the most likely to kill the calf. Then all the warriors and the young men picked out their best and fastest horses, and made ready to start. Among those who prepared for the charge was the poor boy on the old dun horse. But when they saw him, all the rich young braves on their fast horses pointed at him, and said, "Oh, see, there is the horse that is going to catch the spotted calf," and they laughed at him, so that the poor boy was ashamed, and rode off to one side of the crowd, where he could not hear their jokes and laughter.

When he had ridden off some little way, the horse stopped, and turned his head round, and spoke to the boy. He said, "Take me down to the creek, and plaster me all over with mud. Cover my head and neck and body and legs." When the boy heard the horse speak, he was afraid, but he did as he was told. Then the horse said, "Now mount, but do not ride back to the warriors, who laugh at you because you have such a poor horse. Stay right here, until the word is given to charge." So the boy stayed there.

And presently all the fine horses were drawn up in line and pranced about, and were so eager to go that their riders could hardly hold them in; and at last the old crier gave the word, "*Loo-ah*"—Go! Then the Pawnees all leaned forward on their horses and yelled, and away they went. Suddenly, away off to the right, was seen the old dun horse. He did not seem to run. He seemed to sail along like a bird. He passed all the fastest horses, and in a moment he was among the buffalo. First he picked out the spotted calf, and charging up alongside of it, *U-ra-rish!* straight flew the arrow. The calf fell. The boy drew another arrow, and killed a fat cow that was running by. Then he dismounted and began to skin the calf, before any of the other warriors had come up. But when the rider got off the old dun horse, how changed he was! He pranced about and would hardly stand still near the dead buffalo. His back was all right again, his legs were well and fine, and both his eyes were clear and bright.

The boy skinned the calf and the cow that he had killed, and then he packed all the meat on the horse, and put the spotted robe on top of the load, and started back to the camp on foot, leading the dun horse. But even with this heavy load the horse pranced all the time, and was scared at everything he saw. On the way to camp, one of the rich young chiefs of the tribe rode up by the boy, and offered him twelve good horses for the spotted robe, so that he could marry the Head Chief's beautiful daughter; but the boy laughed at him and would not sell the robe.

Now, while the boy walked to the camp leading the dun horse, most of the warriors rode back, and one of those that came first to the village went to the old woman and said to her, "Your grandson has killed the spotted calf." And the old woman said, "Why do you come to tell me this? You ought to be ashamed to make fun of my boy, because he is poor." The warrior said, "What I have told you is true," and then he rode away. After a little while another brave rode up to the old woman and said to her, "Your grandson has killed the spotted calf." Then the old woman began to cry, she felt so badly because everyone made fun of her boy, because he was poor.

Pretty soon the boy came along, leading the horse up to the lodge where he and his grandmother lived. It was a little lodge, just big enough for two, and was made of old pieces of skin that the old woman had picked up, and was tied together with strings of rawhide and sinew. It was the meanest and worst lodge in the village. When the old woman saw her boy leading the dun horse with the load of meat and the robes on it, she was very much surprised. The boy said to her, "Here, I have brought you plenty of meat to eat, and here is a robe, that you may have for yourself. Take the meat off the horse." Then the old woman laughed, for her heart was glad. But when she went to take the meat from the horse's back, he snorted and jumped about, and acted like a wild horse. The old woman looked at him in wonder, and could hardly believe that it was the same horse. So the boy had to take off the meat, for the horse would not let the old woman come near him.

3 /

That night the horse spoke again to the boy and said, "*Wa-ti-hes Chah'-ra-rat wa-ta.* Tomorrow the Sioux are coming—a large war party. They will attack the village, and you will have a great battle. Now, when the Sioux are drawn up in line of battle, and are all ready to fight, you jump on to me, and ride as hard as you can, right into the middle of the Sioux, and up to their Head Chief, their greatest warrior, and count *coup* on him, and kill him, and then ride back. Do this four times, and count *coup* on four of the bravest Sioux, and kill them, but don't go again. If you go the fifth time, maybe you will be killed, or else you will lose me. *La-ku'-ta-chix*—remember." So the boy promised.

The next day it happened as the horse had said, and the Sioux came down and formed a line of battle. Then the boy took his bow and arrows, and jumped on the dun horse, and charged into the midst of them. And when the Sioux saw that he was going to strike their Head Chief, they all shot their arrows at him, and the arrows flew so thickly across each other that the sky became dark, but none of them hit the boy. And he counted *coup* on the Chief, and killed him, and then rode back. After that he charged again among the Sioux, where they were gathered thickest, and counted *coup* on their bravest warrior, and killed him. And then twice more, until he had gone four times as the horse had told him.

But the Sioux and the Pawnees kept on fighting, and the boy stood around and watched the battle. And at last he said to himself, "I have been four times and have killed four Sioux, and I am all right, I am not hurt anywhere; why may I not go again?" So he jumped on the dun horse, and charged again. But when he got among the Sioux, one Sioux warrior drew an arrow and shot. The arrow struck the dun horse behind the forelegs and pierced him through. And the horse fell down dead. But the boy jumped off, and fought his way through the Sioux, and ran away as fast as he could to the Pawnees. Now, as soon as the horse was killed, the Sioux said to each other, "This horse was like a man. He was brave. He was not like a horse." And they took their knives and hatchets, and hacked the dun horse and gashed his flesh, and cut him into small pieces.

The Pawnees and Sioux fought all day long, but toward night the Sioux broke and fled.

4 /

The boy felt very badly that he had lost his horse; and, after the fight was over, he went out from the village to where it had taken place, to mourn for his horse. He went to the spot where the horse lay, and gathered up all the pieces of flesh which the Sioux had cut off, and the legs and the hoofs, and put them all together in a pile. Then he went off to the top of a hill near by, and sat down and drew his robe over his head, and began to mourn for his horse.

As he sat there, he heard a great windstorm coming up, and it passed over him with a loud rushing sound, and after the wind came a rain. The boy looked down from where he sat to the pile of flesh and bones, which was all that was left of his horse, and he could just see it through the rain. And the rain passed by, and his heart was very heavy, and he kept on mourning.

And pretty soon came another rushing wind, and after it a rain; and as he looked through the driving rain toward the spot where the pieces lay, he thought that they seemed to come together and take shape, and that the pile looked like a horse lying down, but he could not see well for the thick rain.

After this, came a third storm like the others; and now when he looked toward the horse he thought he saw its tail move from side to side two or three times, and that it lifted its head from the ground. The boy was afraid, and wanted to run away, but he stayed.

And as he waited, there came another storm. And while the rain fell, looking through the rain, the boy saw the horse raise himself up on his forelegs and look about. Then the dun horse stood up.

5 /

The boy left the place where he had been sitting on the hilltop, and went down to him. When the boy had come near to him, the horse spoke and said, "You have seen how it has been this day; and from this you may know how it will be after this. But *Ti-ra'-wa* has been good, and has let me come back to you. After this, do what I tell you; not any more, not any less." Then the horse said, "Now lead me off, far away from the camp, behind that big hill, and leave me there tonight, and in the morning come for me," and the boy did as he was told.

And when he went for the horse in the morning, he found with him a beautiful white gelding, much more handsome than any horse in the tribe. That night the dun horse told the boy to take him again to the place behind the big hill, and to come for him the next morning; and when the boy went for him again, he found with him a beautiful black gelding. And so for ten nights, he left the horse among the hills, and each morning he found a different colored horse, a bay, a roan, a gray, a blue, a spotted horse, and all of them finer than any horses that the Pawnees had ever had in their tribe before.

Now the boy was rich, and he married the beautiful daughter of the Head Chief, and when he became older, he was made Head Chief himself. He had many children by his beautiful wife, and one day when his oldest boy died, he wrapped him in the

spotted calf robe and buried him in it. He always took good care
of his old grandmother, and kept her in his own lodge until she
died. The dun horse was never ridden except at feasts, and when
they were going to have a doctors' dance, but he was always led
about with the Chief, wherever he went. The horse lived in the
village for many years, until he became very old. And at last
he died.

THE AGING HORSE

POOR OLD HORSE

Anonymous

My clothing was once of the linsey-woolsey fine,
My tail it grew at length, my coat did likewise fine; '
But now I'm growing old; my beauty does decay,
My master frowns upon me; one day I heard him say,
              Poor old horse: poor old horse.

Once I was kept in the stable snug and warm,
To keep my tender limbs from any cold or harm;
But now, in open fields, I am forced for to go,
In all sorts of weather, let it be hail, rain, freeze, or snow.
              Poor old horse: poor old horse.

Once I was fed on the very best corn and hay
That ever grew in yon fields, or in yon meadows gay;
But now there's no such doing can I find at all,
I'm glad to pick the green sprouts that grow behind yon wall.
              Poor old horse: poor old horse.

"You are old, you are cold, you are deaf, dull, dumb and slow,
You are not fit for anything, or in my team to draw.
You have eaten all my hay, you have spoiled all my straw,
So hang him, whip, stick him, to the huntsman let him go."
            Poor old horse: poor old horse.

My hide unto the tanners then I would freely give,
My body to the hound dogs, I would rather die than live,
Likewise my poor bones that have carried you many a mile,
Over hedges, ditches, brooks, bridges, likewise gates and stiles.
            Poor old horse: poor old horse.

THE RELIABLE HORSE

LEVANT
by Hugh Johnson

In "L" Troop of the Nth Cavalry there is a horse that is sixteen years old. He does no work, he eats candy and carrots to his heart's content, and he will never be condemned. The story of these honors is worth knowing. It is unofficial history.

When "L" Troop took the field in the Philippines, its commander was a brand-new second lieutenant, fresh from West Point, for its captain was on distant duty. This might have been a calamity to any troop but "L." The father of Lieutenant Grinnell had commanded the troop before him, and the older sergeants had yanked the boy from beneath the horses' feet on the picket line when he could no more than toddle. He had ridden with them as a lank, awkward twelve-year-old, and slept between their blankets on the Geronimo campaign. They called him Bobbie then, to his face, and Bobbie he would remain to them, even if he became field-marshal-general commanding the allied armies of six nations, as they fondly hoped he some day would. Nothing could have pleased the troop more than his return to it as an officer, and what he did not know about commanding a troop in campaign they would shortly show him.

They did. "L" Troop painted its letter in vivid colors over a large part of the Island of Luzon. It rode through twenty battles, skirmishes, and engagements in the earlier war; it endured a cholera epidemic at Bato-bato, and at last it took station at Bontoc to guard its particular section of a partly pacified country and to await eventualities. It was proud of itself as a whole, but no one was prouder than First Sergeant Dale, who, as the veteran of the troop, the guardian of its traditions, and the rider of the storied horse Levant, was herein forever justified in many extravagant prophecies.

"Didn't we tell 'em—didn't we tell 'em?" he used to chuckle into the silken mane of his horse, for Levant was his chief confidant. "Of *course* the boy's a *soldier*. It's in the blood, an' he's the spit of his daddy before him. They couldn't fool *us*—could they, old Daisy-Crusher? Praise be that we lived to serve under him!" Levant did not understand these effusions, but he *did* know that his sides were plump with fat and his hide was clean and comfortable.

This—or its equivalent—the whole of "L" Troop knew. They were looked after, and they were commanded. When the unreasoning cholera had descended upon them, and a fear that they had not known in the field gripped them uncannily, their lieutenant had gone among them, his cheeks as fresh and smiling, his eye as clear and cool and pleasant as ever; and thus, through it all —"bloody war and sickly season"—they had found him without flaw.

This service-born confidence, you must understand, is the beginning and the end and all between with a company of soldiers. If they have it, the efficiency of the officer is the efficiency of the troop without one iota of discount. "L" Troop believed that it could have whipped the entire armed force of insurrection. Believing so, and led as it was, it was probably right.

But into this confident calm of self-gratulation three horrors descended. In the order of their coming, they were, the rainy season, El General Pedro Geronimo Aguilar Borda y Pradillo, and First Lieutenant Harrison Wentworth.

The rains began as a gentle afternoon shower and settled into a three weeks' deluge. Roads and trails disappeared in rivers and brooklets and lagoons and narrow chasms of liquid mud. The jungle took on new strength of life in the fetid air and threatened to engulf the town. Just when all movement of troops through the swimming country seemed impossible, movement became suddenly imperative. The mail brought Grinnell a simple order:

> The Insurrecto leader, Aguilar, has transferred his activi-
> ties to your section. With the force at your command the
> General looks to you to capture him without delay.
>   *MILTON, Adjutant-General.*

Pedro Aguilar was a little brown guerrilla and his activities were no myth. Day after day, "L" Troop rode on wild chases and day after day it returned disheartened and finally almost hopeless. It received no grace from Aguilar. Now he sacked the hacienda of a friendly Filipino to westward, burning the sugar mills, killing the carabao, and ruining the rice dikes. When the troop arrived at the scene of destruction, he would be blowing up a bridge twenty miles away. It chased him for a month and, at the end of it, seemed no nearer success than when it began. Once it sent a scattering volley after a line of white cotton-clad backs, scuttling through a banana grove, and once it was itself fired into in a narrow gorge, but that was all. Aguilar grew daily bolder. Headquarters became at first insistent, then sarcastic, and finally scathing. The troop thought and dreamed nothing but Aguilar and his capture. Its reputation was at stake and in very apparent danger. The men became peaked and worn and thin and the horses showed signs of grievous suffering. Another organization would have been in a state of incipient mutiny, but these men could still grin and take up new holes in their belts in their ignorance of what was still to come.

First Lieutenant Wentworth came to take the command of the troop from Bobbie Grinnell at a most unfortunate time. For a subaltern, he was an oldish man (perhaps thirty-eight) with a high, narrow forehead and small, close-set, myopic eyes. His captaincy had been too long coming and he was a little soured. He was as neat and "pernickety" as an old maid, his perspective was not broader than a barn door, and he had no sense of humor whatever. He did not like the appearance of Bontoc Sonoyta, and

TROOPER OF THE PLAINS. Frederic Remington.
*Courtesy, The Newark Museum, Newark, N.J.: Gift of
Mr. and Mrs. William V. Griffin.*

he was shocked by the childlike appearance of Bobbie Grinnell.

"You young fellows shouldn't be given command of troops," he told Bobbie, judicially; "you have no experience and you let things go to the dogs. *Look* at these horses."

Grinnell flushed and said nothing. Sergeant Dale was making wry faces, and the men, grooming on the picket line, poised their brushes in midair, expecting to see their lieutenant fall upon and quite obliterate the opinionated interloper. But most of the heart had been taken out of Bobbie. The coming of Wentworth was an official expression of lost confidence, and he had scarcely recovered from the shock when the new lieutenant, passing critically along the line of horses, stopped behind Levant.

"Mister Grinnell," he said decisively (subalterns call each other mister only for discipline or "squelching"), "Mister Grinnell, in the future I will ride this horse."

Now, in most cavalry troops, and certainly in "L," the assignment of any horse to any soldier is considered the beginning of a relation terminable only by death or discharge. Picture, then, the sacrilege here. Dale had trained Levant as an awkward colt recruit. Bobbie was incautious.

"Why, Wentworth—that is—Lieutenant," he stammered, "*that* is Levant—Sergeant Dale's horse. You can't do that. Surely you've heard of Dale and Levant. Why, that would break the old man's heart." The troop had frankly stopped grooming as its lares and penates came tumbling about its ears. Wentworth drew himself to his full height, and fixed Grinnell with a stare, pitying, haughty, and inquiring.

"Mister Grinnell," he began in a weary voice—"*Mister* Grinnell, perhaps you didn't understand me. In the future, *I* will ride *this* horse." Grinnell's fingers straightened to their full length, then they closed in such knotty, painful fists that the cords on the knuckles stood out white and trembling. Once he drew in breath to speak (his face had grown ashen), but turned away, and an hour later shuddered at the thought of what he had been about to do.

"L" Troop's condition became a tragedy. Poor Wentworth was a conscientious man. In theory he was excellent, but he had not served two days with a troop in the field, and he knew as much about men in the abstract as he did about the plumbing system of the sacred city of Lhasa. His idea of discipline was nagging; of firmness, meanness; and of fighting Malay guerrillas, blank and pitiful nothing.

A troop of cavalry is a human machine and this sort of thing may not go on forever. The rainy season was drawing to a close. A burning ball of a sun now popped into a cloudless sky at dawn and seared its way across, sucking the steam from the soaked earth, and literally cooking what it touched. The men off duty lay in their bunks through the sweltering day, fighting swarms of big, vigorous mosquitos, venomous with malaria. The jungle hummed by day and screamed by night with million-throated insect-choruses and Aguilar woke to a fiendish activity like nothing he had done before. A sullen silence fell over the squad rooms. The men no longer laughed and joked. They were growing ugly with that black ugliness that comes to white men in the tropics and outcrops in the horrible things that people at home read about and do not understand. Bobbie, who was as sensitive to the undercurrent of life in the barracks as a delicate thermometer is to heat, wrote to his father:

"If we don't get Aguilar and get rid of Wentworth soon, something—I don't even dare to think what—but something very terrible is going to happen—"

Bobbie did not finish his letter at that sitting. While he was writing, the bugles on the hill sounded a frantic "To Horse" (which is to a troop quite what an alarm is to a fire-company), the barrack yard was alive with half-dressed men dragging saddles and equipment toward the stables, and ten minutes later the troop was formed, with Wentworth, pale and nervous, seated on Levant, in its front. He and Bobbie were scarcely on speaking terms and, anyway, he did not care to tell that he had just received the most audacious message ever penned by a guerrilla Malay to a troop of United States cavalry—namely, to come into the open and fight it out. It was an insult and Wentworth knew it.

He wheeled the troop into column and started down the jungle road at a trot without a word of explanation. This was a grievous error.

For Wentworth had never been under fire. He was going through that stage of mental panic that comes to every man on the eve of his first battle. For no one knows how he may act and every man fears that he *may* act—as he shouldn't. This is to be expected, but it is no state of mind for a troop commander in the face of the enemy. Wentworth forgot his advance guard, and neither Bobbie nor any of the men suspected the imminence of danger. The road dropped into the throat of a little valley between two outlying foothills of the Zambalesian mountains. There was a rustle in the bamboo on each side, and, with no further word of warning, a horizontal sheet of Mauser fire ripped out and emptied six saddles. It was a perfect ambuscade, and the next moment the narrow road was a chaos of rearing, plunging horses and swearing men. A mortally wounded charger, at the head of the column, turned and went careening back through the ruck, screaming and blind with agony. He knocked the remaining semblance of formation into ruin and completed the fearful confusion. From both sides of the road now came a furious fusillade that lacked only accuracy to make it annihilating.

In his panicky state of nerves, Wentworth had shredded

Levant's mouth with the bit and lathered his flanks with bloody foam. The old horse for once failed in his steadiness and completed his rider's panic. Bobbie spurred toward them furiously.

"What's the matter with you?" he yelled. "Why don't you deploy and answer. Don't you see the troop is being murdered?" Wentworth was shaking in frank terror.

"Oh, Grinnell," he chattered, "I know it. They're being killed. Oh, what'll we do? They're all around. Oh, please tell 'em to stop shooting. Tell 'em I surrender. I surrender." He had torn the handkerchief from his neck and was waving it about his head. Bobbie jerked it angrily from his hand.

"Surrender—hell!" he said. "You can't surrender to *them*. They don't know what it means. Surrender if *you* want to. I'm going to fight!" and he turned to take command of the troop.

There are limits, even to the patience of a veteran troop horse, and Levant had quite arrived at his. Just as Bobbie turned, a Mauser bullet whipped like a lash across the old horse's haunches and something within his head seemed to snap. He reared in a mighty effort and came down, boring on the bit, and then, nose poked square to the front, sweat-blinded eyes unseeing, he was off, running like a wild horse, anywhere, anyhow, to escape the stinging pain in his haunches—but straight for the insurrecto lines. Wentworth was no horseman. In the presence of this new peril from his runaway mount (for the thorny bamboo switched his face and tore it cruelly), he forgot all other danger, leaned forward, gripping the mane, and yelled:

"Oh, stop him—please, for the love of heaven, stop him!"

The prayer was answered. Levant came counter of a bamboo fence and stopped because he could go no farther and for no other reason. Wentworth could and did go farther. He smashed against the fence and rolled to the ground. A swarm of little brown men appeared and pounced upon him. They trussed him as peak-backed pigs are trussed for the San Fernando Market. They caught Levant's bridle-reins and they took both to Pedro Aguilar, who was hugely pleased, but who had little time to enjoy his pleasure.

Bobbie somehow formed the troop, unlimbered his pistols and charged the far flank, breaking through and pursuing it until it melted away in the ten-foot-high grass where the horses could not follow. He was returning now to his wounded. Aguilar had no mind to meet a charge on his side of the road, and he had other plans in view. He mounted the captured horse in sinful pride and he saw to it that poor Wentworth was hustled through the brush.

Pedro Aguilar had lost much of his respect for the fighting power of "L" Troop in the preceding weeks. He had prepared the ambuscade, keenly foreseeing exactly what happened. Five miles farther up the gorge he had prepared a place where, if he could lure "L" Troop, he could also destroy it. He had sown the ground cunningly with man traps—automatic arrows, staked foot pits, and fiendish land mines. Above these snares lay his trenches in tiers, where the main force of his command was already waiting. Cautiously he began his feigned retreat.

When Bobbie returned to the road, he found that the other half of the ambuscade had quietly disappeared. He spent perhaps an hour with his wounded. Then he found and took up the trail. But "L" Troop was living under a new regime. It moved cautiously, with its scouts (who had learned their business from the White Mountain Apaches) far to the front, Sergeant Dale commanding. It was these scouts who discovered Aguilar's "position" and Aguilar himself, impudently mounted on Levant, waiting impatiently for the first signs of pursuit, and impudently outlined against the skyline of a little hill. Dale swore. Then a very shrewd look came into his wrinkle-tanned old eyes. He motioned his men to dismount—all save one, who rode with a whispered message back to the troop commander. Bobbie heard it and grinned. Then he halted the troop and called a trumpeter.

At his position on the hilltop, Levant was becoming uneasy. The wind was bringing up odors that disturbed him. Aguilar jerked the reins and told him to be still, but the voice was strange and the words were stranger. Suddenly Levant *was* still—as still as a marble horse on a pedestal—ears pricked sharply forward, nose thrust out, and nostrils dilated. From some place in the flatlands below tinkled a sound, so faint and distant that Aguilar hardly heard it. Levant heard and knew it well. He had heard it twice a day for years. It means the same thing to every horse in the cavalry, and it is the first thing a recruit horse learns, for it calls to grateful grooming, water, and feed. It was stable call, and nine times out of ten it will stop a stampeded herd, and always it will bring the horses in a paddock galloping breakneck to the gate. Levant lunged, and Aguilar did an unwise thing. He struck the old horse over the ears and poll with the flat of his bolo.

"Kitty, *bar* the door!" old Dale always puts it. "It was all off. Fer at that minute, the trumpeter blowed 'Charge,' an' Levant knows the calls as well as he knows me. He was off like a bat from the bad place. He 'charged' all right an' Ageelar! He ain't over bein' scared yet. He makes a fall fer the mane and he hangs on fer all he knows. Levant was a-foggin' like a quarter horse at the stretch—nose an' tail in a straight line an' belly nigh touchin' the ground at every jump. He didn't stop till he got to the troop an' the men had Aggie off a' that an' up before Bobbie quicker 'n the cook can say, 'Come an' git it'."

"L" Troop went wild. There was little food for a feast and only soggy dog tents for comfort in camp that night, but they had more than food and shelter. They made a fire and danced about it like the lesser demons of the pit. They forgot discipline and carried their lieutenant about on their shoulders, mauling him without mercy. They put the old horse in the center of a ceremonial circle, about which they marched, first with yells that dropped to a sort of delirious chant, lapsed into hoarseness, and then to squeaking, when their voices were quite gone.

"No," explains Sergeant Dale, "we didn't attack that position. Aggie *was* the insurrection in our parts. Levant here had captured him, an' that was all we wanted. It was dangerous—but all them ain't the main reasons. You see"—here his eyes closed to shrewd sparkling slits—"we *might*—they was jest that *shade* of chancet, that we'd recapture that Wentworth man—*but* we didn't."

THE WARRIOR HORSE

THOROUGHBREDS
by John Trotwood Moore

Straight at the breastworks, flanked with fire,
Where the angry rifles spat their ire,
And the reeling cannon rocked with flame,
Swift as his namesake, Bullet came.
Young was his rider, fifteen and two,
And yet the battles that he'd been through
Were fifteen and ten—a braver lad
Old Fighting Forrest never had!

And as he rode down the rifled wind
His brown curls bannered the breeze behind.
"O, they are mother's," he had laughed and said
When the men nicknamed him "Trundle Bed"
Two years before—when he first ran away
From mother and school to don the gray.
"But that's all right"—with a toss of his head—
"For Bullet is grown—and he's thoroughbred!"

But that was before the Shiloh fight
Where he led the charge 'gainst Prentiss' right.
And as he came through the smoke and flame
Old Forrest himself was heard to exclaim:
"Just look at Bullet and Trundle Bed!
I tell you, boys, they're both thoroughbred!"
And from that day on it became a law,
"Follow Bullet and you'll go to war!"
Today he rode less erect, I ween,
For he'd had a battle with General Gangrene
In the hospital tent—(a ball in his chest
For riding too far over Kenesaw's crest).

But even while tossing with fever and pain
He had caught a whiff of battle again,
Just smelt it afloat in the sulfurous air,
And he knew, somehow, that Forrest was there
And hard pressed, too—so, 'twixt crutches and crawl,
That night he slipped out to Bullet's stall.
A whinnying welcome—a kiss on his ear,
"I'm alive yet, Bullet—Trundle Bed's here!"
A pattering gallop at first daylight,
The boom of a gun on Johnston's right—
"That's Cleburne, Bullet! What a charming fight!"

Straight at the sheeted and leaden rain
He rode—Alas! not back again!
For the hot fire scorched the curls of brown,
And grapeshot mowed their owner down,
And the heart that beat for mother and home
Was dumb where it wept and wet the loam,
And dim in the dust the blue eyes fine—
But Bullet charged over the Yankee line.

Charged over the line!—then he missed the touch
Of the rider that always had loved him much,
And he wheeled as the gray lines rose and fell
'Neath fire like fire from the pits of hell,
And he rushed again on a backward track
When he saw the Texas brigade fall back.
But whose was the form that caught his eye
With boots to the guns and face to the sky?
And whose was the voice—"Tell mother good-by!"
And why were the curls red? His were brown—
He stopped as if a shot had brought him down!

Hell answered hell in the cannon's roar,
And steel cursed steel—yet he stood before
The form he loved;—for he knew the eyes
Though their June had changed to December skies.
Hell answered hell in the cannon's roar,
And steel cursed steel—yet he whinnied o'er
The form he loved, while the grapeshot tore!

And still he stood o'er the curly head—
For Bullet, you know, was thoroughbred—
Till a solid shot plowed a cruel rent,—
A last loving whinny—and Bullet was spent!

The burying squad in blue next day
Stopped to a man as they wiped away
A tear—for there all calm 'mid the wreck
Was Trundle Bed pillowed on Bullet's neck!

O Union great, O Union strong,
The South, you say, was in the wrong,
And yet, some day, when the foe shall come,
Some day at the beat of an insolent drum,
When the glorious Stars and Stripes unfurl'd
Shall stand for Home in Freedom's world,
The first their blood in the cause to shed
Will be—the sons of the thoroughbred!

THE SAVAGE HORSE.

BLACK EAGLE WHO ONCE RULED THE RANGES

by Sewell Ford

Of his sire and dam there is no record. All that is known is that he was raised on a Kentucky stock farm. Perhaps he was a son of Hanover, but Hanoverian or no, he was a thoroughbred. In the ordinary course of events he would have been tried out with the other three-year-olds for the big meet on Churchill Downs. In the hands of a good trainer he might have carried to victory the silk of some great stable and had his name printed in the sporting almanacs to this day.

But there was about Black Eagle nothing ordinary, either in his blood or in his career. He was born for the part he played. So at three, instead of being entered in his class at Louisville, it happened that he was shipped West, where his fate waited.

No more comely three-year-old ever took the Santa Fe trail. Although he stood but thirteen hands and tipped the beam at scarcely twelve hundred weight, you might have guessed him to be taller by two hands. The deception lay in the way he carried his shapely head and in the manner in which his arched neck tapered from the well-placed shoulders.

A horseman would have said that he had a "perfect barrel," meaning that his ribs were well rounded. His very gait was an embodied essay on graceful pride. As for his coat, save for a white star just in the middle of his forehead, it was as black and sleek as the nap on a new silk hat. After a good rubbing he was so shiny that at a distance you might have thought him starched and ironed and newly come from the laundry.

His arrival at Bar L Ranch made no great stir, however. They were not connoisseurs of good blood and sleek coats at the Bar L outfit. They were busy folks who most needed tough animals that could lope off fifty miles at a stretch. They wanted horses whose education included the fine art of knowing when to settle back on the rope and dig in toes. It was not a question as to how fast you could do your seven furlongs. It was more important to know if you could make yourself useful at a round-up.

" 'Nother bunch o' them green Eastern horses," grumbled the ranch boss as the lot was turned into a corral. "But that black fellow'd make a rustler's mouth water, eh, Lefty?" In answer to which the said Lefty, being a man little given to speech, grunted.

"We'll brand 'em in the mornin'," added the ranch boss.

Now most steers and all horses object to the branding process. Even the spiritless little Indian ponies, accustomed to many ingenious kinds of abuse, rebel at this. A meek-eyed mule, on whom humility rests as an all-covering robe, must be properly roped before submitting.

In branding they first get a rope over your neck and shut off your wind. Then they trip your feet by roping your forelegs while you are on the jump. This brings you down hard and with much abruptness. A cowboy sits on your head while others pin you to the ground from various vantage points. Next someone holds a red-hot iron on your rump until it has sunk deep into your skin. That is branding.

Well, this thing they did to the black thoroughbred, who had up to that time felt not so much as the touch of a whip. They did it, but not before a full dozen cowpunchers had worked themselves into such a fury of exasperation that no shred of picturesque profanity was left unused among them.

Quivering with fear and anger, the black, as soon as the ropes were taken off, dashed madly about the corral looking in vain for a way of escape from his torturers. Corrals, however, are built to resist just such dashes. The burn of a branding iron is supposed to heal almost immediately. Cowboys will tell you that a horse is always more frightened than hurt during the operation, and that the day after he feels none the worse.

All this you need not credit. A burn is a burn, whether made purposely with a branding iron or by accident in any other way. The scorched flesh puckers and smarts. It hurts every time a leg is moved. It seems as if a thousand needles were playing a tattoo on the exposed surface. Neither is this the worst of the business. To a high-strung animal the roping, throwing, and burning is a tremendous nervous shock. For days after branding a horse will jump and start, quivering with expectant agony, at the slightest cause.

It was fully a week before the black thoroughbred was himself again. In that time he had conceived such a deep and lasting hatred for all men, cowboys in particular, as only a high-spirited, blue-blooded horse can acquire. With deep contempt he watched the scrubby little cow ponies as they doggedly carried about those wild, fierce men who threw their circling, whistling, hateful ropes, who wore such big, sharp spurs, and who were viciously handy in using their rawhide quirts.

So when a cowboy put a breaking-bit into the black's mouth there was another lively scene. It was somewhat confused, this scene, but at intervals one could make out that the man, holding stubbornly to mane and forelock, was being slatted and slammed and jerked, now with his feet on the ground, now thrown high in the air and now dangling perilously and at various angles as the stallion raced away.

In the end, of course, came the whistle of the choking, foot-tangling ropes, and the black was saddled. For a fierce half hour he took punishment from bit and spur and quirt. Then, although he gave it up, it was not that his spirit was broken, but because his wind was gone. Quite passively he allowed himself to be ridden out on the prairie to where the herds were grazing.

Undeceived by this apparent docility, the cowboy, when the time came for him to bunk down under the chuck wagon for a few hours of sleep, tethered his mount quite securely to a deep-driven stake. Before the cattleman had taken more than a round dozen of winks the black had tested his tether to the limit of his strength. The tether stood the test. A cow pony might have done this much. There he would have stopped. But the black was a Kentucky thoroughbred, blessed with the inherited intelligence of noble sires, some of whom had been household pets. So he investigated the tether at close range.

Feeling the stake with his sensitive upper lip he discovered it to be firm as a rock. Next he backed away and wrenched tentatively at the halter until convinced that the throat strap was thoroughly sound. His last effort must have been an inspiration. Attacking the taut bucksin rope with his teeth he worked diligently until he had severed three of the four strands. Then he gathered himself for another lunge. With a snap the rope parted and the black dashed away into the night, leaving the cowboy snoring confidently by the campfire.

All night he ran, on and on in the darkness, stopping only to listen tremblingly to the echo of his own hoofs and to sniff suspiciously at the crouching shadows of innocent bushes. By morning he had left the Bar L outfit many miles behind, and when the red sun rolled up over the edge of the prairie he saw that he was alone in a field that stretched unbroken to the circling skyline.

Not until noon did the runaway black scent water. Half mad with thirst he dashed to the edge of a muddy little stream and sucked down a great draught. As he raised his head he saw standing poised above him on the opposite bank, with ears laid menacingly flat and nostrils aquiver in nervous palpitation, a buckskin-colored stallion.

Snorting from fright the black wheeled and ran. He heard behind him a shrill neigh of challenge and in a moment the thunder of many hoofs. Looking back he saw fully a score of horses, the buckskin stallion in the van, charging after him. That was enough. Filling his great lungs with air he leaped into such a burst of speed that his pursuers soon tired of the hopeless chase. Finding that he was no longer followed the black grew curious. Galloping in a circle he gradually approached the band. The horses had settled down to the cropping of buffalo grass, only the buckskin stallion, who had taken a position on a little knoll, remaining on guard.

The surprising thing about this band was that each and every member seemed riderless. Not until he had taken long up-wind sniffs was the thoroughbred convinced of this fact. When certain on this point he cantered toward the band, sniffing inquiringly. Again the buckskin stallion charged, ears back, eyes gleaming wickedly and snorting defiantly. This time the black stood his ground until the buckskin's teeth snapped savagely within a few inches of his throat. Just in time did he rear and swerve. Twice more—for the paddock-raised black was slow to understand such behavior—the buckskin charged. Then the black was roused into aggressiveness.

There ensued such a battle as would have brought delight to the brute soul of a Nero. With forefeet and teeth the two stallions engaged, circling madly about on their hind legs, tearing up great clods of turf, biting and striking as opportunity offered. At last, by a quick, desperate rush, the buckskin caught the thoroughbred fairly by the throat. Here the affair would have ended had not the black stallion, rearing suddenly on his muscle-ridged haunches and lifting his opponent's forequarters clear of the ground, showered on his enemy such a rain of blows from his iron-shod feet that the wild buckskin dropped to the ground, dazed and vanquished.

Standing over him, with all the fierce pride of a victorious gladiator showing in every curve of his glistening body, the black thoroughbred trumpeted out a stentorian call of defiance and command. The band, that had watched the struggle from a discreet distance, now came galloping in, whinnying in friendly fashion.

Black Eagle had won his first fight. He had won the leadership. By right of might he was now chief of this free company of plains rangers. It was for him to lead whither he chose, to pick the place and hour of grazing, the time for watering, and his to guard his companions from all dangers.

As for the buckskin stallion, there remained for him the choice of humbly following the new leader or of limping off alone to try to raise a new band. Being a worthy descendant of the chargers which the men of Cortez rode so fearlessly into the wilds of the New World, he chose the latter course, and having regained his senses, galloped stiffly toward the north, his bruised head lowered in defeat.

Some months later Arizona stockmen began to hear tales of a great band of wild horses, led by a magnificent black stallion which was fleeter than a scared coyote. There came reports of much mischief. Cattle were stampeded by day, calves trampled to death, and steers scattered far and wide over the prairie. By night bunches of tethered cow ponies disappeared. The exasperated cowboys could only tell that suddenly out of the darkness had swept down on their quiet camps an avalanche of wild horses. And generally they caught glimpses of a great black branded stallion who led the marauders at such a pace that he seemed almost to fly through the air.

This stallion came to be known as Black Eagle, and to be thoroughly feared and hated from one end of the cattle country to the other. The Bar L ranch appeared to be the heaviest loser. Time after time were its picketed mares run off, again and again were the Bar L herds scattered by the dash of this mysterious band. Was it that Black Eagle could take revenge? Cattlemen have queer notions. They put a price on his head. It was worth six months' wages to any cowboy who might kill or capture Black Eagle.

About this time Lefty, the silent man of the Bar L outfit, disappeared. Weeks went by and still the branded stallion remained free and unhurt, for no cow horse in all the West could keep him in sight half an hour.

Black Eagle had been the outlaw king of the ranges for nearly two years when one day, as he was standing at lookout while the band cropped the rich mesa grass behind him, he saw entering the cleft end of a distant arroyo a lone cowboy mounted on a dun little pony. With quick intelligence the stallion noted that this arroyo wound about until its mouth gave upon the side of the mesa not a hundred yards from where he stood.

Promptly did Black Eagle act. Calling his band he led it at a sharp pace to a sheltered hollow on the mesa's back slope. There he left it and hurried away to take up his former position. He had not waited long before the cowboy, riding stealthily, reappeared at the arroyo's mouth. Instantly the race was on. Tossing his fine head in the air and switching haughtily his splendid tail, Black Eagle laid his course in a direction which took him away from his sheltered band. Pounding along behind came the cowboy, urging to utmost endeavor the tough little mustang which he rode.

Had this been simply a race it would have lasted but a short time. But it was more than a race. It was a conflict of strategists. Black Eagle wished to do more than merely outdistance his enemy. He meant to lead him far away and then, under cover of night, return to his band.

Also the cowboy had a purpose. Well knowing that he could neither overtake nor tire the black stallion, he intended to ride him down by circling. In circling, the pursuer rides toward the pursued from an angle, gradually forcing his quarry into a circular course whose diameter narrows with every turn.

This, however, was a trick Black Eagle had long ago learned to block. Sure of his superior speed he galloped away in a line straight as an arrow's flight, paying no heed at all to the manner in which he was followed. Before midnight he had rejoined his band, while far off on the prairie was a lone cowboy moodily frying bacon over a sage-brush fire.

But this pursuer was no faint heart. Late the next day he was sighted creeping cunningly up to windward. Again there was a race, not so long this time, for the day was far spent, but with the same result.

When for the third time there came into view this same lone cowboy, Black Eagle was thoroughly aroused to the fact that this persistent rider meant mischief. Having once more led the cowboy a long and fruitless chase the great black gathered up his band and started south. Not until noon of the next day did he halt, and then only because many of the mares were in bad shape. For a week the band was moved on. During intervals of rest a sharp lookout was kept. Watering places, where an enemy might lurk, were approached only after the most careful scouting.

Despite all caution, however, the cowboy finally appeared on the horizon. Unwilling to endanger the rest of the band, and perhaps wishing a free hand in coping with this evident Nemesis,

Black Eagle cantered boldly out to meet him. Just beyond gun range the stallion turned sharply at right angles and sped off over the prairie.

There followed a curious chase. Day after day the great black led his pursuer on, stopping now and then to graze or take water, never allowing him to cross the danger line, but never leaving him wholly out of sight. It was a course of many windings which Black Eagle took, now swinging far to the west to avoid a ranch, now circling east along a watercourse, again doubling back around the base of a mesa, but in the main going steadily northward. Up past the brown Maricopas they worked, across the turgid Gila, skirting Lone Butte desert; up, up, and on until in the distance glistened the bald peaks of Silver range.

Never before did a horse play such a dangerous game, and surely none ever showed such finesse. Deliberately trailing behind him an enemy bent on taking either his life or freedom, not for a moment did Black Eagle show more than imperative caution. At the close of each day when, by a few miles of judicious galloping, he had fully winded the cowboy's mount, the sagacious black would circle to the rear of his pursuer and often, in the gloom of early night, walk recklessly near to the camp of his enemy just for the sake of sniffing curiously. But each morning, as the cowboy cooked his scant breakfast, he would see, standing a few hundred rods away, Black Eagle, patiently waiting for the chase to be resumed.

Day after day was the hunted black called upon to foil a new ruse. Sometimes it was a game of hide and seek among the buttes, and again it was an early morning sally by the cowboy.

Once during a midday stop the dun mustang was turned out to graze. Black Eagle followed suit. A half mile to windward he could see the cow pony, and beside it, evidently sitting with his back toward his quarry, the cowboy. For a half hour, perhaps, all was peace and serenity. Then, as a cougar springing from his lair, there blazed out of the bushes on the bank of a dry watercourse to leeward a rifle shot.

Black Eagle felt a shock that stretched him on the grass. There arrived a stinging at the top of his right shoulder and a numbing sensation all along his backbone. Madly he struggled to get on his feet, but he could do no more than raise his forequarters on his knees. As he did so he saw running toward him

CAPTURE. Henry Mitchell. *Courtesy, Philadelphia Museum of Art.*

from the bushes, coatless and hatless, his relentless pursuer. Black Eagle had been tricked. The figure by the distant mustang, then, was only a dummy. He had been shot from ambush. Human strategy had won.

With one last desperate effort, which sent the red blood spurting from the bullet hole in his shoulder, Black Eagle heaved himself up until he sat on his haunches, braced by his forefeet set wide apart.

Then, just as the cowboy brought his rifle into position for the finishing shot, the stallion threw up his handsome head, his big eyes blazing like two stars, and looked defiantly at his enemy.

Slowly, steadily the cowboy took aim at the sleek black breast behind which beat the brave heart of the wild thoroughbred. With finger touching the trigger he glanced over the sights and looked into those big, bold eyes. For a full minute man and horse faced each other thus. Then the cowboy, in an uncertain, hesitating manner, lowered his rifle. Calmly Black Eagle waited. But the expected shot never came. Instead, the cowboy walked cautiously toward the wounded stallion.

No move did Black Eagle make, no fear did he show. With a splendid indifference worthy of a martyr he sat there, paying no more heed to his approaching enemy than to the red stream which trickled down his shoulder. He was helpless and knew it, but his noble courage was unshaken. Even when the man came close enough to examine the wound and pat the shining neck that for three years had known neither touch of hand nor bridle-rein, the great stallion did no more than follow with curious, steady gaze.

It is an odd fact that feral horse, although while free even wilder and fiercer than those native to the prairies, when once returned to captivity resumes almost instantly the traits and habits of domesticity. So it was with Black Eagle. With no more fuss than he would have made when he was a colt in paddock he allowed the cowboy to wash and dress his wounded shoulder and to lead him about by the halter.

By a little stream that rounded the base of a big butte, Lefty —for it was he—made camp, and every day for a week he applied to Black Eagle's shoulder a fresh poultice of pounded cactus leaves. In that time the big stallion and the silent man buried distrust and hate and enmity. No longer were they captive and captor. They came nearer to being congenial comrades than anything else, for in the calm solitudes of the vast plains such sentiments may thrive.

So, when the wound was fully healed, the black permitted himself to be bridled and saddled. With the cow pony following as best it might they rode toward Santa Fe.

With Black Eagle's return to the cramped quarters of peopled places there came experiences entirely new to him. Every morning he was saddled by Lefty and ridden around a fence-enclosed course. At first he was allowed to set his own gait, but gradually he was urged to show his speed. This was puzzling but not a little to his liking. Also he enjoyed the oats twice a day and the careful grooming after each canter. He became accustomed to stall life and to the scent and voices of men about him, although as yet he trusted none but Lefty. Ever kind and considerate he had found Lefty. There were times, of course, when Black Eagle longed to be again on the prairie at the head of his old band, but the joy of circling the track almost made up for the loss of those wild free dashes.

One day when Lefty took him out Black Eagle found many

other horses on the track, while around the enclosure he saw gathered row on row of men and women. A band was playing and flags were snapping in the breeze. There was a thrill of expectation in the air. Black Eagle felt it, and as he pranced proudly down the track there was lifted a murmur of applause and appreciation which made his nerves tingle strangely.

Just how it all came about the big stallion did not fully understand at the time. He heard a bell ring sharply, heard also the shouts of men, and suddenly found himself flying down the course in company with a dozen other horses and riders. They had finished half the circle before Black Eagle fully realized that a gaunt, long-barrelled bay was not only leading him but gaining with every leap. Tossing his black mane in the wind, opening his bright nostrils and pointing his thin, close-set ears forward he swung into the long prairie stride which he was wont to use when leading his wild band. A half dozen leaps brought him abreast the gaunt bay, and then, feeling Lefty's knees pressing his shoulders and hearing Lefty's voice whispering words of encouragement in his ears, Black Eagle dashed ahead to rush down through the lane of frantically shouting spectators, winner by a half dozen lengths.

That was the beginning of Black Eagle's racing career. How it progressed, how he won races and captured purses in a seemingly endless string of victories unmarred by a single defeat, that is part of the turf records of the South and West.

There had to be an end, of course. Owners of carefully bred running horses took no great pleasure, you may imagine, in seeing so many rich prizes captured by a half-wild branded stallion of no known pedigree, and ridden by a silent, square-jawed cowboy. So they sent East for a "ringer." He came from Chicago in a box-car with two grooms and he was entered as an unknown, although in the betting ring the odds posted were one to five on the stranger. Yet it was a grand race. This alleged unknown, with a suppressed record of victories at Sheepshead, Bennings, and The Fort, did no more than shove his long nose under the wire a bare half head in front of Black Eagle's foam-flecked muzzle.

It was sufficient. The once wild stallion knew when he was beaten. He had done his best and he had lost. His high pride had been humbled, his fierce spirit broken. No more did the course hold for him any pleasure, no more could he be thrilled by the cries of spectators or urged into his old time stride by Lefty's whispered appeals. Never again did Black Eagle win a race.

His end, however, was not wholly inglorious. Much against his will the cowboy who had so relentlessly followed Black Eagle half way across the big territory of Arizona to lay him low with a rifle bullet, who had spared his life at the last moment and who had ridden him to victory in so many glorious races—this silent, square-jawed man had given him a final caress and then, saying a husky good-by, had turned him over to the owner of a great stud farm and gone away with a thick roll of bank notes in his pocket and a guilty feeling in his breast.

Thus it happens that today throughout the Southwest there are many black-pointed fleet-footed horses in whose veins runs the blood of a noble horse. Some of them you will find in well-guarded paddocks, while some still roam the prairies in wild bands which are the menace of stockmen and the vexation of cowboys. As for their sire, he is no more.

This is the story of Black Eagle. Although some of the minor details may be open to dispute, the main points you may hear recited by any cattleman or horse-breeder west of Omaha. For Black Eagle really lived and, as perhaps you will agree, lived not in vain.

THE UNRELIABLE HORSE

HORSES
by Richard Armour

They head the list
    Of bad to bet on,
But I insist
    They're worse to get on.

GETTING CAST
by Maria Louise Pool

When spring began to open some weeks ago, we bought a horse. All winter we had told each other that when spring opened we would certainly buy a horse. The one we purchased was a very good one; he had but one fault. We have always been told that when one has got hold of a horse that has but one fault, one might better hold on to him. So we think we shall hold on to our animal. The man who sold the creature to us informed us with perfect frankness that he had one trick, if "you was a mind to call it a trick. He was as kind as a lamb, kinder if anything; as sound as a dollar and a good roader; would plough and do all kinds of farm work."

Here the man paused, while he gnawed off some tobacco from a piece he took from his pocket, and we waited breathlessly.

"I hope he doesn't kick," said Gertrude, anxiously.

"Oh, law, no; you couldn't make him kick to save your life," was the answer. "The fact is, once in a while he gets cast in the stall. That's all."

"How often is once in a while?"

"Oh, p'raps two or three times a year."

"No oftener?"

" 'Bout that. 'Tain't really nothin' against him. Most anybody wouldn't have mentioned it; but when I trade with women I calkilate to be fair and square every time. That's my motto, fair 'n' square with women."

After this there was a silence, while we all looked very wise. At last my friend inquired what we should do if we took the horse, and he should get cast, for there was no man on the place, and she had always supposed that cast horses needed men.

"Don't need no man a natom," was the reply. "All you've got ter do is jest hitch him ruther high, 'n' then if he does git into trouble, go out there 'n' unhitch him, 'n' cluck to him, 'n' he'll most likely git up himself." \

"But if he doesn't?"

"Don't you worry; he will."

We thought we should never be able to buy of a man who had a more satisfactory motto, so we paid him his price and had the horse turned into the lane to eat grass until night, when we would decoy him into the barn with grain. He was decoyed with great ease, and tied with three or four horse knots. He was so gentle that we congratulated ourselves. Just before we retired for the night we went out to see if the knots had given any. No, they were all as they should be, and the animal turned and looked at us, as if to assure us that he had the same motto as his late master.

When we said good night to each other, we ventured to hope that this night would not prove one of the two or three times when Donald—we had already named our purchase—would get cast.

It was a little after two o'clock when I was startled by hearing a voice say:

"I wish you'd wake. There's a dreadful noise in the barn."

I sat up in bed. At first I did not remember that we had a horse, but when my friend went on to say that she was afraid Donald was cast, I recalled everything.

We lighted a lantern and hurried out, hearing as we went sounds as of a bombardment, accompanied by the crashing of timbers. But before we could unlock the door, all was still, and Gertrude said she supposed he was dead.

"Yes, he is dead," she asserted, when we reached a place where the light would strike the stall. That light revealed the form of the horse on his side, his hind legs stretched out into the floor, a few pieces of freshly torn boards lying over his hips, bedding flung out in profusion.

"I suppose the first thing will be to skin him," I said; and I added that I was glad he had died before I had become attached to him.

Let me remark here that neither of us had ever seen a horse cast, and that we had very little idea as to what the word really meant. Perhaps this remark is unnecessary, however.

Gertrude said she wished we had not set up a horse until

we had set up a boy, and I said I did not see what good a boy could do; to which she responded that he might, at least, climb in among those legs and untie the knots in the halter rope, so that, if Donald were not dead and wanted to get up, he would be able to do so. As for her, it did not seem as though she could pick her way to the horse's head any more than she could walk over red-hot ploughshares.

I had no idea that the horse was so large. We had learned that he weighed 950 pounds, but now I think anyone, even a "jockey," would have set him at about 2,000 pounds, so immense seemed the bulk, which filled the space completely. The partition between this stall and the next was partly down, as I have said, and the horse seemed to be running over, as it were, and threatening to fill that stall also. You who have seen an equine animal cast know what I mean.

It was very gloomy in the barn; the rays of the lantern only appeared to intensify the gloom. Unfortunately our neighbor who lived down the hill was a feeble man who ought not to be routed out in the night; and our neighbor who lived up the hill had been drawn as a juror, and had gone to Dedham to court. Whatever was done we must do ourselves. While we were discussing the feasibility of this and that, Donald suddenly informed us that he was not dead by lifting his head and looking back at us. Then, without any more preliminary movement, all his legs, apparently to the number of eight or ten, began to thrash about and throw bedding at us, while another board of the partition came out and fell on him, whereat he suddenly lay perfectly still again.

We believed now that he was not cast, but that he was having fits, and we began to make an estimate as to how many fits it would require to demolish the entire barn.

I repeated that I was so thankful that I had not become attached to him. Gertrude suggested sharply that it would be much more to the point to wish we had not paid the money for him.

The more we looked at him, the more it seemed the very height of cruelty that he should be hitched at such a time. I said to my friend that I thought she might easily step in quickly, now he was quiet, and unfasten the knots before the next paroxysm began. She replied that she thought I could just run right up to his head and slip off that halter. After these remarks we did not speak for what seemed a good while, and the large festoons of cobwebs hanging from the rafters looked very dismal in the lantern light.

All at once Gertrude began to pin up about her waist the skirt of her wrapper. She gave as a reason for this action that in the adventure before her she did not wish to be hampered by petticoats.

"Are you going in?" I asked in a whisper.

"I am going in," she answered, in the same tone.

I instantly recalled something I had read a good while ago in my history book at school. You will all remember what the Spartan mother said to her son.

It was not a minute before Gertrude was at the horse's head, stooping over and unbuckling the throatlash of the halter. The instant the strap slipped out of the buckle I knew there was going to be an upheaval before she could possibly get out of the stall. She knew it also. She is certainly a very bright woman. In my terror I kept yelling "Whoa! Whoa!" while the horse was thrashing about just as it had done before. It was a situation for a dime novel. I do not know whether my screaming made things any worse or not, but I know it did not make them any better. At the first symptoms Gertrude had crawled under the manger, which was about three feet from the floor. There she crouched all in a heap, until Donald, giving one parting crash to another board, stood up on his feet, and immediately and calmly began to pick up a few stray locks of hay.

Gertrude emerged. She was covered with dirt and very pale. She said it had not been pleasant under the manger, but that she thanked heaven there had been a manger to be under. She also asked me if her hair were any grayer than it had been when she left me. As for me, I began to cry and to be hysterical. I declared that if she had been killed I should have considered myself her murderer, because I had not gone in, instead of allowing her to do so. I embraced her. She replied to my effusiveness by declaring that she was convinced of one fact, and that was that it wasn't fits, but it was getting cast.

And she was right. The next night there was the same noise in the barn, only it occurred a little earlier. We lighted the lantern again, and again went out. More boards down, this time on the other side of the stall. On this occasion it was I who took off Donald's halter and then crept under the manger.·

This day we went after a man in the next village, who "sometimes did a little carpent'rin'." He came and mended the stall. After he was through he went into the lane to see, as he said, "what kind of a critter we had that could rip 'n' tear timber that way." He went on to say that "there wasn't but one hoss 't could do so much damage 't' he ever heard of, 'n' that was the one that used ter b'long ter old Lem Guild in Burnt Swamp. They did say that that animal had cost old Lem nigh on to $300 in carpenter's bills 'fore he could get red of him."

By the time Mr. Smith had finished speaking in this way, he caught sight of Donald, who came walking up to us. He burst out laughing—Mr. Smith, I mean, not Donald.

"It's the same one!" said the man. "I sh'd know him in Egypt." When he had subdued his hilarity so he could articulate with more ease, he advised us to send the horse to some auction where "he wasn't known, 'n' where we shouldn't be obleeged to tell no lies 'bout him. That is, unless we'd ruther keep him. If we did keep him, he'd like the job of bein' our carpenter."

He said he should like to know what the feller that sold the hoss to us said about him.

We answered that he said he had but one fault, that he would get cast two or three times a year.

"Two or three times a year!" cried Mr. Smith, "he don't do nothin' but git cast!"

We said we guessed we wouldn't sell him, and we guessed we could arrange somehow.

"Jes' 's you say, of course," responded Mr. Smith, still grinning in a very offensive way. "Only don't forget; lemme be your carpenter."

Since this first experience we have found that Donald averages to be cast five times a week. We have bought a load of boards—good thick ones, and when one set is completely shattered, with the aid of our boy we put on more boards.

For we have a boy now who comes and spends the nights on a "cot bed" in the chamber over the sink room.

Let me give a brief rehearsal of what occurs five nights in a week. It would be easier for us in every way if we could know when the "off nights" were to be, but we cannot know that. It is usually between twelve and three that Gertrude appears in my door with a lantern and says the horse is cast, and she has just been and roused Henry, the boy.

Then I rise, for thus far it has appeared to us that it would be safer if we both went out with Henry, although there is a distinct duty for but one to perform—Henry runs in by the side of Donald and unties the rope, then creeps directly under the manger. It seems quite proper and fitting for a boy to creep under a manger, but it is not a woman's province. I scramble about halfway up the stairs and wait.

Gertrude flourishes a whip behind the horse, who is one great sprawl among the boards and straw and hay. The moment he begins to move my friend rushes up the stairs to join me. We flee to the stairs since one occasion when Donald's struggles extended so far out into the floor that it appeared as if we were to be involved in them.

It will be seen that our nights are not altogether restful. Henry is a good boy, but he is getting very hard to awaken. We are thinking of taking the stalls away entirely and thus giving Donald the entire first floor of the barn—not hitching him at all. A simple loose box would not be nearly large enough for any creature as large as he is when he is down. Still, he is a very good horse, and, as he has but one fault, when we have succeeded in arranging for that fault I should judge that it would be proper to say that he was perfect; that is, if we ever wished to sell him. Gertrude says that, in case we should wish to part with him, it would be necessary first to kill Henry and then every one who knew about the animal. Although we put the boy under the most impressive of oaths not to tell what kind of midnight orgies we indulged in, we believe that he has told; or why does that peculiar expression come upon the face of each neighbor who asks us how we like our horse—and why does each neighbor ask us that question, not only once, but repeatedly?

Nevertheless, we still think that the motto of the man who sold the horse to us was a good motto.

THE GRACIOUS HORSE

CORKRAN OF THE CLAMSTRETCH
by John Biggs, Jr.

This is a record of genius. I saw him for the first time as he lay beneath an apple tree, endeavoring by muscular twitchings of his upper lip to grab an apple which lay just beyond the reach of his long black nose. Indisputably it was a game which he played, and he ordered it by set rules of his own devising. It was fundamental that he could not move his body, but he might crane or stretch his neck to any impossible posture. I climbed the paddock fence, and moved the apple an inch toward him. He looked at me reproachfully, but seized it nonetheless, and, devouring it with a single crunching bite, rose to his feet, and proceeded inscrutably to stare.

He was a dumpy little horse, resembling a small fat business man, and as soon to be suspected of immortal speed as a stockbroker of a sonnet. His torso was a rotund little barrel. From this his legs, heavy and muscular, stuck out at odd angles. A lean neck rose from the mass, and upon this was plastered a head, many sizes too large, which looked as if it had been thrown at him from a distance and had inadvertently stuck.

His gaze mellowed and he regarded me more leniently. A faint smile began to wreathe his lips; the smile expanded to a soundless tittering. At last, in looking at me, he fairly laughed. This I considered impolite and told him so. He listened courteously, but made no comment other than raising a quizzical hoof. He walked around me and looked carefully at my reverse side. This satisfied him. He returned to the apple tree, yawned broadly, and lay down. Richard Thomas Corkran was at rest.

Tentatively I offered him apples, but his ennui was not to be dispelled. Finally, he slept the sleep of a good and honest horse. I retired to the fence lest I disturb the sacred slumbers.

Genius is an unutterable thing. It is a spark flying from no

visible flame. It is an excitement of the soul; it is a terrific motiva-
tion. It is a vapor that splits the rock of reality.

Richard Thomas Corkran was a strange rhapsody of speed.
He was without circumstance, without explanation. No great
family had crossed a bar sinister upon his unknown escutcheon.
His fathers were indistinguishable clods of work. At the time of
his first race his sides were galled from plough harness. Literally
he was self-made.

He was possesed of an iron will and intelligence. Consum-
mately he understood his metier; never did his greatness over-
whelm him. He remained unmoved, his attitude the epitome of
a successful business. Yet he was capable of a cold and dignified
fury. Always was it merited, but he worked himself to it, for
he had found it to be an efficient symbol. A balanced quietness
was his attitude upon the track, and from it he never deviated.
He raced without the slightest enthusiasm or excitation. Icy imperturbability marked his technique—an imperturbability that
was unaffected. From the tips of his tiny hoofs to his absurd head
he was polite, both to his rivals, whom he scorned, and his attendants, whom he considered unworthy of notice, and this
politeness proceeded from his conscious known superiority.

One thing of all things aroused his wrath, hot and sincere.
He considered himself a free agent, and any molestation of this
right caused anger to boil within him. The hours of his business
were those which he spent upon the track; at all other times
he came and went as he pleased. He would permit no officious
infringement upon his leisure. As to his racing it was indomitably
his own. He considered all human aid simply cooperation. If
it became direction, no matter how tactfully suggested, he was
done. He would not move a hoof toward the track's end. In his
maiden race, a whip had been laid, solely as an incentive, upon
his muscular little thighs. Richard Thomas Corkran had slid to
a stop with stiffened forefeet, and, without heat or expression,
but with icy malevolence, had kicked his sulky to fragments of
wood and steel. Thereafter his driver, by iron order, sat braced
to the sulky, and with loose reins simply fulfilled the requirements
of rule. The race and the trotting of it were solely Richard Thomas
Corkran's.

It was five o'clock when they came to arouse him, and this

partook of a stately, ordered ceremony. There were five men in all, and I presume that he would not have deigned to rise for less. Down the field in careful formation they advanced. First came the head trainer, magnificently unencumbered by blanket, sponge, or currycomb, the veritable master of the bed-chamber, and flanking him, his subalterns, two graceful yellow boys—this touch exotic—carrying combs and skin brushes; next came two buckets, marked with the white initials *R. T. C.*, and then his *own* blanket, plaid-striped, refulgent, the one slight vulgarity necessary to all genius. Last of all was a small white dog, like an animated washrag, propelling itself forward with staccato bounds and barks.

The process halted; the dog continued forward, and barked malevolently in the ear of recumbent greatness, which responded with a slow opening of its left eye. The long thin neck rose from the ground at a right angle, and surveyed the halted host. Richard Thomas Corkran got to his feet and shook his rotund little body. He stood waiting.

As they combed and brushed him, he moved no muscle, but placidly chewed a succession of straws that hung pendulous from his lower lip. It was a gesture nonchalant. At length his black coat was sleeked and glossed. The head trainer stepped forward and felt his chest, his hocks, and pasterns. This he endured with kindness, and, inspection over, trotted toward the watering trough, preceded, however, by the white dog. Pleasurably he played with the water, drinking but little. He blew through his nostrils, causing white bubbles to rise and burst through the turmoil of the surface. The light, finely made racing harness was then put upon him, and adjusted perfectly to each of his expanding muscles, and last the blanket, strapped and belted, making him look like a fat, plaid-cowled monk. The gate was now opened, and he walked gravely from the paddock. Behind him streamed his acolytes in meek procession. Heralding him was the woolly dog. Last was his sulky, wheeled by a Negro boy. Past the judge's house he plodded, and I saw the old jurist rise from the porch to greet him.

The discovery of Richard Thomas Corkran, and his relation to Judge Coleman, a famous county story, deserves record.

At dusk one summer evening Judge Coleman, exercising a favorite mare, herself of note, had, on the Clamstretch, come upon the son of a neighboring farmer, atop the height of an old-fashioned racing sulky, a wooden affair with high shaking wheels. Beneath this relic, for the sulky jutted out almost over his rump, careened an odd little horse, looking in the darkness, so says the judge, like a small, black mouse.

"I'll race you, Tommy," said the judge jokingly to the boy.

"Done," was the reply, and the little horse moved up to the mare's nose.

"Take a handicap, Tommy," said the judge, amused by the boy's confidence.

"*You* take the handicap, judge," said the boy, and the judge, fearful of hurting the boy's feelings, walked his mare some ten yards to the front.

"*Now!*" shouted the boy, and the judge heard with amazement the strong, unbelievably quick beat of the little horse's hoofs as he struck to his stride through the white dust of the road. Past the striving mare he went as if she were haltered to the ground. Three times was this astounding performance repeated, while the straining nostrils of the mare grew red with effort.

The judge pulled to the side of the road.

"What do you use that horse for!" he asked.

"For ploughin'," replied the boy, and he was near tears with pride and rage. "I have to use him for ploughin'."

"What do you call him?" went on the judge.

"Richard Thomas Corkran," replied the boy. "After grand-pop."

Then and there, for an adequate price, Richard Thomas Corkran changed hands, and the judge that night examining him by the light of a stable-lantern discovered the marks of plough-galls upon his flanks.

No attempt was made to teach R. T. C. to race; none was ever needed. When the time came for a race he plodded to the track, and from thence to the starting-point, and thereafter at some time favorable to himself he commenced to trot. No agitation of spectators or contesting horses, no jockeying of drivers, might shake his icy imperturbability, his utter calm. The race done and won, he returned at a walk to his paddock. In two years upon the Grand Circuit he had never missed a meeting nor ever lost a race.

With something of awe I watched him as he passed between the high stone posts of the judge's entrance gate and entered the Clamstretch.

This road is a long white ribbon which runs from the Porter Ferry to the hills. Its crown is covered with clam shells beaten to a soft imponderable dust, and from this it is known as the Clamstretch. It is agreed by county racing authorities that from the center of the ferry gate to the old Weldin Oak is a perfect half mile, and a horse that covers this distance under two minutes is worthy of notice. Richard Thomas Corkran, when the humor was upon him, and trotted the exact half mile in one minute and five seconds.

It is a county saying that colts the day they are born are instructed by their mother mares in the trotting of the Clamstretch.

Beneath the old Weldin Oak and lining the road are rough wooden benches, and before them the ground has been worn bare and hard by many feet. At the side of the road sways a decrepit whitewashed stand, as high as a man's chest, and with two cracker boxes for steps. This is the official stand of the judge of the course when such a formality is necessary.

The customs of the Clamstretch have grown up with time, and are as unbending as bronze. It is decreed that Judge Coleman shall be the ruling authority of the meeting, that the time of trotting shall be from twilight to darkness, and that there shall be as much racing as the light permits.

First the horsemen gather and solemnly trot practice heats, each driver carefully keeping his animal from showing its true worth, though the exact record of each is known to all. Then, with stable boys at the horses' heads, they collect in little groups about the oak, and with tobacco, portentous silences, and great gravity, lay careful bets. But with the entrance of the judge comes drama.

He minces across the bare space before the oak and nods gravely to each friend. From an interior pocket of his immaculate gray coat he draws a small black book, the official record of the Clamstretch. In this book he enters the contesting horses, the names of the owners, and the bets. This finished, the four horsemen selected for the first race pass to the road, briefly inspect their gear, climb to the sulkies, sit magnificently upon the outstretched tails of their horses, and with whips at point, drive slowly toward the gate of the ferry lodge.

The noise of the hoofs dies to abrupt silence as the contestants jockey for position at the start, broken by the sudden thunder of the race. Puffs of white dust, hanging low over the road, rise beneath the drumming hoofs; strained red nostrils flash across the finish. Comes the stentorian voice of the announcer, giving the winner and the time. Gradually the soft light fades; the last race is ended; the judge bids the company a grave good night, and the red point of his cigar disappears in the gloom of the meadow.

There are many names great in the history of racing, whose owners have trotted the broad white road and have been duly inscribed in the black book. From Barnett and Barnetta B., from Almanzer and the Bohemia Girl, forever from R. T. C., the time of the Clamstretch is set, and it is a point of honor between horse and man that when a great king falls he is brought back to trot his last from the lodge gate to the Weldin Oak. From Clamstretch to Clamstretch, is the saying.

I have often witnessed the custom of the Clamstretch, and this time I entered upon it inconspicuously in the magnificent wake of Richard Thomas Corkran. Upon the bare meadow, around the old oak as a nucleus, were gathered many horses. A wild roan mare led the group, a young, untried creature, who kicked and squealed in a nervousness that turned from sudden anger to helpless quaking. A Negro at her head, a shining black hand upon her bit, soothed and quieted her with honey upon his tongue and a sturdy desire to thump her in his heart. Her owner, a bewhiskered farmer, stood just beyond the range of her flying heels and looked at her with dismay.

"Now, pettie," he kept saying. "Now, pettie, that ain't no way to behave. That ain't no way."

A hilarious group of friends, in a half circle behind him, ridiculed his attempts at reconciliation.

"She ain't your pettie," they shouted. "She's some other feller's. . . . Maybe she ain't got none at all. . . . Give her hell, Jim. . . . Soft stuff's no dope."

A large horse, piebald and pretty, looking as if he had been purchased in a toy store, stood next to the virago. Her nervousness was apparently communicated to him, for occasionally he would back and rear. At these times, he raised clouds of dust, which sifted gently over the field, causing a shiver to run down the line of waiting horses.

"Keep 'em horses still," shouted the Negro boys. "Hold onto 'em."

One giant black, a colossal hand upon the muzzle of his horse, a mare as dainty and graceful as a fawn, threw out his great chest with pride.

"My lady's a lady," he crooned softy as the other horses stamped and grew restive. "My lady's a lady." The pretty creature looked at him with wide brown eyes, and shook her head as if softly denying.

An animal at the end of the line held my attention. His hide was the color of running bronze. His head might have been struck for one of the horses of Time, the nostrils flaring and intense, the eyes wild with hint of action. He looked as if he might run with the whirlwind, be bitted to a comet's orbit, and triumph. Sacrilege, it seemed, when I learned that he had never won a race, was quite lacking in the heart that creates a great horse. In him nature was superbly bluffing.

Richard Thomas Corkran stood at some distance from the rank and file. Boredom was unutterably upon him. He seemed looking for a place to lie down and continue his interrupted slumbers, and to be restrained only by the fear that he might be considered *gauche*. Truly there was nothing in which he might be honestly interested. No horse present could give him even the beginnings of a race. His heaviest work had been done upon the grand circuit in the spring and early summer. Vacation and leisure possessed him for this day at least. True, upon the next day he was to trot a race which was, perhaps, the most important of his career. Now, through the courtesy of the judge, he was the *pièce de résistance*, the staple, of the evening. At the end of the racing he would trot a heat in solitary grandeur—one heat, not more, and this heat would be preparation for tomorrow's test. Two horses, strategically placed over the straight half-mile, would pace him, but they would have as little to do with his trotting as the distance posts upon the track. A little knot of

men, gaping and solemn, had already gathered about him, inter-
preting his every bored motion as proof positive of his phenomenal
speed. He accepted this as his due and was in no manner affected
by it.

The men, as always, interested me. A few were professional
horsemen, so marked and molded. They were calm persons, who
spoke without gesture or facial expression. Thought flowed sound-
lessly behind their shrewd eyes. Their attitude was one of continual weighing and balancing of mighty points.

The rest were prosperous farmers, country gentlemen, or
honest artisans from the nearby village, all pleasure-bent. The
regalia of those who were to drive, or hoped to drive, was unique.
They seemed to express their personalities best through high
black boots, striped trousers, and flaming calico shirts. The cli-
macteric pinnacle was usually reached with an inherited racing
cap, scarlet, ochre, brown, yellow, plaid.

Twilight cupped the world, seeming to grant a hush to earth.
The road took on new whiteness, the meadows gradually darkening, touched by the night and the brooding quietness that comes
as the sun goes down.

The first race came to a close—a torrent of young horses.
The wild-eyed virago was among them, and she won by a prodigious stretching of the neck. Thereat, totally unable to withstand triumph, she bucked and squealed, dragging her sulky,
that tormenting appendage, behind her.

"Shure, it's temperamental she is," said a Scotch-Irish farmer
standing beside me. "But she might have walked in on her hands
and won."

The spectacle was dramatic. There was a flurry of horse and
man as a race was called, a rushing to the track's edge by the
spectators, a happy bustling of self-important officials. From the
knots of excited humanity emerged the horses, the drivers with
their whips at trail beneath their elbows, their eyes self-consciously upon the ground. Slender sulkies, gossamer-wheeled,
were pulled out, tested by heavy thumpings, and attached. Carefully the reins were bitted, run back through the guide-rings,
and the drivers swung themselves up. The final touch was the
arranging of the horse's tail, and here technique differed. A good
driver must sit upon his horse's tail. This is beyond question. The
mooted point is whether he shall do so spread or flat. Authority

as usual holds both sides, Richard Thomas Corkran absolutely dissenting, for he would allow no one to sit on his tail but himself.

The horses dwindle to specks upon the long white road. The sound of the hoofs dies to faint pulsing in the ears, a shadow of sound. Silence follows, breathless, expectant, broken by the clarion of the start.

The rhythm becomes a rhapsody of pounding hoofs, quick-timed, staccato. A black swirl up the road falls to detail of straining bodies. A roar crescendoes to high shreds of sound as they flash across the finish. A second of tense silence—pandemonium.

Three races of three heats each were trotted. Darkness was drifting down upon us as the last was finished, and Richard Thomas Corkran walked out upon the track.

His small black body blent with the semidarkness, rendering him almost indistinguishable. The crowd followed him across the track. There was no preparation, no ceremony. The small figure plodded into the graying distance. His pace was scarcely above a walk. He might have been a plough horse returning from a day of labor. The spectators drew back to the road's edge.

The twilight deepened. We waited in silence. A faint drum of hoofs sounded down the wind. Sharper, swifter, it grew. A black line split the darkness, lengthening so quickly as to vanquish eyesight. There was an incredible twinkling of legs as he passed me, a glimpse of square-set methodical shoulders, which moved with the drive of pistons, of a free floating tail spread to the rushing scythe of air. He finished.

Carefully he stopped, not too sharply lest he strain himself. He turned and plodded toward the oak, where hung his blanket, and as its folds fell upon him he returned to peaceful contemplation.

Came the voice of the announcer, a hoarse bellow through the gloom—"Ti-i-ime by the ha-a-alf. Ooone—five—an'—two—fi-i-ifths!!" A roar of applause broke to scattered clapping. Relaxation from the tension expressed itself in laughter, jest, and play. The crowd prepared to go home. The Clamstretch was for that day done.

After dinner Judge Coleman, whose guest I was, and myself walked down the close-cropped green to the paddock fence. A moon had risen, bathing the land in clear pale yellow. Within the paddock and beneath his apple tree lay Richard Thomas Corkran. He rested upon his side, his small torso rising and falling gently with the even flow of his breath. From his upper lip protruded a straw which moved gently as the air was expelled from his nostrils. Untroubled by thoughts of tomorrow's race, he was again sound asleep.

The next morning I saw him leave his paddock for the fair grounds. A large truck, whose side just disclosed the upper edge of his rotund, barreled little body, held him, his three attendants, and his staccato, white, and woolly dog. His placid eye fell upon me as he passed, and I saluted and followed him.

The site of the State Fair was a great fenced field upon the outskirts of a nearby city. Upon one side towered a huge grandstand, facing a broad and dusty half-mile track. In the gigantic oval, thus formed, was a smaller ring, tanbarked and barricaded, used at times as a horse-show ring, across a corner of which was now built a small, precarious wooden platform, where vaudeville teams disported themselves in a bedlam of sound for the free edification of the multitude.

On the outside of the oval of track stretched the Midway, in parlance "Mighty," a herd of tents and rough-board shacks, a staggering line, running to a quiet Negro graveyard, overgrown with yellow grass and flecked with the gray of forgotten tombstones.

Toward the city in larger tents and squat, unsided buildings, were the farming exhibits, and between these and the outer road the racing stables, flanking a hard-beaten square, in whose center leaned a rusty pump, dry for years, and used as a hitching post. Beyond, in a multiplicity of stalls and sties and bins, uncovered to the air, were huge and blooded bulls, monster hogs, and high-crowing, cackling fowl.

Over the wide field hung a haze of dust that stung the nostrils and soaked into the skin, causing a gray change.

I entered through a choked gate into which people streamed as a river banks against a bulwark, a confusion of carriages and cars, walking women with toddling children, red and blue balloons swaying between the ground and the gateposts, flying bits of straw and dust, howling hawkers: a high-pitched excitation of mob.

As I passed through the wooden arch came the sleek backs

of racing-horses, surging toward the eight's posts, and the wild foreground of waving arms as the spectators beat against the rail.

The crowd was a sluggish, slow-moving monster that proceeded with sudden aimless stoppings. It was impossible to change or alter its spasmodic pace. It rippled into every corner of the field; it ran over fences and beat down barricades. It possessed an attribute of quicksilver in that it could never be gathered or held.

Its sound was a great crushing. It winnowed the grass beneath its feet, and the beaten odor came freshly to my nostrils. Its urged over itself and spun slowly back. It never seemed to break or detach itself into individuals. Its tentacles might loop and cling to various protuberances, but its black bulk moved ever on.

I wandered through the maze of exhibits, stopping and listening where I would. The broad river of crowd divided to smaller eddies that swirled endlessly within and between the long rows of buildings and tents.

I passed glittering rows of farming machinery, red-painted, sturdy, clawed feet hooked into the ground. This bushy-bearded farmers tenderly fingered, and fought bitingly and ungrammatically with one another as to its merits.

A small tractor crawled upon its belly through the mud, and struggled and puffed its way over impossible obstacles. It was followed by a hysterical herd of small boys, who miraculously escaped destruction under its iron treads.

I crossed the square where the lean, cowled racing horses were led patiently back and forth by the stable boys. Always the crowd was with me, beating its endless, monotonous forward path. I grew to hate it, longed to tear apart its slow viscosity, to sweep it away and clear the earth.

Inside the buildings I passed between endless counters piled high with pyramids of jelly, saw the broad smiles of the presiding housewives, smelt brown loaves of prize bread. Baskets of huge fruit were allotted place, red apples succulent and glowing, fuzzy peaches white and yellow. The presiding deity of the place—the veritable mother of all food—I found in the center of the shack. Her function was the creation of pie, and this of itself seemed to be sufficient. She was a large woman, red-faced, red-handed, and without a curve to her body. She was composed of but two straight lines, and between these lay her solid ample self. Her round fat arms were bare to the elbow and white with flour. On the table before her was an incalculable area of pie crust, which she kneaded and powdered and cut with deft and stubby fingers. Behind her was a huge charcoal range upon which un-countable pies cooked, and around her were infinite battalions of pies, tremendous legions of pies, gigantic field armies of pies. Ex-aggeration itself fell faint.

Before her, in the consummation of a newer miracle, fed the multitude. All men they were, and they ate steadily, unemo-tionally, as if they might eat eternally. They went from pie to pie to pie. They never ceased, even to wipe their lips. They never stopped to speak. They selected their next pie before they had eaten their last, and reached for it automatically. It was a spectacle so vast as to possess grandeur. Such a woman and such men might have created the world and devoured it in a day.

Around the eaters stood their wives—certainly none could have dared be sweethearts—gaping with that curious feminine lack of understanding—awed but unreasonable—at such prodigies of feeding.

I came next upon monster hogs, buried deep in the straw. Gruntingly they lifted their battleship bulks and waddled to the walls of the pen in response to the pointed sticks of small boys. The air was permeated with animal odor, occasionally split by the fresh smell of cooking pastry and pungent aromatic spices.

With the Midway, sturdy respectability changed to blowsy, tarnished sin. Gaudy placards in primal colors bellied with the wind. All appeal was sensual, to grotesquerie or chance. From the tent of the "Circassian Syrian Dancing Girls" came the beat of a tom-tom, like that of a heavy pulse. Squarely in the passageway a three-shell merchant had placed his light table and was busily at work.

"Step up, ladies!" he called. "Step up, gents. Th' li'l pea against the world! Match it, an' y' win! You take a chance evury day. When yer born you take a chance, when you marry you take a chance, when you die you take an awful chance. Match me! Match me! Match me!"

His fingers moved like the dartings of a snake's tongue. The tiny pea appeared and disappeared.

"You lost! Poor girl. She lost her quarter. The Lord knows how she got it. Time tells an' you ain't old yet . . . !"

Beyond, outside a larger tent, sat a mountainous woman, a tiny fringed ballet skirt overhanging her mammoth legs. She was like some giant, jellied organism. To the crowd which gapingly surrounded her she addressed a continual tittering monologue.

"Step up here, baby. . . . Come up, lady! No, I ain't particular even if I am fat. . . . I don't care who looks at me. I'm a lady, I am. Hell, yes! See that man over there?" She swung a monster finger toward a barker. "He keeps me up here. . . . Sure, he does! You jest let me down an' at him—I'll do him in—I can make twelve of him!"

Further on the crowd clustered thickly around a small tank, from the end of which rose a tall ladder topped by a tiny platform. So high was the ladder that it seemed to melt into a single line. As I watched, a young man climbed upon the edge of the tank. He grimaced and bowed to the crowd.

He stripped off a beflowered green bathrobe, disclosing a body as sleek as a wet seal's, and like a slender black monkey, climbed the ladder. Reaching the platform, he posed with outstretched arms. The crowd stiffly craned their necks.

At the side of the tank appeared another man with a flat, pock-marked face. There ensued an extraordinary dialogue.

"Leopold Benofoski!" shouted the man beside the tank to him in the air, "Is there any last word that you would like to leave your wife and family?"

"No," shouted the man upon the platform.

"Leopold Benofoski!" shouted the interlocuter. "Are you prepared to meet your fate?"

"Yes," said the young man.

"Then dive!" shouted the other, "—and God be with you!" He hid his face with a prodigious gesture of despair.

The young man drew back his arms until he was like a tightened bow. For a second he poised upon tensed legs, then, like a plummet, dropped from the edge of the platform. Incredibly, swiftly he flashed down. I caught the glint of his white legs as he hit the water, a high splash, and he had drawn himself out of the other side. A grimace of shining teeth, and he was gone. The crowd, unmoved, went sluggishly on.

Slowly I worked myself through the area before the grandstand, where the crowd was thickest. There had been an accident upon the track: a young horse, "breaking" because of the hard path worn in the finely combed dirt between the turnstiles of the fence and grandstand, had reared and flung its forelegs into the air. A debacle had followed as the animals close in the ruck had plunged into the leader. Three drivers had been thrown into a thresh of horses. Splintered sulkies and broken shafts lay in the debris, hazed by the cloud of dust. One horse, maddened with fear, had run squealing on, not to be stopped until it had completed the mile. One driver was badly injured.

This had had its effect upon the crowd. An uneasy ripple ran across the grandstand. There was a tinge of hysteria in the movement, a desire to clutch and shiver. As time passed the tension heightened. In the officials' stand I saw the small, staid figure of the judge, peering alertly at the frightened multitude. Then came a consultation of bent heads, and his hand swung up to the cord of the starting bell. The flat clang, for the bell was muffled, beat into the turbulence. A gradual quiet fell.

There followed the announcement of the curtailment of the program to the immediate race of Richard Thomas Corkran.

I cut my way swiftly through the crowd, back to the stables, for I desired to see the little horse leave the paddock.

I found him firmly braced upon stocky legs as they bound his anklets. His refulgent blanket drooped over his rotund torso, and from the striped folds emerged the long, grotesque neck and the absurd hobbyhorse head. As I approaced he eyed me with droll appreciation, for I seemed always subtly to please him.

As the last anklet was buckled he shook himself. It was a methodical testing to see that he was entirely in place. Satisfied, he took a few short steps forward, carefully balancing his weight so that no muscle might be strained. At this juncture the white dog, apparently just released from captivity, bounced forward like a lively rubber ball. Fierce was his attack upon the nose of Richard Thomas Corkran. Devious were his advancings and retreatings. Quietly did the little horse receive this adulation. Again he shook himself.

Now was the spider-web tracery of harness put upon him, the silvered racing bridle and the long thin bit. The blanket readjusted, the paddock gate was opened, and with the small, white dog surging before him, his attendants following, he plodded toward the arena.

As he emerged into the crowd there beat upon him a roar of sound. Like a great wave it ran down the field and reechoed back. It split into individual tendrils that were like pointed spears falling harmless from his small unmoved back. Through the path that opened out before him he slowly went, unnoticing and grave. He entered the weighing ring.

Courteously he stood as his blanket was removed, and he stood bared to the gaze of the three inspecting officials. Then the slender spider-wheeled sulky was pulled up and attached. Suddenly I saw his head lift: the contesting horse had entered the arena.

He was like a legged arrow, a magnificent, straight-lined dart. Thin to the point of emaciation, the bones of his body moved like supple reeds beneath a lustrous skin. Lightly muscled was he, tenuous skeins at his wrists and hocks. He looked as if he might drift before the wind.

He was very nervous. There was a continual thin white line across his nostrils as his high chest took air. A rippling shiver ran through him.

Richard Thomas Corkran was the first to leave the ring. Never had he taken his eyes from his opponent. His small, black muzzle remained fixed, imperturbable. Slowly he plodded out upon the track.

The flat sound of the bell, calling the race, drifted down from above my head. As I fought my way to the rail, the roar of the crowd rose to frenzy. The horses were going by the officials' stand to the starting post.

The challenger went first, his curved neck pulling against the bit, his gait a drifting, slithering stride. After him came Richard Thomas Corkran, a tiny, methodical figure. His head was down. I could see the sulky move gently forward under his easy step.

As they reached the post and turned the tumult died away to a clear and appalling silence. Glancing up the rail, I saw the heads of the crowd leaning forward in motionless expectation.

For an instant they hung unmoving at the post. Then the challenger seemed to lift himself in the air, his forefeet struck out in the beginning of his stride for Richard Thomas Corkran, without warning, had begun to *trot*.

They swept down toward the thin steel wire that overhung the track at the start. In breathless silence they passed, and I heard the shouted—"*Go!*"

Like a dream of immeasurable transiency, they vanished at the turn. I heard the staccato beat of hoofs as they went down the backstretch.

The crowd had turned. To the rail beside me leaped a man, balancing himself like a bird.

"He's ahead!" he shouted wildly. "He's ahead!—ahead!"

I swept him from the fence and climbed upon it myself. Above the bodies of the crowd at the far side of the track I saw two plunging heads. For a second only were they visible. Again they vanished.

They came down the stretch in silence, the spectators standing as though struck into stone. At the three-eighths post they seemed to be equal, but as they drew down the track I saw that the challenger led by a fraction of a foot. His flying hoofs seemed never to strike the ground. He was like some advancing shadow of incredible swiftness.

Richard Thomas Corkran raced with all that was in him. His small legs moved like pistons in perfected cadence.

As the challenger passed I could hear the talking of the driver, low-pitched, tense, driving his horse to a frenzy of effort.

"Boy! Boy! Boy! Let him have it! Let him have it! Take it from him! I'm tellin' you. Go it! Go it! Go it!"

Richard Thomas Corkran's driver sat braced to his sulky, the reins loose upon the horse's back. I caught a glimpse of his grim, strained face above the dust of the advance.

Again there was a wild beating of hoofs up the back of the track.

"He's gotta do it now," shouted some one beside me. "He's gotta do it now. He can't lose! He can't lose!"

At the seven-eighths post the crowd thrust out its arms and began to implore. The waving arms leaped down with the striving horses. The challenger was ahead by yards. His red nostrils flared to the wind. Never had I seen such trotting!

He came under the wire in a great plunge, his driver madly whipping him. Richard Thomas Corkran was defeated!

For seconds the crowd hung mute, seemingly afraid to move or speak. Then from the edge of the grandstand came a single shout. It grew and ran around the field, swelling to an uninterrupted roar that seemed to split itself against the heavens—a tribute to the victor, a greater tribute to the vanquished!

Richard Thomas Corkran plodded slowly around the track to the paddock gates. His head was down as before, and his rotund little body moved steadily onward. At the gates he halted and waited as the winner was led through before him. Then he gravely followed and disappeared into the crowd.

He had met triumph with boredom; he met defeat, as a great gentleman should, with quiet courtesy and good humor. There was nothing of disdain or bitterness upon his small, black muzzle; Richard Thomas Corkran passed to the gods of horse as he had come, imperturbable, alert, sublimely sensible. But in his passing his tiny hoofs were shod with drama. Departing greatness may ask no more!

I saw him later in the paddock. His white, woolly dog was stilled; a Negro rubber sobbed as he held a washing bucket. The little horse stood by himself, his feet as ever firm upon the ground, untouched, unmoved, and quietly resting. The thoughts that he possessed he kept, as always, to himself. I bowed my head and turned away.

THE UNPREDICTABLE HORSE

THE RACING-MAN
by A. P. Herbert

My gentle child, behold this horse—
A noble animal, of *course,*
    But not to be relied on;
I wish he would not stand and snort;
Oh, frankly, he is *not* the sort
    Your father cares to ride on.
His head is tossing up and down,
And he has frightened half the town
    By blowing in their faces,
And making gestures with his feet,
While now and then he stops to eat
    In inconvenient places.
He nearly murdered me today
By trotting in the wildest way
    Through half a mile of forest;
And now he treads upon the kerb,
Consuming some attractive herb
    He borrowed from the florist.
I strike him roughly with my hand;
He does not seem to understand;
    He simply *won't* be bothered
To walk in peace, as I suggest,
A little way towards the West—
    He prances to the No'th'ard.
And yet, by popular repute,
He is a mild, well-mannered brute,
    And very well connected;
Alas! it is the painful fact
That horses hardly ever act
    As anyone expected.

JOCKEY. Hunt Diederich. *Courtesy, The Newark Museum, Newark, N.J.: Gift of Mr. and Mrs. Felix Fuld.*

Yet there are men prepared to place
A sum of money on a race
    In which a horse is running,
An animal as fierce as this,
As full of idle prejudice,
    And every bit as cunning;
And it is marvelous to me
That grown-up gentlemen can be
    So simple, so confiding;
I envy them, but, O my son,
I cannot think that they have done
    A great amount of riding.

THE ELUSIVE HORSE

NORTHWIND

by Herbert Ravenal Sass

It was in the days when Moytoy of Tellequo was High Chief
of the Cherokee Nation that the wild chestnut stallion known
afterward as Northwind left the savannas of the Choctaw country and traveled to the Overhills of the Cherokees. He made
this long journey because the Choctaw horse hunters had been
pressing him hard. A rumor had run through the tribe, started
perhaps by some learned conjurer or medicine man, that the
tall, long-maned chestnut stallion, king of the wild horse herds,
was descended from the famous steed which De Soto rode when,
many years before, he led his Spaniards through the Choctaw
lands far into the Mississippi wilderness and perished there.

This rumor sharpened the eagerness of the younger braves,
for it was well known that De Soto's horse had magic in him.
That spring they hunted the wild stallion more persistently than
ever; and at last, taking two sorrel mares with him, he struck
northeastward, seeking safer pastures.

He did not find them in the Overhills, as the Cherokees
called the high Smokies and the Blue Ridge where they lived
and hunted. At dawn one May morning, as he lay on a bed of
fresh sweet-scented grass near the middle of a natural pasture
known as Long Meadow, a warning came to him. He raised his
head high and sniffed the air, then jumped nimbly to his feet.
For a half minute, however, he did not rouse the two mares
lying on either side of him: and they, if they were aware of his
movement, were content to await his signal.

He gave the signal presently, and the mares rose, their ears
pricked, their nostrils quivering. A light breeze blew across the
meadow from the north. The stallion faced south, for his sensitive nose told him that no foeman was approaching from the
opposite direction. He knew that his ears had not deceived him

and that the sound which he had heard was near at hand. But he did not know the exact quarter from which the sound had come; and though his large eyes were well adapted to the dim light, nowhere could he discern that sinister weaving movement of the tall close-growing grass which would reveal the stealthy approach of bear or puma. So, for some minutes, he waited motionless, his head held high, every faculty keyed to the utmost.

Twenty yards away down the wind, Corane the Raven, young warrior of the Cherokees, crouching low in the grass, watched the wild stallion eagerly. Himself invisible, he could see his quarry more and more plainly as the light grew stronger; and he knew already that the wits of this slim, long-maned chestnut horse, which had come over the mountains from the west, were worthy of his beauty and strength. With all his art—and the Raven prided himself on his skill as a still hunter—and with all the conditions in his favor, he had been baffled. Having located the beds of the wild horses, he had left his own horse, Manito-Kinibic, at the edge of the woods and had crept through the grass as furtively as a lynx. But his approach had been detected when he was yet five lance lengths distant, and since then the stallion had made no false move, had committed no error of judgment.

Corane the Raven knew the wild horses well. Most of them were small and wiry, already approaching the mustang type of later years; but in those early days, before inbreeding had proceeded very far, an occasional stallion still revealed unmistakably the fine qualities of blooded forebears. From his hiding place in the grass the young warrior, naked except for a light loincloth of deer hide, studied the great chestnut carefully, thoughtfully, marveling at the lithe symmetry of his powerful but beautifully molded form, admiring his coolness and steadiness in the face of danger. The stallion showed no sign of fear. He did not fidget or caper nervously. Only his head moved slowly back and forth, while with all his powers of sight, scent, and hearing he strove to locate the precise spot where his enemy was lurking.

The Raven smiled in approval; and presently he applied a test of another kind.

With his long spear he pushed the grass stems in front of him, causing the tops of the tall blades to quiver and wave. The movement was slight, yet even in the pale morning light the wild horse saw it. He watched the spot intently for some moments. Then he moved slowly and cautiously forward, the mares following in his tracks. He moved neither toward the danger nor away from it. Instead, he circled it, and the Raven realized at once what the stallion's purpose was. He intended to get down wind from the suspected spot, so that his nose could tell him whether an enemy hid there, and, if so, what kind of enemy it was.

The young warrior waited, curious to see the outcome. Suddenly the stallion's head jerked upward. He was well down the wind now and a puff of air had filled his nostrils with the man scent. A moment he stood at gaze; and in that moment one of the mares caught the telltale scent, snorted with terror, and bolted at full speed. Close behind her raced the other mare; while the stallion, wheeling gracefully, followed at a slower pace, his eyes searching the grassy plain ahead.

The Raven had risen to his feet and stood in plain view, but the chestnut stallion scarcely glanced at him again. He was no longer a menace. Of greater importance now were other dangers unknown, invisible, yet possibly imminent.

The natural meadows of lush grass and maiden cane were perilous places for the unwary. In them the puma set his ambush; there the black bear often lurked; hidden in that dense cover the Indian horse hunters sometimes waited with their snares. The mares, in a frenzy of panic, were beyond their protector's control. Their nostrils full of the man smell, they had forgotten all other perils. But the stallion had not forgotten. Before the mares had run fifty yards the thing that he feared happened.

Out of the grass a black bulk heaved upward, reared high with huge hairy arms outspread, fell forward with a deep grunting roar on the haunch of the foremost mare. Screaming like a mad thing, the mare reeled, staggered, and went down. In a fraction of a second she was on her feet again, but the big mountain black bear, hurling himself on her hindquarters, crushed them to the ground.

Corane the Raven, racing forward at the sound of the mare's frenzied scream, was near enough to see part of what happened. He saw the wild stallion rear to his utmost height and come down with battering forefeet on the bear's back. He heard the stallion's loud squeal of fury, the bear's hoarse grunt of rage and pain. Next moment the mare was up again and running for her life, the stallion cantering easily behind her.

When the Raven reached the spot the bear had vanished, and the young Indian, marveling at what he had seen, ran toward the wood's edge, where his swift roan, Manito-Kinibic, awaited him.

In this way began the chase of the chestnut stallion—Northwind, as he was afterward known—that long hunt which Corane the Raven made long ago even before the time of Atta-Kulla-Kulla the Wise. It was Dunmore, the trader, who first brought down from the Overhills the story of that hunt and told it one night in Nick Rounder's tavern in Charles Town. Dunmore had it from the Raven himself; and the Raven was known among the white traders and hunters as a truthful man. But he was known also as a man of few words, while Dunmore, great hunter and famous Indian fighter though he was, had a tongue more fluent than a play actor's.

So it was probably Dunmore who put color into the story. The tale appealed to him, for he was a lover of horses; and this story of the feud between Northwind, the wild stallion, and Manito-Kinibic, the Raven's roan, concerned two horses which were paladins of their kind.

For the hunt which began that morning in Long Meadow became in large measure a contest between these two.

It happened that the Raven had returned not long before from a peace mission to the Choctaws, and while in their country he had heard of the wonderful wild horse which was said to have in him the blood of De Soto's steed and which had vanished from the savannas after defying all attemps to capture him. In the Overhills wild horses were rare. When the Raven found the tracks of three of them near Long Meadow about sunset one May day, he thought it worthwhile to sleep that night near the meadow's edge and have a look at the horses in the morning.

So at dawn he tried to stalk them in their beds, and the moment he saw the wild stallion rise from his sleeping place in the grass he knew that the great chestnut horse of which the Choctaws had spoken stood before him. That morning in Long Meadow he knew also that he could not rest until he had taken this matchless wild horse for his own.

It would be a long hunt, for the stallion would not linger

in the Overhills. Small bands of wild horses occasionally crossed the mountains from the west, and always these migrating bands traveled fast, pausing only to feed. Yet, though the hunt might carry him far, Corane the Raven, as he ran swiftly across Long Meadow toward the wood's edge where he had left Manito-Kinibic, had little doubt as to its issue. This wild stallion was a great horse, beautiful, swift, and strong—by far the finest wild horse that the Raven had ever seen.

But there was one other that was his equal in all things except beauty; and that other was Manito-Kinibic, the Raven's roan.

There was no chief of the Cherokees, the Creeks, or the Choctaws who had a horse that could match Manito-Kinibic. His like had never been known in the Overhills. Dunmore, the trader, had seen him and had wondered whence he came: for, though the Raven had taken him from the Chickasaws, whose country lay west of the mountains, it was plain that this big-boned, burly roan was not of the western or southern wild breed, while his name, which in the white man's tongue meant Rattlesnake, had to Dunmore's ear a northern sound.

Thick-bodied, wide-headed, short-maned, heavy-eared, Manito-Kinibic was almost grotesquely ugly, yet in his very ugliness there was a sinister, almost reptilian fascination, heightened by the metallic sheen of his red-speckled coat, the odd flatness of his head, and the fixed, stony glare of his small, deep-set eyes. No warrior of the Cherokees except the Raven could ride him. Few could even approach him, for his temper was as arrogant as that of the royal serpent for which he was named.

There lurked in him, too, a craftiness recalling the subtle cunning which the red men attributed to the rattlesnake, and because of which they venerated the king of serpents almost as a god; and with this craftiness he harbored a savage hatred of the wild creatures which the Indians hunted, so that on the hunt he was even more eager, even more relentless than his rider. It was the Raven's boast that Manito-Kinibic could follow a trail which would baffle many a red hunter; that he could scent a game at a greater distance than the wolf; that his ears were as keen as those of the deer; that he was as crafty as the fox and as ruthless as the weasel; and that he feared no wild beast of the forest, not even the puma itself.

Such was the horse that Corane the Raven rode on his long hunt. From the beginning of that hunt until its end Manito-Kinibic seemed to live for one thing only—the capture of the wild stallion whose scent he sniffed for the first time that morning in Long Meadow after the wild horse's encounter with the bear.

A few minutes after that encounter the Raven reached the wood's edge where he had left the big roan, vaulted upon his back and, riding as swiftly as was prudent through the tall grass and beds of maiden cane, struck the trail of the three wild horses near the spot where they had passed from the meadow at its lower end into the woods.

The trail was plain to the eye. The scent was strong where the wild horses had brushed through the rank grass. From that moment Manito-Kinibic knew what game it was that his rider hunted; and in that moment all the strange, smoldering hatred of his nature was focused upon the wild stallion which, as his nose told him, had passed that way with one or two mares.

Manito-Kinibic leaped forward with long bounds, his nostrils dilated, his ears flattened against his head. Corane the Raven, smiling grimly, let him go. It might be true, as the Choctaws believed, that the wild stallion was sprung from the mighty horse of De Soto himself. But surely this huge, implacable horse that now followed on the wild one's trail must have in his veins the blood of the great black steed which the Evil Spirit bestrode when he stood, wrapped in cloud on the bare summit of Younaguska Peak and hurled those awful arrows of his that flashed like lightning.

Northwind, the chestnut stallion, had passed within sight of Younaguska, highest of the Balsams, which men in these days call Caney Fork Bald; but that somber mountain lay far behind him now, for he had crossed both the main ranges of the mountain bulwark and had begun to descend the eastern slope of the second and lesser range. From Long Meadow he led his mares southeastward at a steady gait, following in general the trend of the valleys and the downward-sloping ridges. The injured mare, though her haunch was raw and bloody where the bear's claws had raked it, kept pace with her companions; and the three traveled fast, pausing only once or twice to drink at some cold, clear, hemlock-shaded stream.

For the most part their course carried them through a virgin forest of oak, chestnut, hickory, and other broad-leaved trees clothing the ridges, the slopes, and most of the valleys. Occasionally the stallion chose his own way, though as a rule he followed the narrow trails made by the deer; but when in the early forenoon he found a broader path through the woods, well marked and evidently often used, he turned into it unhesitatingly and followed it without swerving. The wild horse of the southwestern savannas recognized this path at once. It was one of the highways of the buffalo herds, a road trodden deep and hard through many centuries by thousands of hoofs.

The buffaloes were far less abundant now on the eastern side of the mountains. Although the white men's settlements were still confined to a strip along the coast, white hunters sometimes penetrated the foothills and white traders encouraged the taking of pelts. The deer still abounded in almost incredible numbers, but the eastern buffalo herds were withdrawing gradually across the Appalachians. Small droves, however, still ranged the eastern foothills and kept open the deep-worn paths; and the main buffalo roads across the mountain barrier, wider than the narrow buffalo ruts of the western plains, were still highways for wild creatures of many kinds.

It was one of these main roads that the chestnut stallion and his mares were following, a road which would lead them with many windings down from the mountains into the hills and through the hills to the broad belt of rolling lands beyond which lay the swamps and savannas of the Atlantic plain.

All the forenoon the Raven trailed his quarry. Both to the roan stallion and to his rider the trail was a plain one; and when the tracks of the wild horses turned into the buffalo path the Raven knew that he had only to follow that highway through the woods. With a guttural word he restrained Manito-Kinibic's savage eagerness. So long as the wild horses kept to the buffalo road the task of following them would be simple. The Raven preferred that, for the present, the chestnut stallion should not know that he was being pursued.

Half a bowshot ahead of the young warrior a troop of whitetails crossed the path, following a deer trail leading down the slope to a laurel-bordered stream. Once, at a greater distance, he saw a puma come out of the woods into the path, sit for a moment on its haunches, then vanish at a bound in the forest on the other side. Again and again wild turkeys ran into the woods on either hand, seldom taking wing; and with monotonous regularity ruffed grouse rose a few paces in front of him and whirred swiftly away.

About noon he killed a cock grouse in the path, pinning the bird to the ground with a light cane arrow tipped with bone; and he had scarcely remounted when around a curve of the path appeared the shaggy bulk of a huge buffalo bull. A moment the great beast stood motionless, blinking in astonishment, his massive head hanging low. Then, with surprising nimbleness, he turned and darted around the bend of the trail.

The Raven heard the stamping and trampling of many hoofs and gave Manito-Kinibic his head. The roan bounded forward and almost in an instant reached the bend of the path. At a word from his rider he halted; and the Raven, quivering with excitement, gazed with shining eyes upon a spectacle which sent the blood leaping through his veins—a herd of twenty buffaloes pouring out of the path, crowding and jostling one another as they streamed down the mountainside through the woods, following a deer trail which crossed the buffalo road almost at right angles. Twice the young warrior bent his bow and drew the shaft to the head, and twice he lowered his weapon, unwilling to kill game which he must leave to the wolves.

Afternoon came and still the Raven rode on through the teeming mountain forest, following the deep-worn highway which the migrating herds through unknown centuries had carved across the Overhills. More keenly than ever now his eyes search the path ahead. The wild stallion and his mares had probably grazed abundantly in Long Meadow before their early morning rest had been interrupted; but by this time they should be hungry again, for since leaving Long Meadow they had not stopped to feed. Wherever the Raven saw the forest open a little ahead of him so that grass grew under the far-spaced trees, he halted and listened carefully. Before long in one of those grassy places he should find the three wild horses grazing, and he wished to avoid frightening them.

The path, which heretofore had wound around the mountain shoulders, dipped suddenly into a deep, gorgelike valley at the bottom of which a torrent roared. The forest here was close and dark. The wild horses would not halt in this valley, for there was no grass to be had; and for a time the Raven relaxed his vigilance, letting his eyes stray from the path ahead.

From a tall hemlock on the mountainside a wild gobbler took wing, sailing obliquely across the valley, and the Raven saw an eagle, which had been perching on a dead tulip poplar, launch himself forward in swift pursuit. The young brave turned on his horse's back, gazing upward over his shoulder, eagerly watching the chase.

Without warning, Manito-Kinibic reared, swerved to the right, and plunged forward. His rider, taken utterly by surprise, lurched perilously, yet somehow kept his seat. For an instant, as Manito-Kinibic reared again, the Raven saw a sinewy naked arm raised above a hideous grinning face daubed with vermilion and black. Steel-fingered hands clutched the Raven's leg; on the other side another hand clawed at his thigh. Out from the thicket into the path ahead leaped three more warriors, feathered and plumed with eagle tails and hawk wings, striped and mottled with the red and black paint of war. More dreadful than the hunting cry of the puma, the shrill war whoop of the Muskogees split the air.

But for Manito-Kinibic the Rattlesnake the chase of the chestnut stallion would have ended then. But the Muskogee war party which waylaid Corane the Raven in the pass, hoping to take him alive for slavery or the torture, failed to reckon with the temper and strength of the mighty roan.

In an instant Manito-Kinibic had become a rearing, snorting fury, a raging devil of battering hoofs and gleaming teeth. The Raven saw one Muskogee go down before the plunging roan stallion. He saw another whose shoulder was red with something that was not war paint. He saw the three warriors in the path ahead leap for their lives into the thicket as Manito-Kinibic charged down upon them. Bending low on his horse's neck, he heard an arrow speed over him and, a half second later, another arrow. Then, remembering that he was the son of a war captain, he rose erect, looked back, and flourishing the hand which still held his bow and spear, hurled at his enemies the Cherokee whoop of triumph.

Thenceforward for a time the Raven watched the path behind him rather than the path ahead. The war parties of the

CHEVAL EFFRAYÉ SORTANT DE L'EAU. Eugène
Delacroix. *Courtesy, The Metropolitan Museum of Art: Dick
Fund, 1931.*

Muskogees were often mounted, and the young Cherokee thought it likely that this party had horses concealed in the thickets near the path. They would probably pursue him, but with Manito-Kinibic under him he was safe. Yet for a while he gave the sure-footed roan his head, racing onward as swiftly as the uneven surface of the trail allowed. So it happened that he was driven by necessity into doing the thing which he had intended to avoid.

A mile beyond the scene of the ambush the valley widened. Here, encircled by forested heights, lay a level, sun-bathed meadow, sweet with clover and wild-pea vine. Northwind and his mares had traveled far and fast. Urged on by his restless eagerness to get out of the dark, forbidding mountains—perhaps impelled too, by some mysterious premonition of danger—the chestnut horse had permitted no halt for food. In this beautiful vivid green oasis in the wilderness of woods he halted at last.

The meadow was dotted with grazing deer. Clearly no enemy lurked there. With a joyful whinny Northwind turned aside from the path and led his consorts to the feast.

A half hour later, an instant before the wariest of the whitetails had caught the warning sound, the wild stallion raised his head suddenly, listened intently for a moment, then, with a peremptory summons to the mares, trotted slowly with high head and tail toward the lower end of the meadow. Because wild creatures do not ordinarily rush headlong through the forest, he miscalculated the speed of the intruder whose hoofbeats he had heard. He was still near the middle of the meadow, while the mares, loath to leave the clover beds, were far behind him, when he saw the Raven on Manito-Kinibic dash out of the woods.

The young brave heard the wild stallion's snort of surprise, saw him leap forward and race for the buffalo path, while the mares wheeled and galloped off to the left. In long, beautiful bounds the stallion skimmed over the grass to the meadow's lower end where the path re-entered the forest.

The damage having been done, the Raven let Manito-Kinibic do his best for two or three miles. But the wild horse ran like the north wind which blows across the summit of Unaka Kanoos. It was then that the Raven named him, in honor of that north wind which is the swiftest and keenest of all the winds of the mountains. Until his rider checked him, Manito-Kinibic ran a good race. But they saw the stallion no more that day.

Even among the Cherokees, great hunters and marvelously skillful trackers, it was considered a noteworthy thing that Corane the Raven and Manito-Kinibic the Rattlesnake were able to follow the trail of the chestnut stallion all the way from the eastern slope of the Overhills to the low country of the Atlantic coast, more than two hundred miles as the white man reckons distance. In one respect fortune favored the young warrior. Except for the Muskogee ambush in the mountain pass, he suffered no interference at the hands of man and indeed saw scarcely a human face between the Overhills and the coast. Even when he had reached the white men's country—where, however, the settlements were still small and sparse—the wild horse's fear of human enemies kept both himself and his pursuers out of man's way. The spot where the long chase had its ending was as lonely as the remotest wilderness.

To Northwind, after this long journey, that spot seemed a paradise. To Corane the Raven, viewing it cautiously from the cover of the woods about noon of a warm, cloudless June day, it seemed to combine all the conditions essential for his success. A dry, level meadow, carpeted with short, thick grass and shaped like a broad spearhead, lay between a converging river and a creek which came together at the meadow's lower end. There, and for some distance along the shore, the land sloped sharply to the river, forming a little bluff about ten feet in height, while beyond the river lay vast marshes stretching for miles toward the hazy line of woods on the barrier isles.

The Raven took in these things at a glance; noted, too, with satisfaction, that here and there in the meadow stood clumps of some dense, stiff-branched bush of a kind unknown in the mountains. Then, well pleased, his plan complete to the smallest detail, he let his eyes rest again upon that feature of the scene which was the most important and most gratifying of all.

Almost in the center of the meadow stood Northwind, the wild stallion, alert, arrogant, confident, a picture of lithe, clean-cut beauty and perfectly proportioned strength. But he no longer stood alone. Just beyond him grazed five mares, all of them bays and all of them of one size and build. The Raven knew at once that they were not wild horses, and he surmised that they were strays from the white men's stock. But it mattered little whence they had come. The essential fact was that Northwind had taken them as his own, had become their master and protector.

Two hours before midnight, when the moon, almost at the full, swung high above the marshes beyond the river and the grassy expanse of the meadow was bathed in ghostly light, the Raven led Manito-Kinibic from his hiding place in the woods to the edge of the open. There the young brave halted. The big roan, his nostrils tingling with a scent which set his blood on fire, needed no word of instruction. He knew his part and would play it perfectly. Quivering with eagerness, yet too well trained to give way to the fury that possessed him, Manito-Kinibic moved out into the meadow at a slow walk, his hoofs making no sound.

The Raven waited until the roan had become a dim, uncertain shape in the moonlight. Then, crouching low, the Indian stole to the nearest bush clump, thence to another isolated thicket, and thence by a roundabout course to a third. He was halfway down the meadow when he heard the wild stallion's challenge and knew that Manito-Kinibic's keen nose had led the roan straight to his goal. Bending close to the ground, sometimes creeping on all fours, sometimes crawling like a snake, the Raven moved from bush clump to bush clump toward the sound.

A fresh breeze blew from the sea across the marshes. The wild stallion, resting with his mares near the meadow's lower end where creek and river joined, could neither smell nor hear an enemy approaching from the direction of the woods. Manito-Kinibic was scarcely fifty paces distant when Northwind saw him.

A moment the wild horse stood at gaze, his muscles tense for the long leap which would launch him forward in swift flight. Then fear passed out of him and fury took its place. A glance had shown him what the intruder was—a lone stallion, riderless, unaccompanied by man, roaming at will and evidently seeking the bay mares. Loud and shrill rang Northwind's challenge. Instantly he charged his foe.

Manito-Kinibic the Rattlesnake was a veteran of many battles. The fiercest battle of his career was the one which he fought that night in the moonlit meadow where the long chase of the chestnut stallion had its end. Northwind too had conquered many rivals to make good his mastery of the wild horse herds, but never before had he faced an antagonist as formidable as the burly roan. With Manito-Kinibic lay the advantage of size and weight; with the wild horse the advantage of quickness and agility. In courage neither surpassed the other. In cunning each was the other's match.

Almost at once they took each other's measure and, despite their fury, fought with instinctive skill, each striving to utilize to the utmost those powers in which he excelled. After his first whirlwind charge, Northwind did not charge again. He knew, after that first onset, that he must not hurl himself recklessly against the roan's weight and bulk. This was an enemy too big to be overwhelmed; he must be cut to pieces with slashing hoofs and torn to ribbons with ripping, raking teeth. Hence the wild stallion whirled and circled, feinted and reared, dashed in and leaped clear again, like a skillful rapierman whose opponent wields a broadsword—and wields it well.

For Manito-Kinibic was no blundering bruiser whose sole reliance was his strength. He, too, fought with cunning and skill, maneuvering with a lightness which belied his bulk, parrying and thrusting with an adroitness not much inferior to that of his opponent. But, apparently realizing the advantage which his weight gave him, he strove from the first for close quarters. Furiously, incessantly he forced the fighting, seeking to grip and hold his elusive enemy, rearing high to crush the wild horse with his battering hoofs, plunging forward with all his weight to drive his mighty shoulder against his foe and hurl him to the ground.

It was a fight too furious to last long. A stallion's hoofs and teeth are fearful weapons. A few minutes more must have brought a bloody end to the batle, though no man can say what that end would have been. Suddenly from a bush clump a shadow darted, sped lightly across the grass, and vanished in a tuft of tall weeds. Northwind did not see it because it was behind him. If Manito-Kinibic saw it, he gave no sign.

The battling stallions wheeled and reared, biting and plunging, striking with their forefeet, thrusting, parrying, feinting. Once more the roan hurled himself forward, his small eyes gleaming red, his teeth bared, his heavy hoofs stabbing the air; and once more his slim, long-maned opponent, light as a dancer, lithe as a panther, whirled aside, escaping destruction by an inch.

Again as they fenced for an opening, rearing high, snorting and squealing, the wild horse's back was turned to the tuft of weeds; and again the shadow darted forward, swiftly, noiselessly, gliding over the turf.

Next moment Corane the Raven crouched close behind the chestnut stallion. A half second more, and he had swung his rawhide thong with the skill for which he was famous. Then, with a shout, he leaped for Manito-Kinibic's head.

Northwind was down. He lay on his side, motionless as a dead thing. The rawhide thong, weighted at its ends, was wrapped around his hind legs, binding them tightly together. The greatest miracle was not the skill with which the Raven had thrown his snare. More wonderful still was the quelling of Manito-Kinibic's battle fury, the swiftness with which his master brought the raging roan under control. Yet this was merely the result of teaching, of long, painstaking instruction.

Manito-Kinibic, his neck and shoulders bloody, his flanks heaving, stood quietly, gazing down at his fallen foe with eyes in which the fire of hatred still glowed; but Northwind, his silky sides streaked with red, lay inert, inanimate, seeming scarcely to breathe. He offered no resistance as the Raven, with deft fingers, slipped a strong hobble around the slim forelegs and made it fast above each fetlock. There was no terror, no fierceness in the wild horse's large eyes. Instead they seemed singularly calm and soft, as though the brain behind them were lulled with a vision of places far away and days long ago.

Yet, if the chestnut stallion, a prisoner at last, dreamed of some green daisy-sprinkled forest prairie beyond the mountains, the dream passed quickly. Presently the Raven removed the thong which had held Northwind's hind legs helpless; and instantly the wild horse came to life, panic-stricken, furious, frantic for his freedom.

For a moment he thought himself free. His hind legs were no longer bound. The hobble around his forelegs bound them only loosely. With a snort he heaved upward and leaped away in mad flight—only to pitch headlong to the ground with a force which almost drove the breath from his body. Up he scrambled once more and down again he plunged as his fettered forelegs crumpled under him. Five times he rose and five times he fell before he seemed to realize his impotence.

For several minutes then he lay utterly still. The Raven had remounted Manito-Kinibic. The wild horse could not escape; yet it was well to be prepared for whatever might happen. The ordeal might be over in an hour, or, on the other hand, many hours might pass before Northwind's spirit was broken.

At last he struggled to his feet. The Raven circled him on the roan, watching him keenly. The captive's frenzy seemed to have passed. He was cooler now, steadier on his legs. Sudden anxiety which was almost panic gripped the young Indian. He recalled that once he had seen a hobbled wild horse travel a distance of half a bowshot in short labored bounds before falling; and in a flash he had become aware of a danger hitherto unrealized.

Quickly he slipped from Manito-Kinibic's back and approached Northwind from behind, uncoiling the weighted rawhide thong which he had removed from the wild stallion's hind legs. He would snare those hind legs again and thus make certain of his captive.

By a margin of moments he was too late. Northwind wheeled, bounded forward, and this time he did not fall. He had learned what not one hobbled wild horse in a thousand ever discovered—that while a leap of normal length would throw him every time, he could travel at least a little distance at fair speed if his leaps were very short.

Another bound he made, another and another—stiff-legged, labored, heartbreaking—keeping his balance by a miracle. He was more than halfway to the river's edge when the hobble threw him, and though he fell heavily, almost in an instant he was on his feet again, bounding onward as before.

On the very verge of the low bluff, the Raven, who had remounted as quickly as possible, drove Manito-Kinibic against the chestnut's flank in a last attempt to turn or throw him. Reeling from the blow, Northwind staggered on the brink. Then, rallying his strength for a supreme effort, he plunged sidewise down the steep slope, and the water closed over him.

Some say he was drowned. The Raven never saw him again, though the moon shone brightly on the river. But the water is very deep beside that bluff, and there the ebb tide is very strong and swift. It might have borne him quickly beyond the Indian's vision; and since the hobble allowed his forelegs some freedom of action, he might have made shift to swim.

At any rate, when Dunmore, the trader, told the story of the chestnut stallion that night in Nick Rounder's tavern, an old seafaring man who was present pricked up his ears and asked the trader certain questions. Then, with a great show of wonder and a string of sailor's oaths, he spun a queer yarn.

One midnight, he said, while his ship lay at anchor in a river mouth between two barren islands, the lookout sighted a big chestnut horse coming down the river with the tide. They manned a boat, got a rope over the horse's head, and towed him to the sandy island shore. He seemed almost exhausted, his neck and shoulders were cut and bruised, and how he had come into the river was a mystery, since his forelegs were hobbled. They could not take the horse aboard their vessel; so, after cutting the hobble, they left him lying on the beach, apparently more dead than alive. They expected to see his body there in the morning, but when they weighed anchor at sunrise he was gone.

Dunmore believed the old man's story. At any rate, it fits in with an old legend handed on today in the barrier islands of the Carolina coast.

The story runs that the slim, wiry ponies of those islands, rovers of the beaches and marsh flats, have in them the blood of De Soto's Andalusian horses abandoned nearly four centuries ago in the Mississippi wilderness, six hundred miles away, beyond the mountains. However that may be, the river in which Northwind made his last desperate bid for freedom passes quickly to the sea between two of these barrier isles.

THE BLACK MARE
by MacGregor Jenkins

1/

I stand on the stable floor and look at her critically. Patrick is at her head fondling her soft nose. There is no doubt that the mare is growing old. There are telltale signs that even an owner cannot ignore. But as she stands she is a delight to the eye. Sleek and lithe, with a proud little head that she holds high, smooth, sloping, muscular withers, and four as slender and lovely legs as horse ever had. Her small, nervous ears are sensitive and alert and her eyes clear.

"Looks like a thousand dollars, sir," Patrick comments. "Breeding, that's what it is, sir. Breeding."

I do not reply. I continue my observations in silence. I have adopted my stable technique. My relations with Patrick are unusual. I have absolute confidence in his judgment and follow his advice in every detail of his small domain. But Patrick was born and reared in the old tradition. His comment on the mare is an epitome of his simple creed. As with horses, so with men. "Breeding"—that is the last word. In me he affects, at least, to behold a superior being. His own prestige is heightened by creating an illusion of omniscience in me. He knows in his heart upon what slender foundations this structure has been reared. So he sees to it that by indirection I am shown the way. By suggestion and innuendo he seeks to have me arrive at wise decisions. Early in my relations with him I was guilty of gross improprieties. I performed certain menial tasks which were not mine to perform, I deferred unduly to his judgment, on one or two occasions I abruptly withdrew from delicate negotiations and left them in his hands. These were blunders of the first magnitude. I soon learned my lesson.

In other relationships of life I entertain certain views in regard to a theoretical democracy, the integrity of personality, and, in general, man's equality. These views have been acquired

HORSE IN STABLE. Aelbert Cuyp. *Courtesy, Philadelphia Museum of Art: The William L. Elkins Collection.*

by much reading and little thought, but they stimulate conversation and add to my secret self-esteem. In the stable, however, I find that my role is that of the "quality" with all its pretensions and responsibilities. It is I who must decide, it is I who direct every small detail, and it is from my long inheritance of superior knowledge and experience that comes the sagacious solution of every problem. In the face of Patrick's undisputed superiority in all stable matters it is a difficult role.

But I have adopted a method which seems to satisfy him. I am employing it at the moment. It involves a studied silence and an air of profound reflection during which I count upon receiving from him some subtle hint as to the right decision. This is followed by a brief period of open disagreement with his implied findings and then a dignified acquiescence with them. All this makes our deliberations a little involved and on occasions draws them out to a greater length than they appear to justify, but it maintains the fiction dear to Patrick's honest heart and gives him pleasure. That is enough.

So at this moment we are enacting the little farce. We are attempting to reach a decision in regard to the mare. Is she fit for further competition in the show ring or is she not? Patrick is right about her appearance and I see that he wishes her to attempt the task we have in mind. But aside from my usual affected indecision I am troubled by very real doubts. Time is taking its inexorable toll. No one knows just how old she is. I can only conjecture, even Patrick can only guess.

She has been in my possession for several years and in all that time she has never done a mean or, what is more, a stupid thing in field or stable. In my modest tackroom there is a display of her trophies, ribbons of various colors, blue happily predominating, and my home is adorned with various pieces of plate, some slightly ornate, which further attest her supremacy in her class. But there is one piece which is not there and which I greatly covet. That elusive bit of plate is the Brooks Cup. It was offered by a riding club for the best performance in the Pony Saddle Class for junior riders. It has been in competition for many years; upon it appears a long list of names, some of them twice, but none has achieved the third win which means permanent possession of this much desired trophy. On two occasions the mare has won the event and a third win is all that is necessary to put the cup in a place of honor in our collection.

It would be much simpler for me to arrive at once at a decision and to dismiss the matter, but my relations with Patrick are such as to make prolonged conference seem desirable. Her age is the only factor against further competition. I much prefer to have her retire on the laurels already won rather than to have her end her ring career with defeat. Her owner and rider entertains no doubts as to her ability to meet the test, but youth is happily optimistic and has not yet learned to know the significance of the signs of encroaching years. It is upon maturer shoulders that the burden of decision rests.

"She's perfect, sir," Patrick was saying as his gnarled hand caressed the mare. "All but that one foreleg, the off one, sir. She's a bit tender and she favors it. She has done a power of work in her time and it is beginning to tell. She's not bad, you understand, but she might make a misstep and go down. I'd hate to have her do that. Those ring jumps are tricky and the light is bad for one or two of them. It would be too bad to have her lose, but it's now or never, sir, with this mare; another year and she will not be right. I think she'll go through if she's handled right, but it's for you to decide, sir."

Now this is just what I do not want to do. It is a delicate question and I greatly prefer to have someone else assume the responsibility of a decision. We are joined by the owner, and that makes it more difficult. We both know that it is one of the young woman's minor ambitions to possess that cup, and beneath that desire lie an unbounded affection for and confidence in her little mare. Between them exist an understanding and mutual confidence that reflect credit on them both.

"Put her over the jumps, miss. Nice and easy, and then let her canter around a couple of times," Patrick suggests.

She mounts and rides to a small schooling field I have arranged near by. We watch them go. The mare trots gently to the far end of the field. She picks her way carefully and uses her feet to perfection. There is not the slightest suggestion of uncertainty. Her rider leans forward and caresses her neck. She shakes her head and sidesteps in response. At the end of the field she turns and her delicate ears are erect. Easily she gathers speed, a gentle, rhythmic movement, no haste, no excitement, but every step a little longer and faster as she approaches the first jump. Over she goes, no fumbling, almost no effort, and she lands in her stride to take the next two a bit faster but with equal precision. Then the leisured canter around the improvised track. Neck arched, muzzle in, and tail down, she moves with exquisite grace.

Once more on the stable floor, her eyes are brilliant and her delicate nostrils flex as she stands with what appears to be conscious pride. But critical eyes are upon her. Her sides move gently, she breathes naturally, but there is one blemish and we all see it. That off leg trembles just a hair—the faintest quiver, that is all.

"She took three jumps and a short canter. There are six in the ring and she will have to take them faster," I croak. Patrick is silent, his fingers on the offending leg.

"She's all right," her owner stoutly maintains. "She knows how to handle that leg. She favors it a little, I can feel her do it, but you did not notice it, did you?"

We were compelled to admit that we did not. There had not been a blemish in her performance and certainly she had appeared before a critical audience.

Patrick straightens up and slips the bridle from the mare's head.

"She'll do," he says. "She's better today than most of them. The only one I am afraid of is the Bradley gray. He is young and he is good, but he's green in the ring. Now this mare knows all there is to know. She can show herself and can take care of herself. Now, miss," he added, "if you show her, remember that.

Begging your pardon, miss, let her show herself. Let her do as she likes. You just ride along with her. She'll take you through if you let her have her own way."

Patrick, as usual, has given me my cue. It only remains for me to announce a decision.

"All right, old girl," I say. "We will give you another chance."

"I think you are right, sir," Patrick says with profound respect. The oracle has spoken; it is his now only to obey.

I am greatly relieved. Whatever the result, I have the comforting feeling that I have expressed a doubt. I leave Patrick and the owner in consultation and depart to a field of activity in which I feel a little less uncertain of the probable wisdom of some of my decisions.

2 /

Days of intensive schooling follow. I am not admitted to the sessions and I do not altogether want to be. Doubts assail me and I keep aloof. But from what I can observe from a distance these hours on the schooling field are devoted more to the instruction of the rider than to the exercise of her mount. The mare makes her faultless trips back and forth over the jumps only to be interrupted by Patrick, who corrects some small fault in hands or heels. He raises an authoritative hand and the mare stops. Flushed and bareheaded he stands in the sun looking up at the youthful face above him. I can see his lips move, his hands gesticulate, his body bend forward and back and from side to side. The grave young rider listens with earnest attention and the lesson is resumed. Then follow a few jumps to all appearances exactly like all the others, to be greeted with peals of rich Hibernian laughter and full-throated ejaculations.

"That's the idea, miss! That's the way she wants it!"

For days before the date of the show I haunt the stable. Patrick spends hours with the mare. The leg is anointed with mysterious liquids and bound in snowy bandages. Under his ministrations she takes on greater beauty. Her coat is like satin; with freshly roached mane and fetlocks trimmed, hoofs oiled, and a hair plucked here and there, she looks like a three-year-old.

The mysteries of an equine toilet always fascinate me—the slightly salty odor, the stamp of hoofs, the playful tossing of the head, and the constant hissing which accents every stroke of brush or cloth and which seems to be regarded as an essential part of the ritual. As I sit on an upturned bucket and watch Patrick labor I feel a strange, vicarious delight in the results. I realize that I am experiencing the pleasure of one of the most subtle of human emotions, the pride of ownership. The mere possession of this animal seems in some way to reflect great credit upon myself, upon my sagacity in her purchase, some secret intuition on my part that she was unusual. As a matter of fact, the purchase was quite accidental and could have been accomplished by anyone with a few dollars to spare. Her fearlessness and stamina are no work of my hands, but I like to think they are. Her appearance is due entirely to the untiring industry and skill of an ignorant man whom I employ, and yet I feel a swelling pride in it as if it were I who had accomplished it.

When in reflective mood I am humble and realize that all these pretensions are emptiness and vanity, but in reality they are behind almost all human relationships. A man's home, designed and equipped by a more skillful person, is always regarded by the owner as a monument to his own taste and judgment; the flowers in his garden bloom because he has some gift, denied to others, which brings them to fruition. It is another who has toiled in heat and cold to bring it all about, but in the twilight and with friends the humble servitor is forgotten and the host conducts slightly bored guests from flower to flower with modest implications of his own skill and patience. So it is with his children; be they virtuous or brilliant, beautiful or accomplished, there is down deep in man a prepossession that he is in some way the reason for it all—that the process of inheritance has enriched them by drawing from the treasures of his own mind and heart to make them what they are. And when they betray some doubtful trait he wonders from what remote and alien source it comes.

So I sit on my bucket and revel in this spectacle of strength and beauty before me with all the foolish self-complacence of a normal, sinful man. I sometimes wonder how much of the pleasure I derive from a number of things comes from a real appreciation of them and how much from mere pride in possession. It is a line of meditation that I do not long pursue because it invariably leads to humiliating conclusions.

But the die has been cast and we are once more on the entry

list for the Brooks Cup, and doubts and questionings as to the niceties of human conduct will not help to bring it into our hands. On the morning of the day of the show I wake early with a sense of some impending event of momentous import. I make a hurried visit to the stable and find Patrick in the highest spirits, breaking into occasional burst of song as he bustles about his manifold duties. It is a mood I cannot share. I try to decide whether it is a gaiety born of confidence or a brave attempt to ignore possible disaster. The owner eats a hearty breakfast and does not mention the impending afternoon in the ring. Conversation is a bit difficult, as I am led into the discussion of activities which bear no relation to the one thing that fills my mind. I again marvel at the power of detachment in youth, the bland concentration on bacon and eggs when they are the most unimportant things in the world.

At an early hour Patrick departs, mounted and dressed in his best, not through personal pride, I know, but from a desire properly to represent me. He leads the mare, draped in a new cooler with her owner's initials inconspicuously appearing in one corner. She trots obediently beside Patrick's heavy mount and looks small and delicate in comparison. The owner does not witness the departure, as she is immersed in the morning paper. I think it bravado, but I do not say so.

After an endless morning of effort to compel business to conquer my preoccupations, I give up and go out to an early lunch. I am unfortunate enough to run into Bradley, the owner of the gray. He appears to me to be in a mood of insufferable indifference, and when I ask him (not that I care in the least) if he plans to attend the show he says, "Probably not." He pleads the exactions of his profession as an excuse. I naturally regard this as an indirect criticism of myself, and my opinion of this excellent fellow suffers a decline. I try a game of billiards after lunch, but it fails to interest me and I soon seek refuge in the pages of a sporting magazine. Here I encounter an article on the folly of keeping horses in competition after their prime, with a number of instances of disaster to illustrate its unwisdom. I think the whole article absurd, but it does not add to my confidence or composure.

An hour before the appointed time I take my seat in the gallery of the riding club. There are a dozen others who have come to secure points of vantage and among them I recognize several parents who are probably suffering from the same anxieties as I am, but who are still capable of carrying on light conversation with an air of confidence. Not so with me. I put my elbows on the railing in front of me and lapse into moody contemplation. Somewhere in the remote recesses of the great building the mare is receiving the last touches to her toilet. Patrick is inspecting every strap and buckle, and lively banter is being exchanged by callous grooms. They make small wagers and belittle each other's charges, but after all, I reflect, they cannot care. It is all in a day's work and means nothing to them. They are but taking orders, and the responsibility of success or failure is not theirs.

Abruptly I find myself again indulging in speculation as to the significance of success or failure in this small episode. What does it all amount to after all? Nothing. A dozen canters around a ring, a few jumps, slightly bedraggled decorations, a not altogether tuneful band, and the bestowal of a piece of tawdry plate for doing an entirely unnecessary thing.

But then I think of Patrick, of his devotion, his simple creed of doing his small task as well as he can, of his kindness, loyalty, and patience, his wisdom and his foresight, all exercised, perhaps, for a trivial end, but in themselves important in the general scheme of things. Then the owner, youth with its enthusiasms and its ardors, its blessed isolation from many of the sterner realities, its courage and its mirth. Then the mare, this beautiful creature born for man's service, strength curbed by docility, intelligence governed by the restraint of long training, and an undying spirit of courage and willingness to serve, giving freely of what she has and offering the last of her depleted vigor to serve this strange man who happens to be her master. Perhaps, after all, it is worth while. Perhaps in this little spectacle there lurks a significance which makes it real.

3 /

As a relief from these somewhat complicated reflections I look about me. My nostrils are again assailed by that rich, pungent odor that I love, but now combined with the scent of tanbark, a matchless combination. The ring lies before me smooth and brown; not a mark disfigures its even surface. The jumps, freshly whitewashed, stand in bold relief, one at each end and two on each of the longer sides of the great oval. The farther one near the corner is the distrusted one. There is a shadow there that cannot be corrected, though a near-by window has been draped to lessen it. In the center stands a decorated platform, on three sides are slender posts carrying a heavy rope gleaming with pipe clay. There is a table with piles of brilliant ribbon rosettes and gleaming cups. The walls are hung with bunting and in a lofty gallery a band is assembling. Long shafts of sunlight fall from lofty windows and myriads of dust particles hover in sparkling lanes of brilliancy.

Voices are heard in the distance, heavy doors open and close, spectators arrive in groups and with much discussion find their places. I glance at my watch. It lacks but a few minutes of the appointed hour. Presently the heavy gate of the ring opens and an imposing figure appears. It is the Master. He is resplendent in riding togs and boots; a derby hat sits a bit rakishly upon his auburn locks, and his gloves are immaculate. Most of his days are days of toil, of patient instruction, long hours of drill and dull routine. But today is his day of splendor, of rich apparel and becoming dignity in the observance of an intricate ritual. Most of the contestants have been his pupils, but today he is aloof behind the ramparts of a studied indifference. There must be no sign of favoritism, no confession of his consuming pride in their accomplishments. He is followed by a uniformed bugler borrowed from the band. He approaches the stand with stately tread, leaving the first footprints in the smooth tanbark. He nods to the bugler and a fanfare echoes against the rafters. As it dies away the band blares in martial cadences and the judges appear.

In private life I know them all. My relations with some of them are intimate, but today they seem remote and awful. Dressed in the most approved mode for such an occasion, they appear in pairs and solemnly take their places on the stand. One or two of them are men who combine this pleasant and picturesque duty with real accomplishment in more important walks of life. Others' sole claim to recognition is the skill with which they perform this one humble duty. They are men whose judgment outside of the show ring I should regard as valueless, and yet today I look upon them as beings apart from the ordinary run of humanity, possessing strange powers of divination and incorruptible honesty. Humble as they are in the hurly-burly of human life, today they are Olympians clothed in the majesty of the moment. It is such as they who are to decide the fortunes of the mare and her rider. I am assailed by a cowardly wish that I had been a little more polite to one of them on a recent occasion, but I dismiss this vagrant thought with contempt. I must be as incorruptible as they.

In my impatience I think they indulge in a good deal of unnecessary talk and laughter. One or two of them seem to take their duties with a deplorable lack of seriousness. They fumble the cups and ribbons and consult their programmes. Why do they not get on with their business? Why keep me waiting here with a thousand other duties neglected? I think of the virtuous Bradley and my eye falls upon him as he quietly enters and takes a seat not far from me. I feel better and my regard for him is heightened. He has put the stamp of his professional eminence on the presence of a humbler person here this afternoon.

The judges group themselves at the edge of the stand. Once more the bugle sounds and the gate swings open. The Pony Class is the first event of the afternoon. I am glad. I could not endure sitting through others to wait for it. The little cavalcade appears. It is led by the Bradley gray. A perfect little creature, but evidently a bit nervous and overanxious. He has not become accustomed to the lights and noise. Others follow. It is a good field; not an entry in it would fail of consideration. I wait for the mare. She comes in toward the end of the line. I see at once that she has adopted her ring manner. There is a new spring and lightness in her step, an added toss to her head, and a certain air of breeding as she picks up her dainty feet. I study the rider and find suggestions of a new manner in her as well. She is more relaxed, heels firm but not rigid, hands at rest, back straight but supple. She sits better than usual, lower down in the saddle, and seems more part of her horse than before. There is just the right amount of tension on the snaffle, and a delicate droop in her curb rein. I see the result of the hours on the schooling field.

In single file they make their way around the ring at a walk. Some are restive and crowd forward upon the horse in front of them, some lag and have to be urged on. The mare is evidently beginning to show herself. She keeps a perfect interval from the horse in front of her. She affects a pretty pretense of eagerness, but that is all. Her rider's hands are motionless. There is no need to hold her back or urge her on. As the Bradley gray reaches the gate once more the trumpet sounds the signal to trot. There is a little confusion, the gray breaks into a slow canter and has to be brought back, others do not respond quickly and there are gaps in the line. The mare gives her head a shake and rattles her curb chain. She responds instantly and trots along smoothly with a bit more action than usual and lifts her feet a trifle higher than she does on the road. It is twice around this time and soon the company is in perfect order, with little to choose between them.

Once more the bugle, this time for a canter, and they are off. The gray curvets out of line for a moment, but soon settles down. I watch the mare and her rider. When the bugle sounded I noticed an almost imperceptible movement of the hands and one heel, but it was not necessary. The mare has heard that signal before and knows what it means. With perfect intervals she moves with just action enough to give her grace. Twice round and a signal from the Master brings them to the center of the ring, a long line on either side of the stand. Attendants take their places at the jumps and the real test begins. Each rider wears an arm band with a number on it and these numbers are drawn by the judges. As called, each contestant whirls out of line to take the jumps. One after another, with varying success, they meet the test; they are well schooled and the riders know their business. Some click the top bar, but there are no falls and each in turn comes back to the line.

4 /

There is a stir as the gray goes out. He is known as a good performer and he gives a faultless exhibition. I think he is a bit too eager, that he rushes it a little and his action is not as smooth as it might be, but he has an air which gives him brilliancy. He will be hard to beat. The mare follows him. As she goes out I catch my breath. I am glad she has had a short rest before going, but not long enough to stiffen that leg. That leg, how it haunts me! At the remote end of the ring there is a line of faces above the parapet. Serious, lined faces, tanned and hard. The grooms have this vantage point from which to watch their charges. I see Patrick. He is smiling his charming Irish smile and saying something to the man next him. I wonder what his reflections are. More cheerful than mine, I hope.

The mare goes out with a little flourish. Her rider leans forward and touches her neck and she quiets down. She trots to the end of the ring and breaks into an easy canter as she swings toward the first jump. She is over, clean and neat. She has less to spare than the gray, but enough, and her action looks smoother. If she can only last! The other jumps are but a repetition of the first. I notice that she swings a little on the shadowed jump and does not take it quite straight, but she makes a perfect jump and lands in her stride. She evidently has figured out how to do it. She returns to her place. I put my glasses on her leg. It is motionless and she stands at ease. The others follow and the judges go into a huddle. Soon rider after rider is dismissed, and with them, as they leave the ring, go the hopes and the ambitions of many of the spectators. This weeding-out process is painful and I dread lest the mare go with them. But she does not, and neither do the gray and one other.

There is another long consultation. It is decided that the mare and the gray must make another circuit to aid in the final judgment. I had not counted on this. I am not pleased. The mare did perfectly, but to add another trip over the jumps might be too much for her. The gray goes first. There is just a suggestion of impatience in the air of the rider as he sets out. It is as if to say, "Why all this bother? I have the better horse. We will go through the thing if you want us to and we will show you just what we can do."

He gathers his mount quickly, uses his heels, and dashes away. The gray had been restive during the wait and his rider's mood quickly affects him. One of Patrick's most sage bits of wisdom is the admonition never to telegraph to your horse how you feel unless you want him to feel the same. No creature is more sensitive to mood than a horse. He will at once recognize fear or impatience on the part of his rider. The result is that the gray shares the impatience of his rider. He rushes the first jump and takes off badly, but he steadies and clears the next four without accident. I think he is jumping a bit recklessly and there is a suggestion of swagger on the part of his rider. Five jumps are behind him, only one remains to clinch the victory. As it is approached the gray is urged to an extra effort. The rider is determined to finish in the grand manner. The gray thunders down the long side of the ring and flings himself at the last barrier. I cannot see what happens, but he evidently takes off too soon and is a bit short in his jump. The top rail falls as he hits it; he lands clumsily, trips, and recovers himself. It is a nice bit of footwork, but it unsettles his rider and he is thrown well forward on the gray's neck. He is back in his seat in a moment and canters to take his place beside the mare with as great an air of confidence as he can muster.

I look at the mare and her rider. The young woman is gazing with studious abstraction at the mare's ears and the mare is standing in her most statuesque ring posture. As far as they are concerned the incident might never have happened. They present a charming picture of polite indifference to the world in general and to the gray and his rider in particular. At a nod from the Master they move forward. There is a suggestion of grim determination on the face of the rider and the mare moves with an air of sweet docility. I know they are both prepared for the effort of their ring careers. As the mare breaks into a slow canter they move as one creature. The rider has melted into her saddle and moves not in unison with her mount but as part of her. The mare elects to go a bit farther than she did before to give her a longer start for the jump. Without a suggestion from hand or heel of her rider she turns when she wishes and slowly gathers speed. Gracefully she lifts herself over the first barrier, landing so lightly that she hardly seems to touch the tanbark and is off for the next. When she reaches the fifth, with its treacherous shadow, she turns in toward the wall and clears it with only a few inches to spare.

As she lands she falters for the fraction of a second and I see the rider shift slightly in her saddle. Whatever has happened, the mare recovers herself instantly and now asks for more bridle. The rider gives her her head and sits tight. The mare is now traveling on her own. There is one more jump directly in front of the judges and she elects to approach it in her own way. She is adjusting her stride and is taking her time. Suddenly she is ready. In a few steps she gathers speed. For a moment I fear that the temptation to finish in a blaze of glory may be too strong for both mare and rider. But the lesson of the gray's mishap bears fruit and the mare comes up to the last jump with plenty of speed but easily and without excitement. She sails over it with a long, effortless jump and trots to the center of the ring with an air of utter unconcern.

I have been leaning over the parapet before me at a perilous angle and I now sink back into my seat with a sense of relief. That is done. Whatever the judgment, there is now no chance of mishap and the game little mare has done her best. The final formalities are brief.

As soon as the mare returns to her place beside the gray she poses for the final inspection. She slowly extends herself into the posture which seems to be regarded as orthodox in the ring, for what obscure reason I could never understand. No equine creature ever stood so except in a show ring. It seems to me neither natural nor attractive. But the mare has done it so many times she needs no suggestion. The gray follows, but with repeated signals from toe and heel of his rider. When once posed, the mare does not move a hair. I look at her closely through my glasses. From my point of vantage there appears no tremor in that mistrusted leg. That hoof is a bit lower in the tanbark and she seems to press on it a trifle, but it is hard to tell. I see Patrick's smiling face in the distance and he is talking volubly to a neighbor.

The judges in solemn procession leave the stand and make a deliberate circuit of the motionless horses. Keen eyes note every detail and whispered comments are exchanged. They return to the stand and one of them selects the rosettes, blue, red, and yellow. The Master takes them and a number is called. It is Number Nine and that is the numeral that adorns the arm of the mare's rider. She moves forward and the rosette is placed on her bridle. It seems to me that she obligingly lowers her head to make it easy for the Master. Other ribbons have been placed beneath her delicate ear and she knows the technique. There is generous applause. The red goes to the gray and the yellow to the waiting third, a novice making her first appearance. A judge turns to the table and takes up the Brooks Cup. He carries it to the mare's side and places it in the hands of her rider. He makes some laughing comment and strokes the mare's neck. The band crashes into a stirring march and the three winners make a circuit of the ring, the mare leading.

Never have I seen her so beautiful, never before has she

moved with such grace, never has she held her head so proudly or stepped more daintily. She tosses her head as she turns toward the gate and a fleck of foam clings to her sleek shoulder, accenting the lustrous black of her coat. The gate swings open and she disappears. I see Patrick's head bobbing over the ring parapet as he runs to meet her. As I make my way to the reception room to offer congratulations to the owner I meet Bradley. He grasps my hand cordially.

"Congratulations," he says. "That's a wonderful little mare you have. I wish I had one like her."

"Thanks," I answer, "I am sorry you never will, because there isn't another like her and there never will be."

I decide that on the whole I like Bradley.

5 /

As soon as I reached home I hurried to the stable. Patrick was gazing through the grill of the mare's box stall. She stood with her nose against the grating and they were exchanging confidences. She was covered in her cooler and her leg was freshly bandaged.

Patrick turned as I entered.

"Well, she did it, sir," he said. "I thought she would. But she is through, sir. That leg is gone. It is time. She was dead lame before she was halfway home. I knew it. I saw it go. It was at that tricky jump in the shadow. She landed wrong and she twisted it. She covered it up, but I saw it. She did the last on her nerve—that was all she had left. Did you see her bury that foot in the tanbark when they looked her over? Not a quiver, but I know it hurt her. She landed the cup for the young lady, but she will never step right again. Game, I call it, sir—game. Ah, she's the rare little mare."

"What can we do for her?" I asked.

"Pull her shoes and turn her out. She will be comfortable in a few days. If she does no work she will be well enough."

And so the black mare went to her reward—a verdant hillside with good grass by day and shelter by night, long hours of reflection in the shade, and rest and constant care for the slightest ailment.

But I sometimes wonder what she thinks about. I fancy that

she sometimes hears the band and sees the level tanbark with its white barriers, for she will often trot the length of her enclosure with all the style and beauty of her ring manner, still lithe and graceful and still concealing the stiffness in her leg, proud and game as ever.

And well may she be proud, for she can look back upon a life untouched by cowardice or guile, a life of service and affection, of loyalty and faith. I only hope that when Bradley and I—we have grown to be great friends of late and I owe the pleasure of it to the mare—when Bradley and I have reached the point where the world no longer wants or needs us, when we are old and nurse some hidden infirmity and our shoes are pulled and we are turned out, I trust then we shall find some pleasant pasture where we can be at peace. And may that peace be undisturbed by unpleasant recollections. We both entertain some doubts as to the exact color of the ribbon, if any, which may be awarded us in the final distribution, but there are a few years still to go, and we have at least the record of the mare to guide us.

THE MODEL HORSE

HORSE SENSE
Anonymous

A horse can't pull while kicking.
　　This fact I merely mention.
He can't kick while pulling,
　　Which is my chief contention.

Let's imitate the good old horse
　　And lead a life that's fitting;
Just pull an honest load, and then
　　There'd be no time for kicking.

THE TRIUMPHANT HORSE

CAROLINE, A HORSE
by Arthur Davison Ficke

What lives behind those eloquent eyes
Is neither prescient—souled nor wise—
A glow that faintly lives or dies.

So beautiful! And yet no thought
Into those fibers was inwrought.
As iron is bent, so was she taught

By alternating praise and blow
The few small things her brain can know,
Beyond whose bound she cannot go.

And I, whose strength is nothing, rule
This mighty, breathing, plunging fool
And put her terrible force to school—

I whose vague flickering brain can see
So little of that mystery
Of mighty powers that govern me.

Yet take, O heart, thy moment's pride:
The horse and I, with me to guide—
See how triumphantly we ride!

A STRANGER TO THE WILD
by Charles G. D. Roberts

As the vessel, a big three-masted schooner, struck again and lurched forward, grinding heavily, she cleared the reef by somewhat more than half her length. Then her back broke. The massive swells, pounding upon her from the rear, overwhelmed her stern and crushed it down inescapably upon the rock; and her forward half, hanging in ten fathoms, began to settle sickeningly into the loud hiss and chaos. Around the reef, round the doomed schooner, the lead-colored fog hung thick, impenetrable at half a ship's length. Her crew, cool, swift, ready—they were Gaspé and New Brunswick fishermen, for the most part—kept grim silence, and took the sharp orders that came to them like gunshots through the din. The boats were cleared away forward, where the settling of the bow gave some poor shelter.

At this moment the fog lifted, vanishing swiftly like a breath from the face of a mirror. Straight ahead, not two miles away, loomed a high, black, menacing shore—black, scarred rock, with black woods along its crest and a sharp, white line of surf shuddering along its base. Between that shore and the shattered schooner lay many other reefs, whereon the swells boiled white and broke in dull thunder; but off to the southward was clear water, and safety for the boats. At a glance the captain recognized the land as a cape on the south coast of the Gaspé peninsula, so far from her course had the doomed schooner been driven. Five minutes more, and the loaded boats, hurled up from the seething caldron behind the reef, swung out triumphantly on a long, oil-dark swell, and gained the comparative safety of the open. Hardly had they done so when the broken bow of the schooner, with a final rending of timbers, settled in what seemed like a sudden hurry, pitched nose downward into the smother, and

sank with a huge, startling sigh. The rear half of the hull was left
lodged upon the reef, a kind of gaping cavern, with the surf plunging over it in cataracts, and a mad mob of boxes, bales, and wine
casks tumbling out from its black depths.

Presently the torrent ceased. Then, in the yawning gloom,
appeared the head and forequarters of a white horse, mane
streaming, eyes starting with frantic terror at the terrific scene
that met them. The vision sank back instantly into the darkness.
A moment later a vast surge, mightier than any which had gone
before, engulfed the reef. Its gigantic front lifted the remnant of
the wreck halfway across the barrier, tipping it forward, and
letting it down with a final shattering crash; and the white horse,
hurled violently forth, sank deep into the tumult behind the reef.

The schooner which had fallen on such sudden doom among
the St. Lawrence reefs had sailed from Oporto with a cargo,
chiefly wine, for Quebec. Driven far south of her course by a
terrific northeaster roaring down from Labrador, she had run
into a fog as the wind fell, and been swept to her fate in the grip
of an unknown tide drift. On board, as it chanced, traveling as an
honored passenger, was a finely bred, white Spanish stallion of
Barb descent, who had been shipped to Canada by one of the
heads of the great house of Robin, those fishing princes of Gaspé.
When the vessel struck, and it was seen that her fate was imminent and inevitable, the captain had loosed the beautiful stallion
from his stall, that at the last he might at least have a chance
to fight his own fight for life. And so it came about that, partly
through his own agile alertness, partly by the singular favor of
fortune, he had avoided getting his slim legs broken in the hideous
upheaval and confusion of the wreck.

When the white stallion came to the surface, snorting with
terror and blowing the salt from his wide nostrils, he struck out
desperately, and soon cleared the turmoil of the breakers. Over
the vast, smooth swells he swam easily, his graceful, high head
out of water. But at first, in his bewilderment and panic, he swam
straight seaward. In a few moments, however, as he saw that he
seemed to be overcoming disaster very well, his wits returned,
and the nerve of his breeding came to his aid. Keeping on the
crest of a roller, he surveyed the situation keenly, observed the
land, and noted the maze of reefs that tore the leaden surges into
tumult. Instead of heading directly shoreward, therefore—for

HORSE AND ZEBRA ON A BEACH. Giorgio de Chirico. *Courtesy, Newark Museum, Newark, N.J.: Gift of Mr. and Mrs. William V. Griffin.*

every boiling whiteness smote him with horror—he shaped his course in on a long slant, where the way seemed clear.

Once well south of the loud herd of reefs, he swam straight inshore, until the raving and white convulsion of the surf along the base of the cliff again struck terror into his heart; and again he bore away southward, at a distance of about three hundred yards outside the breakers. Strong, tough-sinewed, and endowed with the unfailing wind of his far-off desert ancestors, he was not aware of any fatigue from his long swim. Presently, rounding a point of rock which thrust a low spur out into the surges, he came into a sheltered cove where there was no turf. The long waves rolled on past the point, while in the cove there was only a measured, moderate rise and fall of the gray water, like a quiet breathing, and only a gentle backwash fringed the black-stoned, weedy beach with foam. At the head of the cove a shallow stream, running down through a narrow valley, emptied itself between two little red sandspits.

Close beside the stream the white stallion came ashore. As soon as his feet were quite clear of the uppermost fringe of foam, as soon as he stood on ground that was not only firm, but dry, he shook himself violently, tossed his fine head with a whinny of exultation, and turned a long look of hate and defiance upon the element from which he had just made his escape. Then at a determined trot he set off up the valley, eager to leave all sight and sound of the sea as far as possible behind him.

Reared as he had been on the windy and arid plateau of northern Spain, the wanderer was filled with great loneliness in these dark woods of fir and spruce. An occasional maple in its blaze of autumn scarlet, or a clump of white birch in shimmering, aerial gold, seen unexpectedly upon the heavy-shadowed green, startled him like a sudden noise. Nevertheless, strange though they were, they were trees, and so not altogether alien to his memory. And the brook, with its eddying pools and brawling, shallow cascades, that seemed to him a familiar, kindly thing. It was only the sea that he really feared and hated. So long as he was sure he was putting the huge surges and loud reefs farther and farther behind him, he felt a certain measure of content as he pushed onward deeper and deeper into the serried gloom and silence of the spruce woods. At last, coming to a little patch of brookside meadow where the grass kept short and sweet and green even at this late season, he stopped his flight, and fell to pasturing.

Late in the afternoon, the even gray mass of cloud which for days had veiled the sky thinned away and scattered, showing the clear blue of the north. The sun, near setting, sent long rays of cheerful light down the narrow valley, bringing out warm, golden bronzes in the massive, dull green of the fir and spruce and hemlock, and striking sharp flame on the surfaces of the smooth pools. Elated by the sudden brightness, the white stallion resumed his journey at a gallop, straight toward the sunset, his long mane and tail, now dry, streaming out on the light afternoon breeze that drew down between the hills. He kept on up the valley till the sun went down, and then, in the swiftly deepening twilight, came to a little grassy point backed by a steep rock. Here where the rippling of the water enclosed him on three sides, and the rock, with a thick mass of hemlocks surmounting it, shut him in on the fourth, he felt more secure, less desolate, than when surrounded by the endless corridors of the forest; and close to the foot of the rock he lay down, facing the mysterious gloom of the trees across the stream.

Just as he was settling himself, a strange voice, hollow yet muffled, cried across the open space "*Hoo-hoo, hoo-hoo, woo-hoo-hoo!*" and he bounded to his feet, every nerve on the alert. He had never in his life before heard the voice of the great horned owl, and his apprehensive wonder was excusable. Again and yet again came the hollow call out of the deep dark of the banked woods opposite. As he stood listening tensely, eyes and nostrils wide, a bat flitted past his ears, and he jumped half around, with a startled snort. The ominous sound, however, was not repeated, and in a couple of minutes he lay down again, still keeping watchful eyes upon the dark mass across the stream. Then, at last, a broad-winged bird, taking shape softly above the open, as noiseless as a gigantic moth, floated over him, and looked down upon him under his rock with round, palely luminous eyes. By some quick intuition he knew that this visitor was the source of the mysterious call. It was only a bird, after all, and no great thing in comparison with the eagles of his own Pyrenean heights. His apprehensions vanished, and he settled himself to sleep.

Worn out with days and nights of strain and terror, the exile slept soundly. Soon, under the crisp autumn starlight, a red fox crept down circumspectly to hunt mice in the tangled dry grasses of the point. At sight of the strange white form sleeping carelessly at the foot of the rock he bounded back into cover, startled quite out of his philosophic composure. He had never before seen any such being as that; and the smell, too, was mysterious and hostile to his wrinkling, fastidious nostrils. Having eyed the newcomer for some time from his hiding place under the branches, he crept around the rock and surveyed him stealthily from the other side. Finding no enlightenment, or immediate prospect of it, he again drew back, and made a careful investigation of the stranger's tracks, which were quite unlike the tracks of any creature he knew. Finally he made up his mind that he must confine his hunting to the immediate neighborhood, keeping the stranger under surveillance till he could find out more about him.

Soon after the fox's going a tuft-eared lynx came out on the top of the rock, and with round, bright, cruel eyes glared down upon the grassy point, half hoping to see some rabbits playing there. Instead, she saw the dim white bulk of the sleeping stallion. In her astonishment at this unheard-of apparition, her eyes grew wider and whiter than before, her hair stood up along her back, her absurd little stub of a tail fluffed out to a fussy pompon, and she uttered a hasty, spitting growl as she drew back into the shelter of the hemlocks. In the dreaming ears of the sleeper this angry sound was only a growl of the seas which had for days been clamoring about the gloom of his stall on the ship. It disturbed him not at all.

At about two o'clock in the morning, as that mystic hour when Nature seems to send a message to all her animate children, preparing them for the advent of dawn, the white stallion got up, shook himself, stepped softly down to the brook's-edge for a drink, and then fell to cropping the grass wherever it remained green. The forest, though to a careless ear it might have seemed as silent as before, had in reality stirred to a sudden, ephemeral life. Far off, from some high rock, a she-fox barked sharply. Faint, muffled chirps from the thick bushes told of junkos and chickadees waking up to see if all was well with the world. The mice set up a scurrying in the grass. And presently a high-antlered buck stepped out of the shadows and started across the open toward the brook.

The dark buck, himself a moving shadow, saw the stallion first, and stopped with a loud snort of astonishment and defiance. The stallion wheeled about, eyed the intruder for a moment doubtfully, then trotted up with a whinny of pleased interrogation. He had no dread of the antlered visitor, but rather a hope of companionship in the vast and overpowering loneliness of the alien night.

The buck, however, was in anything but a friendly mood. His veins aflame with the arrogant pugnacity of the rutting season, he saw in the white stranger only a possible rival, and grew hot with rage at his approach. With an impatient stamping of his slim forehoofs, he gave challenge. But to the stallion this was an unknown language. Innocently he came up, his nose stretched out in question, till he was within a few feet of the motionless buck. Then, to his astonishment, the latter bounced suddenly aside like a ball, stood straight up on his hind legs, and struck at him like lightning with those keen-edged, slim forehoofs. It was a savage assault, and two long, red furrows—one longer and deeper than the other—appeared on the stallion's silky white flank.

In that instant the wanderer's friendliness vanished, and an avenging fury took its place. His confidence had been cruelly betrayed. With a harsh squeal, his mouth wide open and lips drawn back from his formidable teeth, he sprang at his assailant. But the buck had no vain idea of standing up against this whirlwind of wrath which he had evoked. He bounded aside, lightly but hurriedly, and watched for an opportunity to repeat his attack.

The stallion, however, was not to be caught again; and the dashing ferocity of his rushes kept his adversary ceaselessly on the move, bounding into the air and leaping aside to avoid those disastrous teeth. The buck was awaiting what he felt sure would come, the chance to strike again; and his confidence in his own supreme agility kept him from any apprehension as to the outcome of the fight.

But the buck's great weakness lay in his ignorance, his insufficient knowledge of the game he was playing. He had no idea that his rushing white antagonist had any other tactics at command. When he gave way, therefore, he went just far enough to escape the stallion's teeth and battering forefeet. The stallion, on the other hand, soon realized the futility of his present method of attack against so nimble an adversary. On his next rush, therefore, just as the buck bounced aside, he wheeled in a short half-circle, and lashed out high and far with his steel-shod heels. The buck was just within the most deadly range of the blow. He caught the terrific impact on the base of the neck and the forward point of the shoulder, and went down as if an explosive bullet had struck him. Before he could even stir to rise, the stallion was upon him, trampling, battering, squealing, biting madly; and the fight was done. When the wanderer had spent his vengeance, and paused, snorting and wild-eyed, to take breath, he looked down upon a mangled shape that no longer struggled or stirred or even breathed. Then the last of his righteous fury faded out. The sight and smell of the blood sickened him, and in a kind of terror he turned away. For a few hesitating moments he stared about his little retreat and then, finding it had grown hateful to him, he forsook it, and pushed onward up the edge of the stream, between the black, impending walls of the forest.

About daybreak he came out on the flat, marshy shores of a shrunken lake, the unstirred waters of which gleamed violet and pale gold beneath the twisting coils and drifting plumes of white vapor. All around the lake stood the grim, serried lines of the firs, under a sky of palpitating opal. The marshes, in their autumn coloring of burnt gold and pinky olive, with here and there a little patch of enduring emerald, caught the wanderer's fancy with a faint reminder of home. Here was pasture, here was sweet water, here was room to get away from the oppressive mystery of the woods. He halted to rest and recover himself; and in the clear, tonic air, so cold that every morning the edges of the lake were crisped with ice, the aching red gashes on his flank speedily healed.

He had been at the lake about ten days, and was beginning to grow restlessly impatient of the unchanging solitude, before anything new took place. A vividly conspicuous object in his gleaming whiteness as he roamed the marshes, pasturing or galloping up and down the shore with streaming mane and tail, he

had been seen and watched and wondered at by all the wild
kindreds who had their habitations in the woods about the lake.
But they had all kept carefully out of his sight, regarding him
with no less terror than wonder; and he imagined himself utterly
alone, except for the fishhawks, and the southward journeying
ducks, which would drop with loud quacking and splashing into
the shallows after sunset, and the owls the somber hooting of
which disturbed him every night. Several times, too, from the extreme head of the lake he heard a discordant call, a great braying
bellow, which puzzled him, and brought him instantly to his feet
by a note of challenge in it; but the issuer of this hoarse defiance
never revealed himself. Sometimes he heard a similar call, with a
difference—a longer, less harshly blatant cry, the under note of
which was one of appeal rather than of challenge. Over both he
puzzled in vain; for the moose, bulls and cows alike, had no wish
to try the qualities of the great white stranger who seemed to
have usurped the lordship of the lake.

At last, one violet evening in the close of the sunset, as he
stood fetlock deep in the chill water, drinking, a light sound of
many feet caught his alert ear. Lifting his head quickly, he saw a
herd of strange-looking, heavy-antlered, whitish-brown deer
emerging in long line from the woods and crossing the open toward the foot of the lake. The leader of the caribou herd, a massive bull, nearly white, with antlers almost equal to those of a
moose, returned the stallion's inquiring stare with a glance of
mild curiosity, but did not halt an instant. It was plain that he
considered his business urgent; for the caribou, as a rule, are
nothing if not curious when confronted by any strange sight. But
at present the whole herd, which journeyed, in the main, in single
file, seemed to be in a kind of orderly haste. They turned questioning eyes upon the white stallion as they passed, then looked
away indifferently, intent only upon following their leader on his
quest. The stallion stood watching, his head high and his nostrils
wide, till the very last of the herd had disappeared into the woods
across the lake. Then the loneliness of his spacious pasture all at
once quite overwhelmed him. He did not want the company of
the caribou, by any means, or he might have followed them as
they turned their backs toward the sunset; but it was the dwell-
ings of men he wanted, the human hand on his mane, the prov-

endered stall, the voice of kindly command, and the fellowship of his kindred of the uncleft hoof. In some way he had got it into his head that men might be found most readily by traveling toward the southwest. Toward the head of the lake, therefore, and just a little south of the sunset's deepest glow, he now took his way. He was done with the lake and the empty marshes.

From the head of the lake he followed up a narrow stillwater for perhaps half a mile, crashing his way through a difficult tangle of fallen, rotting trunks and dense underbrush, till he came out upon another and much smaller lake, very different from the one he had just left. Here were no meadowy margins; but the shores were steep and thick-wooded to the water's edge. Diagonally thrust out across the outlet, and about a hundred yards above it, ran a low, bare spit of white sand, evidently covered at high water. Over the black line of the woods hung a yellow crescent moon, only a few nights old and near setting.

Coming suddenly from the difficult gloom of the woods, where the noise of his own movements kept his senses occupied to the exclusion of all else, the wanderer stopped and stood quite still for a long time under the shadow of a thick hemlock, investigating this new world with ear and eye and nostril. Presently, a few hundred yards around the lake shore, to his left, almost opposite the jutting sand spit, arose a noisy crashing and thrashing of the bushes. As he listened in wonder, his ears erect and eagerly interrogative, the noise stopped, and again the intense silence settled down upon the forest. A minute or two later a big, high-shouldered, shambling, hornless creature came out upon the sand spit, stood blackly silhouetted against the moonlight, stretched its ungainly neck, and sent across the water that harsh, bleating cry of appeal which he had been hearing night after night. It was the cow moose calling for her mate. And in almost instant answer arose again that great crashing among the underbrush on the opposite shore.

With a certain nervousness added to his curiosity, the white stallion listened as the crashing noise drew near. At the same time something in his blood began to tingle with the lust of combat. There was menace in the approaching sounds, and his courage arose to meet it. All at once, within about fifty yards of him, and just across the outlet, the noise ceased absolutely. For perhaps ten minutes there was not a sound,—not the snap of a twig or the splash of a ripple,—except that twice again came the call of the solitary cow standing out against the moon. Then, so suddenly that he gave an involuntary snort of amazement at the apparition, the wanderer grew aware of a tall, black bulk with enormous antlers which took shape among the undergrowth not ten paces distant.

The wanderer's mane rose along his arched neck, his lips drew back savagely over his great white teeth, fire flamed into his eyes, and for a score of seconds he stared into the wicked, little, gleaming eyes of the bull moose. He was eager for the fight, but waiting for the enemy to begin. Then, as noiselessly and miraculously as he had come, the great moose disappeared, simply fading into the darkness, and leaving the stallion all a-tremble with apprehension. For some minutes he peered anxiously into every black thicket within reach of his eyes, expecting a rushing assault from some unexpected quarter. Then, glancing out again across the lake, he saw that the cow had vanished from the moonlit point. Bewildered, and in the grasp of an inexplicable trepidation, he waded out into the lake belly-deep, skirted around the south shore, climbed the steep slope, and plunged straight into the dark of the woods. His impulse was to get away at once from the mysteries of that little, lonely lake.

The deep woods, of course, for him were just as lonely as the lake, for his heedless trampling and conspicuous coloring made a solitude all about him as he went. At last, however, he stumbled upon a trail. This he adopted gladly as his path, for it led away from the lake and in a direction which his whim had elected to follow.

Moving now on the deep turf, with little sound save the occasional swish of branches that brushed his flanks, he began to realize that the woods were not as empty as he had thought. On each side, in the soft dark, he heard little squeaks and rustlings and scurryings. Rabbits went bounding across the trail, just under his nose. Once a fox trotted ahead of him, looking back coolly at the great, white stranger. Once a small, stripe-backed animal passed leisurely before him, and a whiff of pungent smell annoyed his sensitive nose. Wide wings winnowed over him now and then, making him jump nervously; and once a pouncing sound, followed by a snarl, a squeal, and a scuffle, moved him to so keen an excitement that he swerved a few steps from the trail in his anxiety to see what it was all about. He failed to see anything, however, and after much stumbling was relieved to get back to the easy trail again. With all these unusual interests the miles and the hours seemed short to him; and when the gray of dawn came filtering down among the trees, he saw before him a clearing with two low-roofed cabins in the middle of it. Wild with delight at this evidence of man's presence, he neighed shrilly, and tore up to the door of the nearest cabin at full gallop, his hoofs clattering on the old chips which strewed the open.

To his bitter disappointment, he found the cabin, which was simply an old lumber-camp, deserted. The door being ajar, he nosed it open and entered. The damp, cheerless interior, with no furnishing but a rusty stove, a long bench hewn from a log, and a tier of bunks along one side, disheartened him. The smell of human occupation still lingered about the bunks, but all else savored of desertion and decay. With drooping head he emerged, and crossed over to the log stable. That horses had occupied it once, though not recently, was plain to him through various unmistakable signs; but it was more in the hope of sniffing the scent of his own kind than from any expectation of finding the stable occupied that he poked his nose in through the open doorway.

It was no scent of horses, however, which now greeted his startled nostrils. It was a scent quite unfamiliar to him, but one which, nevertheless, filled him with instinctive apprehension. At the first whiff of it he started back. Then, impelled by his curiosity, he again looked in, peering into the gloom. The next instant he was aware of a huge black shape leaping straight at him. Springing back with a loud snort, he wheeled like lightning, and lashed out madly with his heels.

The bear caught the blow full in the ribs, and staggered against the door-post with a loud, grunting cough, while the stallion trotted off some twenty yards across the chips and paused, wondering. The blow, in all probability, had broken several of the bear's ribs, but without greatly impairing his capacity for a fight; and now, in a blind rage, he rushed again upon the intruder who had dealt him so rude a buffet. The stallion, however, was in no fighting mood. Depressed as he was by the desolation of the

cabin, and daunted by the mysterious character of this attack
from the dark of the stable, he was now like a child frightened of
ghosts. Not the bear alone, but the whole place, terrified him.
Away he went at full gallop across the clearing, by good fortune
struck the continuation of the loggers' road, and plunged onward
into the shadowy forest.

For a couple of miles he ran, then he slowed down to a trot,
and at last dropped into a leisurely walk. This trail was much
broader and clearer than the one which had led him to the camp,
and a short, sweet grass grew along it, so that he pastured com-
fortably without much loss of time. The spirit of his quest, however, was now so strong upon him that he would not rest after
feeding. Mile after mile he pressed on, till the sun was high in
the clear, blue heavens, and the shadows of the ancient firs were
short and luminous. Then suddenly the woods broke away before
him.

Far below he saw the blue sea sparkling. But it was not the
beauty of the sea that held his eyes. From his very feet the road
dropped down through open, half-cleared burnt lands, a stretch
of rough pasture fields, and a belt of sloping meadow, to a little
white village clustering about an inlet. The clutter of roofs was
homelike to his eyes, hungry with long loneliness; the little white
church, with shining spire and cross, was very homelike. But
nearer, in the very first pasture field, just across the burnt land,
was a sight that came yet nearer to his heart. There, in a corner of
the crooked snake fence, stood two bay mares and a foal, their
heads over the fence as they gazed up the hill in his direction. Up
went mane and tail, and loud and long he neighed to them his
greeting. Their answer was a whinny of welcome, and down across
the fields he dashed at a wild gallop that took no heed of fences.
When, a little later in the day, a swarthy French-Canadian farmer
came up from the village to lead his mares down to water, he was
bewildered with delight to find himself the apparent master of a
splendid white stallion, which insisted on claiming him, nosing
him joyously, and following at his heels like a dog.

HORSES AND SHEEP AT PASTURE. Adriaen van de
Velde. *Courtesy, The John G. Johnson Collection, Philadelphia.*

THE SOVEREIGN HORSE

THE DOCTOR'S HORSE
by Mary E. Wilkins

The horse was a colt when he was purchased with the money paid
by the heirs of one of the doctor's patients, and those were his
days of fire. At first it was opined that the horse would never do
for the doctor: he was too nervous, and his nerves beyond the
reach of the doctor's drugs. He shied at every wayside bush and
stone; he ran away several times; he was loath to stand, and many
a time the doctor in those days was forced to rush from the bed-
sides of patients to seize his refractory horse by the bridle and

soothe and compel him to quiet. The horse in that untamed youth of his was like a furnace of fierce animal fire; when he was given rein on a frosty morning the pound of his iron-bound hoofs on the rigid roads cleared them of the slow-plodding country teams. A current as of the very freedom and invincibility of life seemed to pass through the taut reins to the doctor's hands. But the doctor was the master of his horse, as of all other things with which he came in contact. He was a firm and hard man in the pursuance of his duty, never yielding to it with love, but unswervingly stanch. He was never cruel to his horse; he seldom whipped him, but he never petted him; he simply mastered him, and after a while the fiery animal began to go the doctor's gait, and not his own.

When the doctor was sent for in a hurry, to an emergency case, the horse stretched his legs at a gallop, no matter how little inclined he felt for it, perhaps on a burning day of summer. When there was no haste, and the doctor disposed to take his time, the horse went at a gentle amble, even though the frosts of a winter morning were firing his blood and every one of his iron nerves and muscles was strained with that awful strain of repressed motion. Even on those mornings the horse would stand at the door of the patient who was ill with old-fashioned consumption or chronic liver disease, his four legs planted widely, his head and neck describing a long downward curve, so expressive of submission and dejection that it might have served as a hieroglyphic for them, and no more thought of letting those bounding impulses of his have their way than if the doctor's will had verily bound his every foot to the ground with unbreakable chains of servitude. He had become the doctor's horse. He was the will of the doctor, embodied in a perfect compliance of action and motion. People remarked how the horse had sobered down, what a splendid animal he was for the doctor, and they had thought that he would never be able to keep him and employ him in his profession.

Now and then the horse used to look around at the empty buggy as he stood at the gate of a patient's house, to see if the doctor were there, but the will which held the reins, being still evident to his consciousness, even when its owner was absent, kept him in his place. He would have no thought of taking advantage of his freedom; he would turn his head and droop it in that curve of utter submission, shift his weight slightly to another foot, make a sound which was like a human sigh of patience, and wait again. When the doctor, carrying his little medicine chest, came forth, he would sometimes look at him, sometimes not; but he would set every muscle into an attitude of readiness for progress at the feel of the taut lines and the sound of the masterly human voice behind him.

Then he would proceed to the house of the next patient, and the story would be repeated. The horse seemed to live his life in a perfect monotony of identical chapters. His waiting was scarcely cheered or stimulated by the vision and anticipation of his stall and his supper, so unvarying was it. The same stall, the same measure of oats, the same allotment of hay. He was never put out to pasture, for the doctor was a poor man, and unable to buy another horse and to spare him. All the variation which came to his experience was the uncertainty as to the night calls. Sometimes he would feel a slight revival of spirit and rebellion when led forth on a bitter winter night from his stolidity of repose, broken only by the shifting of his weight for bodily comfort, never by any perturbation of his inner life. The horse had no disturbing memories, and no anticipations, but he was still somewhat sensitive to surprises. When the flare of the lantern came athwart his stall, and he felt the doctor's hand at his halter in the deep silence of a midnight, he would sometimes feel himself as a separate consciousness from the doctor, and experience the individualizing of contrary desires.

Now and then he pulled back, planting his four feet firmly, but he always yielded in a second before the masterly will of the man. Sometimes he started with a vicious emphasis, but it was never more than momentary. In the end he fell back into his state of utter submission. The horse was not unhappy. He was well cared for. His work, though considerable, was not beyond his strength. He had lost something, undoubtedly, in this complete surrender of his own will, but a loss of which one is unconscious tends only to the degradation of an animal, not to his misery.

The doctor often remarked with pride that his horse was a well-broken animal, somewhat stupid, but faithful. All the timid women folk in the village looked upon him with favor; the doctor's wife, who was nervous, loved to drive with her husband behind this docile horse, and was not afraid even to sit, while the doctor was visiting his patients, with the reins over the animal's

back. The horse had become to her a piece of mechanism absolutely under the control of her husband, and he was, in truth,
little more. Still, a furnace is a furnace, even when the fire runs
low, and there is always the possibility of a blaze.

The doctor had owned the horse several years, though he
was still young, when a young woman came to live in the family.
She was the doctor's niece, a fragile thing, so exposed as to her
network of supersensitive nerves to all the winds of life that she
was always in a quiver of reciprocation or repulsion. She feared
everything unknown, and all strength. She was innately suspicious
of the latter. She knew its power to work her harm, and believed
in its desire to do so. Especially was she afraid of that rampant
and uncertain strength of a horse. Never did she ride behind one
but she watched his every motion; she herself shied in spirit at
every wayside stone. She watched for him to do his worst. She
had no faith when she was told by her uncle that this horse was
so steady that she herself could drive him. She had been told
that so many times, and her confidence had been betrayed. But
the doctor, since she was like a pale weed grown in the shade,
with no stimulus of life except that given at its birth, prescribed
fresh air and, to her consternation, daily drives with him. Day
after day she went. She dared not refuse, for she was as compliant
in her way to a stronger will as the horse. But she went in an
agony of terror, of which the doctor had no conception. She sat
in the buggy all alone while the doctor visited his patients, and
she watched every motion of the horse. If he turned to look at
her, her heart stood still.

And at last it came to pass that the horse began in a curious
fashion to regain something of his lost spirit, and met her fear of
him, and became that which she dreaded. One day as he stood
before a gate in late autumn, with a burning gold of maple
branches over his head and the wine of the frost in his nostrils,
and this timorous thing seated behind him, anticipating that
which he could but had forgotten that he could do, the knowledge and the memory of it awoke in him. There was a stiff north-
wester blowing. The girl was huddled in shawls and robes; her
little, pale face looked forth from the midst with wide eyes, with a
prospectus of infinite danger from all life in them; her little, thin
hands clutched the reins with that consciousness of helplessness

and conviction of the horse's power of mischief which is sometimes like an electric current firing the blood of a beast.

Suddenly a piece of paper blew under the horse's nose. He
had been unmoved by firecrackers before, but today, with that
current of terror behind him firing his blood, that paper put him
in a sudden fury of panic of self-assertion, of rage, of all three
combined. He snorted; the girl screamed wildly. He started; the
girl gave the reins a frantic pull. He stopped. Then the paper
blew under his nose again, and he started again. The girl fairly
gasped with terror; she pulled the reins, and the terror in her
hands was like a whip of stimulus to the evil freedom in the horse.
She screamed again, and the sound of that scream was the climax.
The horse knew all at once what he was—not the doctor, but a
horse, with a great power of blood and muscle which made him
not only his own master, but the master of all weaker things. He
gave a great plunge that was rapture, the assertion of freedom—
freedom itself—and was off. The faint screams of the frightened
creature behind him stimulated him to madder progress. At last
he knew, by her terrified recognition of it, his own sovereignty of
liberty.

He thundered along the road; he had no more thought of
his pitiful encumbrance of servitude, the buggy, than a free soul
of its mortal coil. The country road was cleared before him; plod-
ding teams were pulled frantically to the side; women scuttled
into dooryards; pale faces peered after him from windows. Now
and then an adventurous man rushed into his path with wild
halloos and a mad swinging of arms, then fled precipitately before
his resistless might of advance. At first the horse had heard the
doctor's shouts behind him, and had laughed within himself,
then he left them far behind. He leaped, he plunged, his iron-
shod heels touched the dashboard of the buggy. He heard splint-
ering wood. He gave another lunging plunge, then he swerved
and leaped a wall. Finally he had cleared himself of everything
except a remnant of his harness. The buggy was a wreck, strewn
piecemeal over a meadow. The girl was lying unhurt, but as still
as if she were dead; but the horse which her fear had fired to new
life was away in a mad gallop over the autumn fields, and his
youth had returned. He was again himself—what he had been
when he first awoke to a consciousness of existence and the joy of

bounding motion in his mighty nerves and muscles. He was no longer the doctor's horse, but his own.

The doctor had to sell him. After that his reputation was gone, and, indeed, he was never safe. He ran away with the doctor. He would not stand a moment unless tied, and then pawed and pulled madly at the halter, and rent the air with impatient whinnies. So the doctor sold him, and made a good bargain. The horse was formed for speed, and his lapse from virtue had increased his financial value. The man who bought him had a good eye for horseflesh, and had no wish to stand at doors on his road to success, but to take a beeline for the winning post. The horse was well cared for, but for the first time he felt the lash and heard curses; however, they only served to stimulate to a fiercer glow the fire which had awakened within him. He was never his new master's horse as he had been the doctor's. He gained the reputation of speed, but also of vicious nervousness. He was put on the racecourse. He made a record at the county fair. Once he killed his jockey. He used to speed along the road drawing a man crouched in a tilting gig. Few other horses could pass him. Then he began to grow old.

At last, when the horse was old, he came into his first master's hands again. The doctor had grown old, older than the horse, and he did not know him at first, though he did say to his old wife that he looked something like that horse which he had owned which ran away and nearly killed his niece. After he said that, nothing could induce the doctor's wife to ride behind him; but the doctor, even in his feeble old age, had no fear, and the sidelong fire in the old horse's eye, and the proud cant of his neck, and his haughty resentment at unfamiliar sights on the road pleased him. He felt a confidence in his ability to tame this untamed thing, and the old man seemed to grow younger after he had bought the horse. He had given up his practice after a severe illness, and a young man had taken it, but he began to have dreams of work again. He never knew that he had bought his own old horse until after he had owned him some weeks. He was driving him along the country road one day in October when the oaks were a ruddy blaze, and the sumacs like torches along the walls, and the air like wine with the smell of grapes and apples. Then suddenly, while the doctor was sitting in the buggy with loose reins, speeding along the familiar road, the horse stopped; and he stopped before the house where had used to dwell the man afflicted with old-fashioned consumption, and the window which had once framed his haggard, coughing visage reflected the western sunlight like a blank page of gold. There the horse stood, his head and long neck bent in the old curve. He was ready to wait until the consumptive arose from his grave in the churchyard, if so ordered. The doctor stared at him. Then he got out and went to the animal's head, and man and horse recognized each other. The light of youth was again in the man's eyes as he looked at his own spiritual handiwork. He was once more the master, in the presence of that which he had mastered. But the horse was expressed in body and spirit only by the lines of utter yielding and patience and submission. He was again the doctor's horse.

THE HARD-WORKING HORSE

OLD MAJOR
by Bianca Bradbury

No one of us can keep him in his stall,
No fettered feet can stop his wandering,
When April walks long the pasture wall,
And his old blood is stirring in the spring
To the rhythm of the harrow and the plow.
There is a faithfulness in all his ways,
And gaunt and lonely and bewildered now
He plods behind his master and the bays,
And stamps and whinnies all along the lanes
For his own harness and his story row.
And if some April we shall find his reins
Are gone and his stall empty, we will know
That somewhere past the dim, celestial bars
Old Major plows in faith his field of stars.

THE MARTYRED HORSE

HORSES ARE HORSES
by Joseph Tenenbaum

1 /

First Lieutenant Ferenczi had a horse—a horse of rare distinction —one in a million.

It was the lieutenant's boast—repeated *ad nauseam*—that he had won him in a fair fight: shot down a Cossack and took his horse.

The horse was a magnificent bay with the mane of a lion. There was a white beauty spot between his two dreamy eyes. His nostrils quivered sensitively. Under a smooth, satin skin, the muscles rolled and played in a changing network. His legs were straight, clean, nervous. We called him "The Cossack," and the name was well chosen. He was as temperamental as a southern storm, and as whimsical as a prima donna. He was proud, obstinate, and supercilious. He hated the kind of familiarity that one bestows on plebeian horses. He was an aristocrat. Once offended by a vulgar slap on the haunches, he never forgot it. Not even a fistful of sugar could win back his favor.

No one could ride him at first, and only Ferenczi, a son of the vast Hungarian pusta, and perhaps the best horseman in the division, was able to conquer him after a long and obstinate struggle. Once conquered by the iron will and supple body of the lieutenant, the Cossack became his friend; but no one else could boast of his good graces.

I remember an instance of the Cossack's fastidiousness. One day, we wanted to make a little, lazy excursion in an old-fashioned post chaise. We harnessed two horses, my old mare and the Cossack. It would be an exaggeration to say that my mare had either grace or aristocracy about her; but she had bulk and muscle. She strained at the harness until the dashboard creaked; but the Cos-

sack set back his ears and dug his hoofs into the soil; he refused
to budge. I flicked him with the whip, and that being ineffective,
beat upon his flanks in earnest. He shot his head sidewards and
backwards, and gave me a steady, malevolent look over his shoulder. Then he began to move. Well, thought I, Cossack or no Cossack, an Austrian officer must be obeyed. On he galloped in a
pleasant rhythmic trot. Until we reached a narrow river, over
which a bridge ran almost on a level with the water. In the middle of the bridge, the Cossack stopped. I began to fret. What the
devil had come over him again? But this time, argument was of
no avail. I lost my temper and, cursing him roundly, flayed him
with the whip. This was worse than useless. I exhausted myself

THE WHITE HORSE. Jean Géricault. *Courtesy, Philadelphia Museum of Art: The William L. Elkins Collection.*

and it apparently amused him. At last I got down, with the intention of seizing him by the bridle and pulling him along. The moment I was on the bridge, off he was, together with the mare. Ferenczi sat helplessly laughing on the cart; he had the time of his life. I remained standing on the bridge. From that day on, the Cossack had a mortal hatred for me.

"That horse of mine," said Ferenczi, grinning when he came back from the ride, "is a born anti-Semite."

Well, what can you expect from a Cossack?

2 /

It is a pitch-dark night.

We are advancing into enemy territory. I ride in front of the battalion along a black forest road. The troops come crawling behind us, exhausted and sleepy. For some reason or other, we expect no encounter; and, seated on my horse, I fall into a half doze. The hoofs beat a monotonous tattoo on the fallen branches underfoot. No one speaks; the only human sound we hear is an occasional snore. Then, of a sudden, the horses become restive. They rear and sidle. They neigh loudly, and the disconcerting equine melody echoes back from a thousand gnarled trees. We rub our eyes. A shrill whistle sounds; a whizz, a rattle; bullets begin to fly. Off the path and right in among the trees we go. Dismount! Take cover! Every man for himself! The silence of the forest gives way to a crackling tumult. We fire, God knows at whom, God knows why; but we fire, and the night becomes hideous with the racket of sustained fusillades, coming from nowhere and everywhere.

And so the night passes in this fantastic way. The dawn begins to creep up grayly through the ragged branches above us and to the front. And with the growing light, we realize our ghastly mistake. We have been shooting mostly at each other. Dead and dying are scattered under the trees; our own men! Very few Russians are among the dead. Apparently, a Cossack patrol spied us, shot at us and was off and away.

3 /

We stand looking at each other in rage and stupefaction, sunk in a mad despair. A horse comes dashing through the trees. The Cossack! Where's Ferenczi? The Cossack horse answers clearly. He dances around me, swishing his tail. He sniffs at me beseechingly. He takes my elbow between his teeth and pulls me. And when I move in the direction he indicates, he lets go and gallops ahead of me, over roots, over fallen trunks; he stops, looks back to see if I am following, and then gallops on with feverish impatience.

Panting, I follow until I find Ferenczi sitting on the ground and bandaging his foot. He cannot stand up.

"It's good to see you, Cap," he said.

"But what are you doing out here?" I asked; he was more than a mile ahead of us.

"It's that God-damn Cossack! The moment he heard the sound of Russians, he set off at a gallop. Gave me no chance to dismount. I didn't dare to jump off in the dark among these trees. But I got wounded and fell out of the saddle. I must have broken my leg on top of it; I can't move. Can you beat that?" He looked at the Cossack, red with anger. "Just a plain traitor. That's all."

I looked at his wound with an expert eye and he continued his lingual barrage.

"What a swine a horse can be! Got me into trouble with his mad gallop; threw me off when I was wounded. He wouldn't leave me and wouldn't stand still either. Danced hither and thither like a crazy donkey. Running away and coming back as if waiting for me to mount him, so he could join his brother Cossacks with a prisoner on the saddle. Damn him! I felt like shooting him; and I feel like doing it right now."

The Cossack horse stood by, watching us out of guilty eyes. Nervous tremors spread over his skin, like the ripples on a lake into which a stone had been flung. His nostrils quivered as if begging forgiveness. He thumped on the ground, and with one of his forelegs, he scooped out the equine alphabet in the soil. He licked the lieutenant's broken leg, as if to ease his pain. He was obviously downhearted. He forgot his pride. I was genuinely sorry for him.

"Aye, leave him alone, the Cossack," I interceded with the

lieutenant. "After all, he is a Russian, too; born on the vast
Ukrainian steppes, raised to freedom and wide expanse; not used
to a foreign yoke. How do you know what came over him that
dark night? He may have heard the neighing of an old comrade,
a brother, a sister, or mayhap his own mother, coming all the way
from the depths of Russia. You can't blame him for wanting to
join his brood. Wouldn't you have done the same?

"Well, who knows the mind of a horse?" I added soothingly,
while adjusting an improvised splint of two broken twigs to his
shattered leg.

"I can very well picture to myself the blind, tantalizing struggle that took place in that narrow, tormented brain of the horse.
There, his own blood and flesh calling him, tempting, luring; the
aching longing for his own kind; the obscure and powerful memories of childhood; the powerful temptation to be free again; free
from captivity; a Cossack colt under a Cossack rider, untrammeled,
swift and wild like the wind in the pampas. . . . And at the same
time, his devotion to his new master began weighing upon him
heavier and heavier, nailing him down to his post with a sense of
duty; the utter shame of it to leave his master and run away like a
coward at the critical moment when this master of his lay
wounded, helpless, perhaps dying. . . . Why, how can you?"

"Oh, hang it, Doctor!"

My patient lost his nerve.

"Gently, please, it hurts."

I began to lift the lieutenant from the ground. He made a
fierce grimace.

"Watch it," he muttered again. "That leg hurts like hell."

The Cossack sat down on his hind legs, resting on his forelegs. He sat quietly, attentively, watching every move of mine,
imploring me with his looks, like an intelligent being, not to hurt
his lieutenant. I was through with my orthopedics. I managed to
get Ferenczi up again. He hobbled alongside of me, using my
shoulder as a crutch. Then the Cossack also struggled to his feet
and paced back thoughtfully, almost sadly.

4 /

But Ferenczi was not to be appeased so easily. It was not so much
the wound that worried him as his hurt pride. The Cossack had

shown how incomplete his mastery was. He had betrayed a double instead of a single loyalty—a hyphenated allegiance. And what could be more exasperating to a sensitive and boastful horseman? The more Ferenczi thought of it, the angrier he became.

He complained of his wound and his twisted leg like an irritable old maid. Every step was torture to him.

"If not for that crazy brute, I wouldn't be suffering," he blurted. "God damn it, Captain, be careful the way you drag me along."

"It wouldn't do you any harm to behave like a soldier," I said, exasperated by his fussiness.

"It's the horse, the damn horse," he said, gritting his teeth. "It's all his fault. The vile beast!"

He jerked himself out of my grip suddenly, as if he were slipping. I tried to sustain him, but did not succeed. The infuriated lieutenant had got hold of his revolver. He aimed.

There was a sudden shrill buzz in the air, a crack! The Cossack stood dead still and twisted his head around. From the jaws, red blood flowed. He sank slowly to his haunches. He tried to get up again, but his forefeet helplessly dug into the soil. His eyes, uncomprehending, filled with fear and surprise, turned toward Ferenczi. Then he toppled over. The Cossack was done for. . . .

"That leg of mine hurts like the devil," Ferenczi said peevishly.

I started. "You're pretty raw, Lieutenant," I said to him coldly.

He began to rave. "See here, Cap, I asked you to look after me, not give me lectures. Just get me to the field station, that's all."

He regretted those words the moment he had uttered them. After all, I was the doctor, and he the helpless patient. He tried to excuse himself.

"Come on, Doctor, what's making you stare like that? It's only a dead horse. There are horses enough in the world, aren't there?"

"There are," I said.

"And what are horses?" he asked, with a shrug of the shoulders.

"That's right," I agreed. "Horses are horses."

THE UNMOUNTABLE HORSE

SAD SAM
by Fred Gipson

It was 1938 and folks of Refugio were pulling off a little two-bit rodeo for South Texas ranch people. Nobody had come with the expectation of seeing the last show of one of the greatest rodeo broncs ever to throw a rider. But when in the middle of a calf-roping contest the announcer halted the show to call an exhibition bronc ride—"Buck West coming out on Sad Sam!"—there wasn't a handful of people who didn't sit up and take notice.

The handlers led Sad Sam into the bucking chutes for saddling and the old horse sure didn't represent the popular notion of an outlaw bronc known from Pendleton, Oregon, to New York's Madison Square Garden. He was just a big old rawboned bay with a black mane and tail, spur-scarred from head to foot and shaggy as a brush-frazzled saddle blanket. He was tub-footed, jug-headed, and had a right ear drooping at a forlorn angle. He stood with the air of dejection that had caused the great bull-dozer Mike Hastings to name him Sad Sam seventeen years before.

Up in the stands, an old Nueces River rider slapped a grizzly-faced partner on the leg. "Now, Wash," he said, "this'll do to watch and recollect. Buck West's over-matched hisself this time. Sad Sam'll throw him clean up into the judge's stand."

Wash wasn't convinced. "Ten year back," he said, "you'd a-been right. But Buck'll ride him now. Buck's rode in the big time. And Sad Sam's too old and stove-up from dragging a fresno * in a slush pit."

"He's dead-old," agreed Nueces. "Twenty-one, they tell me. And Long Tom Heard just unhooked him last night from another week in harness. But you watch; he'll hang Buck's chin on the moon!"

* Five-six foot wide scoop with sharp leading edge used in oil fields.

From the top bar of the chute, Buck West slapped a regulation bucking saddle down on the old horse's back and Sad Sam didn't even flinch. Most broncs will fall back on their haunches and fight every step of the way into the chutes, then try to climb out over the top; but Sad Sam hadn't even tightened the halter shank the chute man led him by. For all the spectators could tell, Buck West might have been saddling some old plug for a bunch of kids to play on.

The rider eased himself down onto the horse. Sad Sam didn't move. West jammed his boots into the stirrups and rocked his saddle to make certain he was all set. He caught up his bucking rein to the right length, pulled off his hat, then nodded to the chute man: "Give us air."

The man jerked the tie-ropes loose and yanked the chute gates apart. Buck West swung his feet forward and slammed his spur rowels into the big bay's shoulders. That opened the ball. Sad Sam lunged out of the chute, bogged his head and exploded into the arena, coughing and roaring like a meat-hungry lion.

There was no fancy sunfishing or pinwheeling or rolling his belly up to the sun. Sad Sam didn't have a trick in his bag for catching a man off balance and loosening him in the saddle. His was just old hard, straightaway bucking, but the kind to rattle every leather on a saddle and every bone in the body of the man straddling it.

Buck West didn't last till he got started. He lost his right stirrup on the third jump, his left stirrup on the fourth, and by the time the bawling bay had made his fifth leap, the big-time show rider couldn't have found his saddle seat with a forked stick. He left Sad Sam in a spread-eagle dive that ended when his bare head slapped against the bottom of an arena fence post.

The pickup men spurred out to cut the horse off before he could paw the unconscious man to death. Sad Sam had stopped pitching the instant he'd felt Buck West's weight leave the saddle. Now he stood within three steps of the fallen rider, staring down at him with a sort of sad, worried look, as if he half wished he hadn't thrown him so hard. Sad Sam wasn't a man killer.

They carted Buck West off to a hospital, and up in the grandstands the Nueces River rider crowed to his partner. "Now, what'd I tell you!" he said. "Why, Wash, it takes a damned good

FOUR HORSES. Thomas Eakins. *Courtesy, Philadelphia Museum of Art.*

rider just to keep his seat on a fence and watch that old Sad Sam pitch!"

Those words just about summed up the opinion of every bronc rider in America back when Sad Sam followed the circuits of the big rodeos. In those days, nearly every great bronc buster, the near-great, and plenty of mail-order rodeo hands had a try at riding Sad Sam—and they all lived to regret it.

The first time anybody paid any attention to Sad Sam was in Fort Worth in the early spring of 1921, when W. T. Johnston, who furnished stock for the big rodeos of America every year, was shaping up his string of bucking horses for the coming rodeo season. Johnston had thirty head of new horses from Wyoming. They were big horses, outlaws and man haters, most of them, wicked as sin.

Johnston ordered his men to saddle and mount each one, but to quit the saddle as soon as a horse was pitching good. That way, a bronc got to thinking he was throwing his rider every time. Later, in a rodeo arena, a horse trained like that would put all he had into unloading his rider.

But the first of Johnston's rodeo hands to mount a big, sleepy-headed four-year-old bay horse that stood hipshot in the chute while being saddled—that rider never got a chance to quit the saddle. He was wiping up the arena with his shirt-tail before he knew what had happened. The surprised buster got up and hat-whipped the dust out of his clothes. "Offhand," he observed, "I'd say it won't take a lot of training to make a rodeo bronc out of that bent-eared rascal."

Which was more truth than the rodeo hand realized. Nobody ever had to train Sad Sam to pitch; mighty few could stay on him long enough to get set to jump off.

Sad Sam made the rounds of the rodeos that year—Boston, New York, Chicago, and others not so big. Nobody paid him any particular attention. He was just another rodeo bronc, a little uglier than most, a little more comical-looking, maybe. But being a deadhead any time he wasn't coming out of the chutes with a rider, Sad Sam soon got to be a favorite of the chute hands. They could walk into a corral full of bad horses and catch him where he stood. They found they could belly up across his back and he'd help them corner the others to tie on the halter shanks. It got so that if you'd lead Sad Sam in or out of a railroad car first, all the rest would follow like pack mules trailing a bell mare. But the minute you threw a leg across his back to straddle him, he'd land you in the misty Beyond.

That didn't make him especially noteworthy at first, however. Not among such famous names as Corkscrew, Gates of the Mountain, Fiddle Face, and Buzzard Roost. These rodeo broncs had class; they were bad. They were making rodeo history all over the United States. You couldn't tell about a bronc new to the game like Sad Sam. Plenty of good beginners never lasted out the first season. But by the wind-up of his second season, it gradually came to the riders and rodeo directors that nobody had ever stayed on him till the whistle blew. And that was mighty hard to understand. It's common knowledge among bronc peelers that a straightaway bucker is the easiest kind of horse to ride. But as the bronc rider Jack Laidley put it, "That old horse just fair and square beats a man to death in a saddle."

The fans came to recognize and like the bay bronc. He was such a big old ugly, comical-acting horse to pack such a belly-load of dynamite. They liked the way he gave a rider every chance to get set in his tree before the show started, then made a windmill out of him. They liked the godawful roar he cut loose with when he left the chutes. Best of all, they loved that remorseful look Sad Sam invariably turned on a rider he'd just finished stacking up.

The busters who rode at Sad Sam, though—they felt different about it. All the affection they had for that bronc wouldn't have made a great long love story. The first time a man drew Sad Sam for a ride, he'd try to bluff it out. Here was his chance, he'd say, to show the rest of the bronc twisters how to take the starch out of that old bay horse. But after that first time, he'd just swear at his luck and go off. He wouldn't be in the prize money that day.

Pete Knight, who one time held the world championship for bronc riding, drew Sad Sam for a ride in New York, in Boston, and in Chicago. Pete was all man, big and strong as a bull. He'd bet you a $20 bill he could hook one forefinger over a doorsill and chin himself three times before his boots ever touched the floor. And he'd win your money. Pete sat a bucking saddle as if it had grown to the seat of his pants. But Pete wasn't man enough to draw money riding Sad Sam. Every time, Sad Sam put Pete to eating gravel before the whistle blew.

Year after year, Sad Sam made the circuits of the big shows. New York; Boston; Chicago; Blackfoot, Idaho; Kingman, Kansas; Salinas, California; the Pendleton Roundup. Five years is a long time for a bronc horse to last in a rodeo arena. Outlaws from the start, most of them kill or cripple themselves in the chutes, fighting to the last against the man creatures they've hated from the beginning. But Sad Sam never fought a man in the chutes or tried to hurt a rider after he had him on the ground. All he ever turned on a man was that fool look that made the spectators roar with laughter.

Among the best judges of good riding, it's generally accepted that Chief Corral came closest to making a ride on Sad Sam. Chief Corral is a little dark-skinned Osage from Oklahoma with plenty of championship ribbons. He drew Sad Sam in Chicago, and that was a ride to make a spectator bite the tip end off his heart. When the chute men turned Sad Sam out, he bellowed his usual deafening roar; and Chief Corral let out an ear-splitting panther scream to match it. Chief's silver-mounted spurs flashed in rhythm to the horse's leaps, back and forth, from shoulder to flank, raking hair every time. Once, twice, three times.

Sad Sam must have sensed that he was mounted by a real rider this time. He warped his backbone, put all he had into making a whip-cracker out of it. And for a while there, it looked as if the little Indian could take all the big bay horse had to dish out.

For six or seven seconds, the Osage was sitting pretty and Sad Sam's fans held their breath. Then suddenly something happened to the rhythm of those raking spurs. Chief swept them to the front for another rake at Sad Sam's hide and Sad Sam wasn't between them. Chief Corral was still squalling like a panther when he hit the dirt.

But age stacks up on a horse, same as on a man; and in 1930 Sad Sam got so he wouldn't buck at night. The floodlights seemed to baffle him. Any time a man mounted him in daylight, understand, there was still hell to pay and no water hot. But more and more of the big shows were being held at night and that finished Sam for the big time. Johnston sold him, along with some other cut-back rodeo broncs.

Sad Sam ended up with the Heard cousins, Long Tom and Short Tom, who hauled oil field equipment. Sad Sam never fought the work. He bucked with the harness a few times, then caught on. In charge of Dobe Lewis, a little black teamster who had horse savvy to spare, he worked to a fresno, gouging out slush pits for the new oil wells brought in. All the little Negro had to do was holler once, and Sad Sam would crawl up in that collar and dig in with his feet and grunt and heave till something moved. And he'd fall asleep the moment little Dobe hollered "Whoa!"

It looked as if the old rodeo bronc's show days were done.

Then one evening when the fresno teams plodded in, here came little Dobe driving his four-up team, sitting crossways on Sad Sam's back.

Long Tom Heard stepped out of his office and hollered at the little teamster. "Damn, Dobe!" he yelled, "don't you know you can't ride that Sad Sam horse?"

"Yassah," Dobe said. "I knows about dat. But me'n old Sam, boss, we's got us an understanding. I don't puts no foot across old Sam's back and old Sam, he don't throws me!"

Watching Dobe ride Sad Sam into the barns set Long Tom to wondering how much fight was left in the old horse. That night he and Short Tom decided to put on a little home-town rodeo there in Refugio the following Sunday. That country was full of ranch-hand brush-poppers who'd mount any bronc just to see if they could ride it. If those old broncs could still pitch, a rodeo would furnish good entertainment for the oil-field workers and might make some money, to boot.

From both angles, that little two-bit rodeo was a success. Some of the broncs would still pitch and some wouldn't; but everybody had a rip-roaring good time. And every brush-popper who took a hot seat on Sad Sam hit the dirt—some inside the arena, some out. So the Heards put on little rodeos all over South Texas for several years. They'd work Sad Sam and his mates in harness all week, then throw them into a bronc-busting show of a Sunday. And still nobody rode Sad Sam. He was getting old; he'd have to give it up some time, but he wasn't through when an ambitious kid from Mathis, Texas, who had built himself up a pretty big reputation as a rider, tried to top him out in the Refugio arena. Nobody knew for sure just what went wrong. When they turned Sad Sam out of the chute the kid threw away his bucking rein, grabbed for the saddlehorn with both hands and froze to it. That, coupled with the fact that he hooked his spurs in the saddle girth and tried to make a tight-legged ride of it, set him so rigidly in the saddle that there was no give to him anywhere. Which was a bad mistake on any hard-pitchng horse like Sad Sam. Right away, the kid's head began to flop back and forth like the popper on a bullwhip. If the pickup men hadn't been onto their jobs and dragged him off in a hurry, the chances are Sad Sam would have broken the kid's neck right there in the saddle.

In 1940, two years after Sad Sam had sent Buck West to the hospital for a week from that Refugio arena, Rocky Reagan put on a rodeo at Beeville and called on Long Tom Heard for the use of the old bay to fill out his bucking string. Sad Sam was twenty-three now; all over him were patches of white hair and patches where there was no hair at all, spur marks left by hundreds of riders, none of whom had ever managed to ride him.

But shaggy and decrepit-looking as he was, Reagan's riders didn't like the looks of him when they recognized him. Wouldn't a man feel a fool if that beat-up crowbait just happened to unload him!

They cornered Reagan in his office. "Reagan," the spokesman said, "you'll either take that old Sad Sam out of the bunch we ride or we'll take out on your show!"

Well, they had Reagan up a tree. You can't put on a bronc show without riders. Sad Sam was taken out.

Long Tom Heard wouldn't put Sad Sam back in harness after that. He figured that a horse twenty-three years old who could still bluff out a bunch of tough rodeo hands didn't deserve hard work. He loaded the old bronc into a trailer and hauled him off to his Berclair Ranch on Blanco Creek where he turned Sad Sam out on the pasture.

There, where the grass grew tall, where the water was good and shade handy, Sad Sam took his ease till the fall of 1944. One day Jack Harvey, a Negro ranch hand, rode in. "Well, Mistah Tom," he said, "I guess the cowhands can rest easy now. Old Sad Sam, he's passed on."

Jack said it looked as if the old bronc had lain down in the bed of the creek to take a roll in that pretty white sand and had died when he turned over the first time.

Today, none of the ranch hands want to come right out and say that nobody ever rode Sad Sam. They know how much truth there is in that old range saw:

> There ain't no man what can't be throwed;
> There ain't no hoss what can't be rode.

But they'll just be dogged if *they* can recollect a man who ever stayed with Sad Sam till the whistle blowed!

THE PATIENT HORSE

LANKO'S WHITE MARE
by H. E. Bates

Every morning just after daybreak Lanko, the quoits man, led out the white mare along with the other horses from the fair and watered her. She was a conspicuous figure, the only white horse in a long line of handsome grays, chestnuts, blacks, and piebalds.

On Lanko's head there were white hairs, also, and in spite of his flashing dark eyes, he was slow and steady when he walked.

He and the mare never went too fast for each other and he never grew impatient with her, but on the contrary understood her perfectly, trusting her to walk wherever he wished merely by a touch on her side. She in turn knew his touch unmistakably, for he had given it her with the same unfailing gentleness and care for nearly fifteen years.

One morning, in order to be ready to depart with the rest, Lanko was in haste to return to the fairground. He was a little farther behind the other horses than usual. In the fairground it-

THE HORSE FAIR. Rosa Bonheur. *Courtesy, The Metropolitan Museum of Art: Gift of Cornelius Vanderbilt, 1887.*

self, ever since before dawn, there had been commotion: the rattling of buckets, shrill voices, the jingle of harness, the heavy cough of great engines making their steam. Coming out of the gates, Lanko had had an argument with the "Fat Lady" man, a trivial and foolish argument, but which nevertheless had aroused a spark of anger in his eyes and had thrown him behind the rest.

For the first time when taking the white mare to drink he felt impatient; in the chilly morning air, with the sounds of departure behind him and the clatter of hoofs in front, the distance to the drinking place seemed immense. He knew that the white mare did not understand this. Her pace did not once quicken, she did not notice the absence of her fellow creatures. Yet he felt that because she had been understanding and obedient for nearly fifteen years she must understand now.

"We're late!" he told her. He slapped her ribs.

Her pace did not alter. After a moment Lanko ran a little in front of her and beckoned her, pulling the halter gently. She seemed to recognize his presence, but without responding or increasing her pace even a little. He began to run at her side, slapping her ribs again, as if to encourage her to imitation. But she would not run, or disturb herself, or even turn her head.

Lanko began to grow puzzled. A little more than halfway to the drinking place he saw the rest of the horses begin to return. This was an unprecedented thing: he had been there, day after day, for fifteen years with the rest. Now he would be forced to meet them returning, would have to stand aside while the handsome, many-colored crowd cantered past. In his mood of half disappointment, half consternation, he even desisted from urging the mare onward, and they fell into their habitual pace again, neither one too fast for the other, as if their patient and mutual understanding had suffered no break.

In a moment the long line of blacks and piebalds, roans and browns began to trot past him. He awoke from his mood of disappointment. He drew the white mare to the roadside, holding her there while the rest cantered disdainfully past, the men flaunting their arms, whistling and shouting, demanding what had become of him in a good-natured tirade which he could not understand. It seemed to him an hour before the mass of clattering hoofs filed past; he had not thought before that so many horses could come from the fair.

The last of the men, suddenly distasteful and aggravating to him in their red and check shirts, shouted: "She's only a filly!— Make her gallop—you'll never get away!" They turned on the bare backs of their horses and laughed at him.

Their reproaches stung him. With sudden anger he struck the mare's ribs again. It was a blow under which he had expected her to leap forward, as if startled by a shot. Instead she moved onward slowly, patient and steady, with habitual faith and obedience. Enraged by this, Lanko ran before and behind her, entreating, urging, beckoning her, pulling her halter, striking her ribs with even heavier blows than before, but without ever inducing her to change her pace. He pulled at her head and glared into her eyes.

Like this he managed to get her to the drinking pool at last, leading her down to the edge by the halter, pulling down her head until it touched the water. This was his every morning custom, a gesture of tender assistance, as towards a child. The white mare always responded, always drank her fill. But on this morning she only sniffed the water, gazed downward as if at her own reflection in the surface, then lifted her head and turned away.

Lanko was puzzled. The pool was muddy from the feet of the other horses, but he had seen her drink during fifteen years the foulest and most stagnant of waters. She too had suffered hardships. He patted her head in understanding of this. In a moment she would drink, he thought, if only he were patient, if only he waited.

For nearly a minute he was true to this resolve: he stood caressing the silk of her nostrils as he had so often done, humoring her, talking to her, full of patience for her. But she did not drink. All the time her head dropped a little towards the water, as if she were making up her mind, as if she were dreaming. The ripples her feet had made in the surface ran far away, grew faint, and then died—she remained so still.

"Drink! for God's sake! Drink, and let's get away!"

His words were half command, half entreaty. But she did not move, though it seemed to him she must understand why he had brought her there, simply because for fifteen years, morning by morning, she had understood and obeyed.

Lanko grew desperate again. "Drink!" He slapped her ribs. It was as if she were dead to all feeling—she did not respond, did not even quiver.

"Drink, damn you, drink!" he shouted suddenly. He pulled down her head to the water again, wetting her lips. Without even a mouthful she raised it again and turned away.

He led her to another part of the pool and repeated the gesture to which she had never failed to respond, suppressing momentarily all impatience and anger. But there, as before, he drew from her only the response, as it seemed to him, of a stupid and stubborn will.

Here his anger grew uncontrollable—he wrenched the halter upward and from the bank dragged at the white mare's head until she followed him. "If you won't drink you must go thirsty, damn you!"

Suddenly he thought: I shall be last. They'll be harnessed up and gone. I shall be crowded out.

Again he shouted to the mare, threatening her.

The mare remained still, staring emptily ahead. Lanko turned and looked at her, and then, angered by this long succession of futile words, of unanswered gestures and tenderness, strode forward and with his uplifted knee kicked her in the ribs.

There was a pause. Then Lanko, though able to see how startled she was, how deeply she felt the blow, pushed her hindquarters desperately. To his immense relief she responded and began to move off. But she seemed slower even than usual, heavier in body; her feet touched the ground uncertainly, her head had drooped a little.

It began to be urged upon Lanko very slowly, in spite of his joy at seeing her move again, that his difficulties with her were not ended. Matters grew worse as he recalled the mornings when she had trotted back from drinking, when the longest journeys in summer had not seemed to tire her.

His anger abated a little and he walked at her side with all his old patience, exactly in time with her, patting her side gently in order to remind her of his presence.

Some caravans were already leaving the fairground as he arrived there. It was a relief to find that he would not be crowded out: looking at the sky he thought he would be away before the sun was far up.

The white mare stood very still while he fetched her harness. This morning, as always before, he dropped it over her back with practiced quickness and ease, with a great jingle of buckles and bells. To his astonishment the white mare started forward as if struck and seemed to shudder under the weight. "Whoa!" She shivered involuntarily again. His astonishment and impatience increasing, he put on her bridle, but having buckled it, caressed her silky nostrils and spoke to her softly. She seemed to understand. Gently, little by little, he backed her into his little covered cart bearing his pots and pans, his food, and the red and white striped awnings and poles of his stall.

They joined the long line of brightly painted caravans and the engines drawing the roundabouts. The white mare was quiet. She moved steadily, as if the shouting and rattle of departure had awoken her against herself. Lanko walked at her side, relieved but silent, chewing a straw. Now and then, when the mare seemed to hesitate and slacken her pace again, he stroked her side, encouraging her. It was autumn and the red of the trees, the heavy dew sparkling on the dying grass, and the frosty smell in the air reminded him how often he and the mare had traveled this way, how she had never failed him, and how always, as on this morning, the jingle of the bells on her bridle had filled him with happiness.

Soon afterwards the sun broke out, shedding a soft, sudden light on that long line gleaming like a multicolored snake over the road. It seemed to bring out also not only color but smell, so that besides the scent of frosty leaves and decay, Lanko suddenly caught all the odors that were precious to him—the smell of horses and straw, of cooked herrings, of onions and cabbage, of oil, and the smoke belched out far ahead. It seemed difficult to believe he was not young again, so fresh and strong were these smells, as if coming to him for the first time.

Suddenly he was aroused out of these memories by the white mare. Her bells had ceased jingling. She had become perfectly still.

Lanko caressed her head with one hand and patted her side with the other. He consoled her, as he consoled himself, with the whisper that they had not far to go. She went on again, and with the habit of fifteen years he fell in with her slow, patient and uncomplaining step.

"Good girl—good girl," he said.

The tinkle of her bells was once more a delight to him. His deep, dark-browed eyes shone. In the sunshine the mare's coat gleamed like silk.

The journey did not seem long to him, but sometimes the mare seemed to lose all courage and would stop again, shivering, staring ahead and breathing hard, so that her sides rose and fell under his hand. Each time by consoling and caressing her he managed to make her go again. Gradually, however, her pauses grew more frequent, her breathing so difficult as to be almost agonizing, and her struggles to draw the cart more terrible.

Lanko dropped behind the rest of the line. Now, however, the thought that he would be crowded out at the pitching did not trouble him. He began to see now, even though with intense reluctance, that the mare was not stubborn or stupid or capricious, but ill. He began to reproach himself for having kicked her, even for having struck her. His efforts to atone for this were desperately tender.

"Good girl, good girl! Ain't far now, steady! ain't far."

They arrived at last. In the only remaining pitch, in one corner of the ground, he unharnessed the mare. As before she stood very still, uncomplaining, until he had finished. Then suddenly, as if only the burden of the harness and the existence of the cart behind her had borne her up since morning, she sank down upon the grass at his feet.

Lanko knelt down too, impelled by astonishment and fear. Her head was still upright but the nostrils were faintly distended and from the mouth hung a little foam, like the slobbering of a child. The look in her eyes, sick and remote, began, even then, to grow deeper. It drove away very slowly but certainly all the intelligence, all the softness and understanding that had gathered there during all the years of her life. Lanko opened her mouth and touched her tongue. Her mouth seemed to him full of the deathly heat of a fever.

He stared at her for a long moment. She seemed to him to grow no worse. It was not yet afternoon and he began to console himself with the thought that she would be able to rest there all day and all night—even for nearly a week, if need be. "Good girl, good girl," he whispered to her.

An inspiration seized him. He fetched water in a bucket and held it to her lips in the profound hope that he had found her remedy. As in the morning, at the pool, however, she would not drink. In desperation he cajoled and pleaded with her; she seemed to him to turn away at last with all the weariness and distaste of a deadly sickness.

Afternoon drew on. The painted poles of the stalls and the tops of the great roundabouts began to show themselves against the sky. Lanko unpacked his belongings, then let them remain where they had fallen on the grass. He could not think of trade, and, after lighting a fire, boiled up a concoction which it seemed to him, if only he could persuade or force the mare to drink it, must ease her before morning. All the time the mare crouched in the grass, the deathly sickness of her eyes growing steadily more terrible.

The faith in the remedy he had spent so long in preparing made Lanko approach her at last with both an entreaty and a smile on his lips. "Good girl—drink—good girl." He opened her mouth.

When he brought the medicine to her lips they closed suddenly again. He tried to be patient, to be calm. Again he stroked her soft nostrils and put his head against hers. In this way he told her not to be afraid, that he was only nursing her. But her lips would not remain open. Again and again they closed, feverish and clammy with foam, trembling as if both from fear and sickness. Sweat came out on Lanko's brow, he also trembled. "Good girl, good girl!" he repeated.

Now she seemed to make no conscious effort to withstand him—it was as if the fever seized and held her mouth closed, until she was rigid and terrified beneath it. She became exhausted quickly, with the result that while she had no power to withstand Lanko she had also none to repulse the tenacity of the sickness.

The medicine grew cold at Lanko's side. For a little while he felt helpless, full only of a dejected wonder that the strong, patient, silky body of the white mare should sink to this. Once again, and now more bitterly, he reproached himself for the blows and the single kick he had given her that morning. That might have begun it, he thought. Suddenly this enraged him, quickened him into life.

He left the mare, and running off, seized the first man he knew. It was the "Fat Lady" man, the one with whom he had begun the argument so trivial and ridiculous that neither could remember on what subject it had been. Lanko seized him.

"Come and look at my old mare a minute!"

They went and knelt at the mare's side. She seemed to have sickened, even in those few moments, more rapidly and terribly than ever before. "Look at her, look at her!"

The other spent a long time regarding her. Unable at last to bear this any longer, Lanko said:

300] THE PERSONALITY OF THE HORSE

"What is it? What do you think it is?"

Before them the mare grew visibly weaker, breathing with pathetic effort. The "Fat Lady" man answered in low tones:

"You don't know—it might be anything."

Lanko began to talk with intense desperation, explaining it all. "I couldn't get her to drink this morning, not anyhow. Then on the road she kept lagging and stopping." His voice fell a little. "After that, just as we got here she fell down and hasn't been up since. She can't get up."

The "Fat Lady" man indicated the medicine and said slowly: "We'll try her with that again—see if that'll do anything."

Lanko heated the concoction again and brought it to the white mare's lips. He had become more than ever patient, fuller of sympathy and care. "Open her mouth—gently," he asked. The "Fat Lady" man was tender also. Very slowly he forced open the lips which, having no longer the power to hold their own spittle, let it run down his wrists and arms in a pitiful flow. To his attentions there came no resistance, no struggle. Into the mouth held open thus, without strength or spirit, Lanko poured some of the medicine. Along the mare's neck ran a ripple or two; he poured in a little more, making more ripples in her silky flesh, and so on until she had drunk it all. The "Fat Lady" man let the lips close again. "Good girl, good girl," Lanko whispered.

Both men rose to their feet. "You can't do no more than that," the "Fat Lady" man whispered. "Let her be—keep her still. Put something over her."

"What is it? What do you think it is?"

"You don't know—it might be anything."

He went off, and over the mare Lanko laid sacks and a blanket or two. Again he told himself he must be patient and calm—so long as she kept up her head, even though with the sickness staring from her eyes, there was hope.

Dusk began falling; the grass was clothed in mists. In the fair itself lights sprang up from the vans; here and there was a paraffin flare.

The covered flanks of the mare gleamed softly in the dark, motionless, uncomplaining, expressive of her quiet and stoical spirit. To his joy her head did not droop again. At her side he sat and watched looking at her as if to say: "Tell me what I can do?—Good girl, good girl."

Out of the surrounding darkness began to come figures. One by one they bent and looked at the mare as she half lay, half sat in the grass, and then to Lanko expressed their opinions. He knew them all, he recognized the voices of the men who had jeered good-naturedly at him that morning by the drinking pool. Their dark, check-shirted, red-shirted, swarthy figures blacked out the light of his fire. He saw the coconut man, the "Aunt Sallies," the shooting men, the skittle-board and bagatelle owners, the watch and clock men, little Jews with rings on their fat fingers, the joy-wheel proprietor, the peacock man, his wife with long rings in her ears. The "Fat Lady" herself came, too. Each of them looked at the white mare, some even touched her, all of them spoke to Lanko kindly, answering his persistent and desperate little enquiries with tact, with bluff, in whatever manner seemed to them best for keeping alive his hope in her ebbing life.

In each of them he found something for which to be thankful. He discovered too that his spirits did not droop, that he had now such faith in the mare as never before. It even seemed to him that so far from drooping her head had raised itself a little. In the darkness, also, the sickness seemed to have been driven from her eyes.

The men continued their advice, their calm bluff, the sympathies of their understanding yet undeceived minds. "You can't tell—know better in the morning—might be over in a week or a day." They spoke with the difficult care of men seeking to conceal a painful truth. Then one by one they wandered off slowly, as if reluctantly, into the darkness.

Lanko and the white mare were alone again. Her head had drooped, her flanks were steadier, she seemed at rest, he thought. He fell into reminiscences about her—of her early days, when she too had cantered, had borne her head with an arched, beautifully shadowed neck, when he had had to cut her tail in order to keep it from dragging on the ground. In those days he had decorated her not only with bells, but with colored ribbons and cords and painted banners. She had traveled everywhere with him, in springtime, in summer and autumn, and in winter had camped with him or had been stabled in some village while he traded. In his mind he could see her anywhere—on the road, in the meadows, at the fairs—with her white reflection in the drinking-pools where they went.

Suddenly he looked up. It was very dark, his fire became momentarily dim, but he saw that her head had fallen. Very slowly he crawled on his hands and knees towards her. He saw that what he had for so long dreaded and hoped against had taken place and was still going on. He could see, even as he came up to her, that her head was lowering in fast, spasmodic jerks, her mane falling across her black eyes, the sickly foam once again dripping from her lips. He leaned forward and took her head in his hands, striving to hold it erect in spite of its heaviness, smoothing back her mane as he might have done a child's hair. He wiped the foam from her lips with the sleeve of his coat. He spoke to her. He exerted his strength in order to keep her head from sinking a fraction. "Good girl, good girl," he whispered.

Suddenly she sank beyond his grasp. As if unable to realize the swiftness of it all, he raised her head again and held it in his arms. She was still warm. She raised a murmur. This sound, either of protest or pain, seemed to strike him like something cold, in the center of his breast. It crept to his heart. Her head sank to the ground. There was silence. He could not even call to her.

But into her soft, silky flanks, still warm for him with the memory of a life recently there, and gleaming in the grass with the rest of her like some pale, appealing ghost, he suddenly buried his face. His lips opened as if to say something, but nothing came, and they closed without a sound.

On the dark grass the white mare lay silent too.

THE BARGAIN HORSE

FOR SALE, A HORSE
by Charles Edward Taylor

In good condition,
Cheap, on account of competition,
Well-broken, easy on his bridle,
Which curb or snaffle never idle.
A very little child can ride him,
And carry three or four beside him.
Why plod when you can ride so cheaply?
There is no need to ponder deeply.
I'll warrant he'll not bite nor kick you;
I've not the slightest wish to stick you!
However short you are, you're suited,
For low-stand men can mount when booted.
Come, buy my steed with manner gracious.
He'll aid your reading of Horatius.

THE FEMININE HORSE

THE TENNESSEE GIRL AND
THE PACING MARE
by John Trotwood Moore

The Tennessee girl and the pacing mare are a pair I can never separate in my thoughts. When I think of the one I see the other, and when I see the other I think of the one. They go together much better than Jonathan and David, or Damon and Pythias;

and they travel along life's road with a great deal less friction than either would go with a male companion. They are a pair of females entirely bent on femininity.

The bottom may drop out of the universe; political parties may rise and fall; hades may boil out of Mount Vesuvius, and horses of the male persuasion may break the records of the world, but the Tennessee girl and the old mare are only bent on preserving the chastity of the female race as they shuffle along down a sunshiny pike to carry a hank of yarn and a brace of spring chickens to another pair of the same gender living about three miles further on.

The girl is demure, modest and sweet. The old mare is demure, modest and fleet. The girl is shyer than a sixteen-year-old nymph clad in a petticoat of sea foam, before the mirror of the Olympian gods. The old mare is more timid than a fawn in a herd of buffalo. The Seventh Regiment Band, in full regalia, could not march by the damsel with enough éclat to make her peep out from under her sunbonnet long enough to see the color of their uniforms; and forty thousand of them could not make the old mare look around unless their martial music happened to stampede the shuffling sorrel offspring ambling behind her—then she'd ride over the regiment to get to it. So would the girl.

But the sorrel offspring does not really belong in this duo. He is looked on as a necessary evil which is liable to happen in the early spring days of April or May. When the hazy gleam settles over the landscape in the twinkling glow of autumn's aftermath, he goes out of their life and existence. Perhaps he has grown too large; perhaps too saucy; perhaps too much of a man to be allowed the companionship of this pair who worship at the shrine of Vesta and yet live in the hope of one day making it uncomfortable for a male man and his unregenerate offspring when cleaning-up day comes round! In the fall, then, the colt will be missing. But the girl rides on and says nothing; while the old mare merely paces along in a gradually increasing ratio of avoirdupois till next spring. Then you may meet a trio again.

The Tennessee girl is a born rider. No silk hat with half a white goose feather adorns her shapely head. No long riding skirt streams under her horse's flanks, or flutters out behind to frighten the steeds of unsuspecting passers-by. No gloves that reach to her elbows. No silver-mounted English whip that abruptly stops in its make-up about the place you think the whip ought to begin; no goggle glasses, hair in a Psyche knot, and look *à la hauteur*— no; that isn't the Tennessee girl on the old mare; that's the city girl that's riding for fun. The girl we are talking about never got on a horse for fun in her life.

A snow-white sunbonnet with a few stray curls peeping out from under. It is tied with a double bow-knot under the chin and two streamers play in the wind behind. A blue calico skirt comes down nearly far enough to hide a pretty foot that's got good hold on a solid steel stirrup. Where is the other foot, you ask? Come, don't be too inquisitive. The Tennessee girl has two; the other, with its necessary attachment, has got a grip on the pommel of the saddle—and a Comanche princess can't stick there tighter. A pair of woolen mittens cover chubby hands that know how to hold bridle reins—and there she goes, one hundred and forty-five pounds of solid "gal" in a saddle her great-grandmother rode over "from North Callina in."

The Tennessee girl is the best female rider—ah! beg your pardon, equestrienne they call it now—in the world. And yet nobody ever saw such riding! She rolls in the saddle with every motion of the old mare. She is the most unstable-looking thing in the saddle, to be as solid as she is, I ever saw. She sits her horse like a forty-ton flatboat on the roll of a wave, and yet she goes ahead like a graceful yacht in mid-ocean on the crest of a billow. She will fool you to death. It is painful for a tenderfoot to behold her ride. His first thought will be to rush up and save her from falling off; his second to stand and see her fall—a mishap no one has ever yet seen, not unless the double girth broke. Down the pike she goes—while the spectator is waiting to pick her up— following every curve and rolling with every roll of the pacing mare, all the time in unison, toppling but never falling, swaying but never breaking, easy, jolly, joyous, forgetful, unthinking, un- affected; she can ride out of a storm like Diana, pace home in a curve-line of beauty, or gallop with her brother over the field like a princess of the Montezumas.

And don't you discount on the old pacing mare. As sleepy as she looks and as unconcerned and all that, she is the deadest game thing under heaven! She carries the blood of the desert— the memory of fifty Derbys in her veins! She is the same the world over, and would just as soon throw speed amid the sand hills of Sahara as among the roses of Andalusia. She'll bring race mules if bred to a jack, throw "B B" breadwinners if mated with mustangs, and give us world-beating Pointers when bred to her equal. She carries the girls to church like a three-year-old, takes the old lady to meetin' like a forty-year-old, carries the old man on a nightly fox hunt like Tam O'Shanter's "Meg" with a witch at her tail, and yet brings him home, when he gets drunk, at daylight, as slowly and solemnly as the burial of Sir John Moore. She will kill a dozen mules in a plow, would make a sway-back elephant ashamed of himself when she backs her ears and throws herself in the collar of a stalled wagon, and on general principles will pull anything she is hitched to, from a log wagon to a sucker's leg, and in her friskier moods will throw anything from a race horse to a horse race!

She eats less, works more, lives longer, says less, than any animal under the sun, and springs more unexpected speed from unexpected places than a dozen jack-rabbits in a sedge field! She is homely in her old-fashioned ways, yet glorious in her grit! Leggy in her angularity, yet beautiful in her strength. Solemn in her Scotch-Irish honesty, yet brilliantly humorous when she takes the bit and tries to pace a 2:10 clip in her old age. Modest and gentle as a nun's dream of her first love, yet as fiery and aggressive as a helmeted knight in an honor quarrel. Homely she may be, plain, painfully plain, and yet to me, when I know what is slumbering there, she is

> Moulded as trim as a gatling gun,
> And full to the brim of its fire!

Nothing can stop the Tennessee girl and the old mare. Nature, recognizing their claims, keeps the sun shining, the sweet birds singing, the winds playing and the brooks dancing when the precious pair start down the pike. Even the tollgates—brazen evidences of corporations and cruel obstructionists of freedom and unrestrained progress—fail to stop them.

"Your toll, please," said the gatekeeper, as a pair of them came to a halt, recently, when the gate swung up.

"But do we have to pay toll?" asked the fair rider, with a look so full of pretty injured innocence as to make the hard-hearted collector inwardly swear he would never collect another toll as long as he lived.

"Certainly, Miss; five cents, if you please; here are the regulations"—

| A carriage and horses . . . 25c |
| A wagon and team . . . 15c |
| A buggy and horse . . . 10c |
| A man and horse . . . . 5c |

"A man and a horse! Why, we are a gal and a mare," said the Tennessee girl, as she rode on through, after casting a withering look on the abject keeper, who was trying to skulk off and hang himself.

THE SPORTING HORSE

THE MALTESE CAT
by Rudyard Kipling

They had good reason to be proud, and better reason to be afraid, all twelve of them; for, though they had fought their way, game by game, up the teams entered for the polo tournament, they were meeting the Archangels that afternoon in the final match; and the Archangels' men were playing with half a dozen ponies apiece. As the game was divided into six quarters of eight minutes each, that meant a fresh pony after every halt. The Skidars' team, even supposing there were no accidents, could only supply one pony for every other change; and two to one is heavy odds. Again, as Shiraz, the gray Syrian, pointed out, they were meeting the pink and pick of the polo ponies of Upper India; ponies that had cost from a thousand rupees each, while they themselves were a cheap lot gathered, often from country carts, by their masters who belonged to a poor but honest native infantry regiment.

"Money means pace and weight," said Shiraz, rubbing his black silk nose dolefully along his neat-fitting boot, "and by the maxims of the game as I know it—"

"Ah, but we aren't playing the maxims," said the Maltese Cat. "We're playing the game, and we've the great advantage of knowing the game. Just think a stride, Shiraz. We've pulled up from bottom to second place in two weeks against all those fellows on the ground here; and that's because we play with our heads as well as with our feet."

"It makes me feel undersized and unhappy all the same," said Kittiwynk, a mouse-colored mare with a red browband and the cleanest pair of legs that ever an aged pony owned. "They've twice our size, these others."

Kittiwynk looked at the gathering and sighed. The hard, dusty Umballa polo ground was lined with thousands of soldiers, black and white, not counting hundreds and hundreds of carriages, and drags, and dogcarts, and ladies with brilliant-colored parasols, and officers in uniform and out of it, and crowds of natives behind them; and orderlies on camels who had halted to watch the game, instead of carrying letters up and down the station, and native horse dealers running about on thin-eared Biluchi mares, looking for a chance to sell a few first-class polo ponies. Then there were the ponies of thirty teams that had entered for the Upper India Free-for-All Cup—nearly every pony of worth and dignity from Mhow to Peshawar, from Allahabad to Multan; prize ponies, Arabs, Syrian, Barb, country-bred, Deccanee, Waziri, and Kabul ponies of every color and shape and temper that you could imagine. Some of them were in mat-roofed stables close to the polo ground, but most were under saddle while their masters, who had been defeated in the earlier games, trotted in and out and told each other exactly how the game should be played.

It was a glorious sight, and the come-and-go of the little quick hoofs, and the incessant salutations of ponies that had met before on other polo grounds or racecourses, were enough to drive a four-footed thing wild.

But the Skidars' team were careful not to know their neighbors, though half the ponies on the ground were anxious to scrape acquaintance with the little fellows that had come from the North, and, so far, had swept the board.

"Let's see," said a soft, golden-colored Arab, who had been playing very badly the day before, to the Maltese Cat, "didn't we meet in Abdul Rahman's stable in Bombay four seasons ago? I won the Paikpattan Cup next season, you may remember."

"Not me," said the Maltese Cat politely. "I was at Malta then, pulling a vegetable cart. I don't race. I play the game."

"O-oh!" said the Arab, cocking his tail and swaggering off.

"Keep yourselves to yourselves," said the Maltese Cat to his companions. "We don't want to rub noses with all those goose-rumped half-breeds of Upper India. When we've won this cup they'll give their shoes to know us."

"We shan't win the cup," said Shiraz. "How do you feel?"

"Stale as last night's feed when a muskrat has run over it," said Polaris, a rather heavy-shouldered gray, and the rest of the team agreed with him.

"The sooner you forget that the better," said the Maltese Cat cheerfully. "They've finished tiffin in the big tent. We shall be wanted now. If your saddles are not comfy, kick. If your bits aren't easy, rear, and let the saises know whether your boots are tight."

Each pony had his sais, his groom, who lived and ate and slept with the pony, and had betted a great deal more than he could afford on the result of the game. There was no chance of anything going wrong, and, to make sure, each sais was shampooing the legs of his pony to the last minute. Behind the saises sat as many of the Skidars' regiment as had to leave to attend that match—about half the native officers, and a hundred or two dark, black-bearded men with the regimental pipers nervously fingering the big be-ribboned bagpipes. The Skidars were what they call a Pioneer regiment; and the bagpipes made the national music of half the men. The native officers held bundles of polo sticks, long cane-handled mallets, and as the grandstand filled after lunch they arranged themselves by ones and twos at different points round the ground, so that if a stick were broken the player would not have far to ride for a new one. An impatient British cavalry band struck up "If you want to know the time, ask a p'leeceman!" and the two umpires in light dust coats danced out on two little excited ponies. The four players of the Archangels' team followed, and the sight of their beautiful mounts made Shiraz groan again.

"Wait till we know," said the Maltese Cat. "Two of 'em are playing in blinkers, and that means they can't see to get out of the way of their own side, or they may shy at the umpires' ponies.

They've all got white web reins that are sure to stretch or slip!"

"And," said Kittiwynk, dancing to take the stiffness out of her, "they carry their whips in their hands instead of on their wrists. Hah!"

"True enough. No man can manage his stick and his reins, and his whip that way," said the Maltese Cat. "I've fallen over every square yard of the Malta ground, and I ought to know." He quivered his little flea-bitten withers just to show how satisfied he felt; but his heart was not so light. Ever since he had drifted into India on a troopship, taken, with an old rifle, as part payment for a racing debt, the Maltese Cat had played and preached polo to the Skidars' team on the Skidars' stony polo ground. Now a polo pony is like a poet. If he is born with a love for the game he can be made. The Maltese Cat knew that bamboos grew solely in order that polo balls might be turned from their roots, that grain was given to ponies to keep them in hard condition, and that ponies were shod to prevent them slipping on a turn. But, besides all these things, he knew every trick and device of the finest game of the world, and for two seasons he had been teaching the others all he knew or guessed.

"Remember," he said for the hundredth time as the riders came up, "we must play together, and you must play with your heads. Whatever happens, follow the ball. Who goes out first?"

Kittiwynk, Shiraz, Polaris, and a short high little bay fellow with tremendous hocks and no withers worth speaking of (he was called Corks) were being girthed up, and the soldiers in the background stared with all their eyes.

"I want you men to keep quiet," said Lutyens, the captain of the team, "and especially not to blow your pipes."

"Not if we win, Captain Sahib?" asked a piper.

"If we win, you can do what you please," said Lutyens, with a smile, as he slipped the loop of his stick over his wrist, and wheeled to canter to his place. The Archangels' ponies were a little bit above themselves on account of the many-colored crowd so close to the ground. Their riders were excellent players, but they were a team of crack players instead of a crack team; and that made all the difference in the world. They honestly meant to play together, but it is very hard for four men, each the best of the team he is picked from, to remember that in polo no brilliancy of hitting or riding makes up for playing alone. Their captain shouted his orders to them by name, and it is a curious thing that if you call his name aloud in public after an Englishman you make him hot and fretty. Lutyens said nothing to his men because it had all been said before. He pulled up Shiraz, for he was playing "back," to guard the goal. Powell on Polaris was halfback, and Macnamara and Hughes on Corks and Kittiwynk were forwards. The tough bamboo-root ball was put into the middle of the ground one hundred and fifty yards from the ends, and Hughes crossed sticks, heads up, with the captain of the Archangels, who saw fit to play forward, and that is a place from which you cannot easily control the team. The little click as the cane shafts met was heard all over the ground, and then Hughes made some sort of quick wrist stroke that just dribbled the ball a few yards. Kittiwynk knew that stroke of old, and followed as a cat follows a mouse. While the captain of the Archangels was wrenching his pony round Hughes struck with all his strength, and next instant Kittiwynk was away, Corks following close behind her, their little feet pattering like raindrops on glass.

"Pull out to the left," said Kittiwynk between her teeth, "it's coming our way, Corks!"

The back and halfback of the Archangels were tearing down on her just as she was within reach of the ball. Hughes leaned forward with a loose rein, and cut it away to the left almost under Kittiwynk's feet, and it hopped and skipped off to Corks, who saw that, if he were not quick, it would run beyond the boundaries. That long bouncing drive gave the Archangels time to wheel and send three men across the ground to head off Corks. Kittiwynk stayed where she was, for she knew the game. Corks was on the ball half a fraction of a second before the others came up, and Macnamara, with a back-handed stroke, sent it back across the ground to Hughes, who saw the way clear to the Archangels' goal, and smacked the ball in before any one quite knew what had happened.

"That's luck," said Corks, as they changed ends. "A goal in three minutes for three hits and no riding to speak of."

"Don't know," said Polaris. "We've made 'em angry too soon. Shouldn't wonder if they try to rush us off our feet next time."

"Keep the ball hanging then," said Shiraz. "That wears out every pony that isn't used to it."

Next time there was no easy galloping across the ground.

All the Archangels closed up as one man, but there they stayed, for Corks, Kittiwynk, and Polaris were somewhere on the top of the ball, marking time among the rattling sticks, while Shiraz circled about outside, waiting for a chance.

"We can do this all day," said Polaris, ramming his quarters into the side of another pony. "Where do you think you're shoving to?"

"I'll—I'll be driven in an ekka if I know," was the gasping reply, "and I'd give a week's feed to get my blinkers off. I can't see anything."

"The dust is rather bad. Whew! That was one for my off hock. Where's the ball, Corks?"

"Under my tail. At least a man's looking for it there. This is beautiful. They can't use their sticks, and it's driving 'em wild. Give old blinkers a push and he'll go over!"

"Here, don't touch me! I can't see. I'll—I'll back out, I think," said the pony in blinkers, who knew that if you can't see all round your head you cannot prop yourself against a shock.

Corks was watching the ball where it lay in the dust close to his near fore, with Macnamara's shortened stick tap-tapping it from time to time. Kittiwynk was edging her way out of the scrimmage, whisking her stump of a tail with nervous excitement.

"Ho! They've got it," she snorted. "Let me out!" and she galloped like a rifle bullet just behind a tall lanky pony of the Archangels, whose rider was swinging up his stick for a stroke.

"Not today, thank you," said Hughes, as the blow slid off his raised stick, and Kittiwynk laid her shoulder to the tall pony's quarters, and shoved him aside just as Lutyens on Shiraz sent the ball where it had come from, and the tall pony went skating and slipping away to the left. Kittiwynk, seeing that Polaris had joined Corks in the chase for the ball up the ground, dropped into Polaris's place, and then time was called.

The Skidars' ponies wasted no time in kicking or fuming. They knew each minute's rest meant so much gain, and trotted off to the rails and their saises, who began to scrape and blanket and rub them at once.

"Whew!" said Corks, stiffening up to get all the tickle out of the big vulcanite scraper. "If we were playing pony for pony we'd bend those Archangels double in half an hour. But they'll bring out fresh ones and fresh ones, and fresh ones after that—you see."

"Who cares?" said Polaris. "We've drawn first blood. Is my hock swelling?"

"Looks puffy," said Corks. "You must have had rather a wipe. Don't let it stiffen. You'll be wanted again in half an hour."

"What's the game like?" said the Maltese Cat.

"Ground's like your shoe, except where they've put too much water on it," said Kittiwynk. "Then it's slippery. Don't play in the center. There's a bog there. I don't know how their next four are going to behave, but we kept the ball hanging and made 'em lather for nothing. Who goes out? Two Arabs and a couple of country-breds! That's bad. What a comfort it is to wash your mouth out!"

Kitty was talking with the neck of a leather-covered soda-water bottle between her teeth and trying to look over her withers at the same time. This gave her a very coquettish air.

"What's bad?" said Gray Dawn, giving to the girth and admiring his well-set shoulders.

"You Arabs can't gallop fast enough to keep yourselves warm —that's what Kitty means," said Polaris, limping to show that his hock needed attention. "Are you playing 'back,' Gray Dawn?"

"Looks like it," said Gray Dawn, as Lutyens swung himself up. Powell mounted the Rabbit, a plain bay country-bred much like Corks, but with mulish ears. Macnamara took Faiz Ullah, a handy short-backed little red Arab with a long tail, and Hughes mounted Benami, an old and sullen brown beast, who stood over in front more than a polo pony should.

"Benami looks like business," said Shiraz. "How's your temper, Ben?" The old campaigner hobbled off without answering, and the Maltese Cat looked at the new Archangel ponies prancing about on the ground. They were four beautiful blacks, and they saddled big enough and strong enough to eat the Skidars' team and gallop away with the meal inside them.

"Blinkers again," said the Maltese Cat. "Good enough!"

"They're chargers—cavalry chargers!" said Kittiwynk indignantly. "They'll never see thirteen three again."

"They've all been fairly measured and they've all got their certificates," said the Maltese Cat, "or they wouldn't be here. We must take things as they come along, and keep our eyes on the ball."

The game began, but this time the Skidars were penned to

their own end of the ground, and the watching ponies did not approve of that.

"Faiz Ullah is shirking as usual," said Polaris, with a scornful grunt.

"Faiz Ullah is eating whip," said Corks. They could hear the leather-thonged polo quirt lacing the little fellow's well-rounded barrel. Then the Rabbit's shrill neigh came across the ground. "I can't do all the work," he cried.

"Play the game, don't talk," the Maltese Cat whickered; and all the ponies wriggled with excitement, and the soldiers and the grooms gripped the railings and shouted. A black pony with blinkers had singled out old Benami, and was interfering with him in every possible way. They could see Benami shaking his head up and down and flapping his underlip.

"There'll be a fall in a minute," said Polaris. "Benami is getting stuffy."

The game flickered up and down between goal post and goal post, and the black ponies were getting more confident as they felt they had the legs of the others. The ball was hit out of a little scrimmage, and Benami and the Rabbit followed it; Faiz Ullah only too glad to be quiet for an instant.

The blinkered black pony came up like a hawk, with two of his own side behind him, and Benami's eye glittered as he raced. The question was which pony should make way for the other; each rider was perfectly willing to risk a fall in a good cause. The black who had been driven nearly crazy by his blinkers trusted to his weight and his temper; but Benami knew how to apply his weight and how to keep his temper. They met, and there was a cloud of dust. The black was lying on his side with all the breath knocked out of his body. The Rabbit was a hundred yards up the ground with the ball, and Benami was sitting down. He had slid nearly ten yards, but he had had his revenge, and sat cracking his nostrils till the black pony rose.

"That's what you get for interfering. Do you want any more?" said Benami, and he plunged into the game. Nothing was done because Faiz Ullah would not gallop, though Macnamara beat him whenever he could spare a second. The fall of the black pony had impressed his companions tremendously, and so the Archangels could not profit by Faiz Ullah's bad behavior.

But as the Maltese Cat said, when time was called and the

four came back blowing and dripping, Faiz Ullah ought to have been kicked all round Umballa. If he did not behave better next time, the Maltese Cat promised to pull out his Arab tail by the root and eat it.

There was no time to talk, for the third four were ordered out.

The third quarter of a game is generally the hottest, for each side thinks that the others must be pumped; and most of the winning play in a game is made about that time.

Lutyens took over the Maltese Cat with a pat and a hug, for Lutyens valued him more than anything else in the world. Powell had Shikast, a little gray rat with no pedigree and no manners outside polo; Macnamara mounted Bamboo, the largest of the team, and Hughes took Who's Who, alias The Animal. He was supposed to have Australian blood in his veins, but he looked like a clotheshorse, and you could whack him on the legs with an iron crowbar without hurting him.

They went out to meet the very flower of the Archangels' team, and when Who's Who saw their elegantly booted legs and their beautiful satiny skins he grinned a grin through his light, well-worn bridle.

"My word!" said Who's Who. "We must give 'em a little football. Those gentlemen need a rubbing down."

"No biting," said the Maltese Cat warningly, for once or twice in his career Who's Who had been known to forget himself in that way.

"Who said anything about biting? I'm not playing tiddly-winks. I'm playing the game."

The Archangels came down like a wolf on the fold, for they were tired of football and they wanted polo. They got it more and more. Just after the game began, Lutyens hit a ball that was coming towards him rapidly, and it rose in the air, as a ball sometimes will, with the whirr of a frightened partridge. Shikast heard, but could not see it for the minute, though he looked everywhere and up into the air as the Maltese Cat had taught him. When he saw it ahead and overhead he went forward with Powell as fast as he could put foot to ground. It was then that Powell, a quiet and level-headed man as a rule, became inspired and played a stroke that sometimes comes off successfully on a quiet afternoon of long practice. He took his stick in both hands, and standing up in his stirrups, swiped at the ball in the air, Munipore fashion.

There was one second of paralyzed astonishment, and then all four sides of the ground went up in a yell of applause and delight as the ball flew true (you could see the amazed Archangels ducking in their saddles to get out of the line of flight, and looking at it with open mouths), and the regimental pipes of the Skidars squealed from the railings as long as the piper had breath.

Shikast heard the stroke; but he heard the head of the stick fly off at the same time. Nine hundred and ninety-nine ponies out of a thousand would have gone tearing on after the ball with a useless player pulling at their heads, but Powell knew him, and he knew Powell; and the instant he felt Powell's right leg shift a trifle on the saddle-flap he headed to the boundary, where a native officer was frantically waving a new stick. Before the shouts had ended Powell was armed again.

Once before in his life the Maltese Cat had heard that very same stroke played off his own back, and had profited by the confusion it made. This time he acted on experience, and leaving Bamboo to guard the goal in case of accidents, came through the others like a flash, head and tail low, Lutyens standing up to ease him—swept on and on before the other side knew what was the matter, and nearly pitched on his head between the Archangels' goal posts as Lutyens tipped the ball in after a straight scurry of a hundred and fifty yards. If there was one thing more than another upon which the Maltese Cat prided himself it was on this quick, streaking kind of run half across the ground. He did not believe in taking balls round the field unless you were clearly overmatched. After this they gave the Archangels five minutes' football, and an expensive fast pony hates football because it rumples his temper.

Who's Who showed himself even better than Polaris in this game. He did not permit any wriggling away, but bored joyfully into the scrimmage as if he had his nose in a feedbox, and were looking for something nice. Little Shikast jumped on the ball the minute it got clear, and every time an Archangel pony followed it he found Shikast standing over it asking what was the matter.

"If we can live through this quarter," said the Maltese Cat, "I shan't care. Don't take it out of yourselves. Let them do the lathering."

So the ponies, as their riders explained afterwards, "shut up." The Archangels kept them tied fast in front of their goal, but it cost the Archangels' ponies all that was left of their tempers; and ponies began to kick, and men began to repeat compliments, and they chopped at the legs of Who's Who, and he set his teeth and stayed where he was, and the dust stood up like a tree over the scrimmage till that hot quarter ended.

They found the ponies very excited and confident when they went to their saises; and the Maltese Cat had to warn them that the worst of the game was coming.

"Now we are all going in for the second time," said he, "and they are trotting out fresh ponies. You'll think you can gallop, but you'll find you can't; and then you'll be sorry."

"But two goals to nothing is a halter-long lead," said Kittiwynk, prancing.

"How long does it take to get a goal?" the Maltese Cat answered. "For pity sake, don't run away with the notion that the game is half-won just because we happen to be in luck now. They'll ride you into the grandstand if they can; you must not give 'em a chance. Follow the ball."

"Football as usual?" said Polaris. "My hock's half as big as a nose bag."

"Don't let them have a look at the ball if you can help it. Now leave me alone. I must get all the rest I can before the last quarter."

He hung down his head and let all his muscles go slack; Shikast, Bamboo, and Who's Who copying his example.

"Better not watch the game," he said. "We aren't playing, and we shall only take it out of ourselves if we grow anxious. Look at the ground and pretend it's flytime."

They did their best, but it was hard advice to follow. The hoofs were drumming and the sticks were rattling all up and down the ground, and yells of applause from the English troops told that the Archangels were pressing the Skidars hard. The native soldiers behind the ponies groaned and grunted, and said things in undertones, and presently they heard a long-drawn shout and a clatter of hurrahs!

"One to the Archangels," said Shikast, without raising his head. "Time's nearly up. Oh, my sire and—dam!"

"Faiz Ullah," said the Maltese Cat, "if you don't play to the last nail in your shoes this time, I'll kick you on the ground before all the other ponies."

"I'll do my best when my times comes," said the little Arab sturdily.

The saises looked at each other gravely as they rubbed their ponies' legs. This was the first time when long purses began to tell, and everybody knew it. Kittiwynk and the others came back with the sweat dripping over their hoofs and their tails telling sad stories.

"They're better than we are," said Shiraz. "I knew how it would be."

"Shut your big head," said the Maltese Cat; "we've one goal to the good yet."

"Yes, but it's two Arabs and two country-breds to play now," said Corks. "Faiz Ullah, remember!" He spoke in a biting voice.

As Lutyens mounted Gray Dawn he looked at his men, and they did not look pretty. They were covered with dust and sweat in streaks. Their yellow boots were almost black, their wrists were red and lumpy, and their eyes seemed two inches deep in their heads, but the expression in the eyes was satisfactory.

"Did you take anything at tiffin?" said Lutyens, and the team shook their heads. They were too dry to talk.

"All right. The Archangels did. They are worse pumped than we are."

"They've got the better ponies," said Powell. "I shan't be sorry when this business is over."

That fifth quarter was a sad one in every way. Faiz Ullah played like a little red demon; and the Rabbit seemed to be everywhere at once, and Benami rode straight at anything and everything that came in his way, while the umpires on their ponies wheeled like gulls outside the shifting game. But the Archangels had the better mounts—they had kept their racers till late in the game—and never allowed the Skidars to play football. They hit the ball up and down the width of the ground till Benami and the rest were outpaced. Then they went forward, and time and again Lutyens and Gray Dawn were just, and only just, able to send the ball away with a long splitting backhander. Gray Dawn forgot that he was an Arab; and turned from gray to blue as he galloped. Indeed, he forgot too well, for he did not keep his eyes on the ground as an Arab should, but stuck out his nose and scuttled for the dear honor of the game. They had watered the ground once or twice between the quarters, and a careless waterman had emptied the last of his skinful all in one place near the Skidars' goal. It was close to the end of play, and for the tenth time Gray Dawn was bolting after a ball when his near hind foot slipped on the greasy mud and he rolled over and over, pitching Lutyens just clear of the goalpost; and the triumphant Archangels made their goal. Then time was called—two goals all; but Lutyens had to be helped up, and Gray Dawn rose with his near hind leg strained somewhere.

"What's the damage?" said Powell, his arm round Lutyens.

"Collarbone, of course," said Lutyens between his teeth. It was the third time he had broken it in two years, and it hurt him.

Powell and the others whistled. "Game's up," said Hughes.

"Hold on. We've five good minutes yet, and it isn't my right hand," said Lutyens. "We'll stick it out."

"I say," said the captain of the Archangels, trotting up. "Are you hurt, Lutyens? We'll wait if you care to put in a substitute. I wish—I mean—the fact is, you fellows deserve this game if any team does. Wish we could give you a man or some of our ponies— or something."

"You're awfully good, but we'll play to a finish, I think."

The captain of the Archangels stared for a little. "That's not half bad," he said, and went back to his own side, while Lutyens borrowed a scarf from one of his native officers and made a sling of it. Then an Archangel galloped up with a big bath sponge and advised Lutyens to put it under his armpit to ease his shoulder, and between them they tied up his left arm scientifically, and one of the native officers leaped forward with four long glasses that fizzed and bubbled.

The team looked at Lutyens piteously, and he nodded. It was the last quarter, and nothing would matter after that. They drank out the dark golden drink, and wiped their mustaches, and things looked more hopeful.

The Maltese Cat had put his nose into the front of Lutyens' shirt, and was trying to say how sorry he was.

"He knows," said Lutyens, proudly. "The beggar knows. I've played him without a bridle before now—for fun."

"It's no fun now," said Powell. "But we haven't a decent substitute."

"No," said Lutyens. "It's the last quarter, and we've got to make our goal and win. I'll trust the Cat."

"If you fall this time you'll suffer a little," said Macnamara.
"I'll trust the Cat," said Lutyens.

"You hear that?" said the Maltese Cat proudly to the others.
"It's worth while playing polo for ten years to have that said of
you. Now then, my sons, come along. We'll kick up a little bit,
just to show the Archangels this team haven't suffered."

And, sure enough, as they went on to the ground the Maltese
Cat, after satisfying himself that Lutyens was home in the saddle,
kicked out three or four times, and Lutyens laughed. The reins
were caught up anyhow in the tips of his strapped hand, and he
never pretended to rely on them. He knew the Cat would answer
to the least pressure of the leg, and by way of showing off—for
his shoulder hurt him very much—he bent the little fellow in a
close figure-of-eight in and out between the goalposts. There was
a roar from the native officers and men, who dearly loved a piece
of dugabashi (horse-trick work), as they called it, and the pipes
very quietly and scornfully droned out the first bars of a common
bazaar tune called "Freshly Fresh and Newly New," just as a
warning to the other regiments that the Skidars were fit. All the
natives laughed.

"And now," said the Cat, as they took their place, "remember
that this is the last quarter, and follow the ball!"

"Don't need to be told," said Who's Who.

"Let me go on. All those people on all four sides will begin
to crowd in—just as they did at Malta. You'll hear people calling
out, and moving forward and being pushed back, and that is
going to make the Archangel ponies very unhappy. But if a ball
is struck to the boundary, you go after it, and let the people get
out of your way. I went over the pole of a four-in-hand once, and
picked a game out of the dust by it. Back me up when I run, and
follow the ball."

There was a sort of an all-round sound of sympathy and
wonder as the last quarter opened, and then there began exactly
what the Maltese Cat had foreseen. People crowded in close to
the boundaries, and the Archangels' ponies kept looking sideways
at the narrowing space. If you know how a man feels to be
cramped at tennis—not because he wants to run out of the court,
but because he likes to know that he can at a pinch—you will
guess how ponies must feel when they are playing in a box of
human beings.

"I'll bend some of those men if I can get away," said Who's Who, as he rocketed behind the ball; and Bamboo nodded without speaking. They were playing the last ounce in them, and the Maltese Cat had left the goal undefended to join them. Lutyens gave him every order that he could to bring him back, but this was the first time in his career that the little wise gray had ever played polo on his own responsibility, and he was going to make the most of it.

"What are you doing here?" said Hughes, as the Cat crossed in front of him and rode off an Archangel.

"The Cat's in charge—mind the goal!" shouted Lutyens, and bowing forward hit the ball full, and followed on, forcing the Archangels towards their own goal.

"No football," said the Cat. "Keep the ball by the boundaries and cramp 'em. Play open order and drive 'em to the boundaries."

Across and across the ground in big diagonals flew the ball, and whenever it came to a flying rush and a stroke close to the boundaries the Archangel ponies moved stiffly. They did not care to go headlong at a wall of men and carriages, though if the ground had been open they could have turned on a sixpence.

"Wriggle her up the sides," said the Cat. "Keep her close to the crowd. They hate the carriages. Shikast, keep her up this side."

Shikast with Powell lay left and right behind the uneasy scuffle of an open scrimmage, and every time the ball was hit away Shikast galloped on it at such an angle that Powell was forced to hit it towards the boundary; and when the crowd had been driven away from that side, Lutyens would send the ball over to the other, and Shikast would slide desperately after it till his friends came down to help. It was billiards, and no football, this time— billiards in a corner pocket; and the cues were not well chalked.

"If they get us out in the middle of the ground they'll walk away from us. Dribble her along the sides," cried the Cat.

So they dribbled all along the boundary, where a pony could not come on their right-hand side; and the Archangels were furious, and the umpires had to neglect the game to shout at the people to get back, and several blundering mounted policemen tried to restore order, all close to the scrimmage, and the nerves of the Archangels' ponies stretched and broke like cobwebs.

Five or six times an Archangel hit the ball up into the middle of the ground, and each time the watchful Shikast gave Powell his chance to send it back, and after each return, when the dust had settled, men could see that the Skidars had gained a few yards.

Every now and again there were shouts of " 'Side! Off side!" from the spectators; but the teams were too busy to care, and the umpires had all they could do to keep their maddened ponies clear of the scuffle.

At last Lutyens missed a short easy stroke, and the Skidars had to fly back helter-skelter to protect their own goal, Shikast leading. Powell stopped the ball with a backhander when it was not fifty yards from the goalposts, and Shikast spun round with a wrench that nearly hoisted Powell out of his saddle.

"Now's our last chance," said the Cat, wheeling like a cockchafer on a pin. "We've got to ride it out. Come along."

Lutyens felt the little chap take a deep breath, and, as it were, crouch under his rider. The ball was hopping towards the right-hand boundary, an Archangel riding for it with both spurs and a whip; but neither spur nor whip would make his pony stretch himself as he neared the crowd. The Maltese Cat glided under his very nose, picking up his hind legs sharp, for there was not a foot to spare between his quarters and the other pony's bit. It was as neat an exhibition as fancy figure-skating. Lutyens hit with all the strength he had left, but the stick slipped a little in his hand, and the ball flew off to the left instead of keeping close to the boundary. Who's Who was far across the ground, thinking hard as he galloped. He repeated, stride for stride, the Cat's maneuvers with another Archangel pony, nipping the ball away from under his bridle, and clearing his opponent by half a fraction of an inch, for Who's Who was clumsy behind. Then he drove away towards the right as the Maltese Cat came up from the left; and Bamboo held a middle course exactly between them. The three were making a sort of Government-broad-arrow-shaped attack; and there was only the Archangels' back to guard the goal; but immediately behind them were three Archangels racing all they knew, and mixed up with them was Powell, sending Shikast along on what he felt was their last hope. It takes a very good man to stand up to the rush of seven crazy ponies in the last quarters of a cup game, when men are riding with their necks for sale, and the ponies are delirious. The Archangels' back missed his stroke, and pulled aside just in time to let the rush go by. Bamboo and Who's Who shortened stride to give the Maltese Cat room, and Lutyens got the goal with a clean, smooth, smacking stroke that was heard all over the field. But there was no stopping the ponies. They poured through the goalposts in one mixed mob, winners and losers together, for the pace had been terrific. The Maltese Cat knew by experience what would happen, and, to save Lutyens, turned to the right with one last effort that strained a back-sinew beyond hope of repair. As he did so he heard the right-hand goalpost crack as a pony cannoned into it—crack, splinter, and fall like a mast. It had been sawed three parts through in case of accidents, but it upset the pony nevertheless, and he blundered into another, who blundered into the left-hand post, and then there was confusion and dust and wood. Bamboo was lying on the ground, seeing stars; an Archangel pony rolled beside him, breathless and angry; Shikast had sat down dog-fashion to avoid falling over the others, and was sliding along on his little bobtail in a cloud of dust; and Powell was sitting on the ground, hammering with his stick and trying to cheer. All the others were shouting at the top of what was left of their voices, and the men who had been split were shouting too. As soon as the people saw no one was hurt, ten thousand native and English shouted and clapped and yelled, and before any one could stop them the pipers of the Skidars broke on to the ground, with all the native officers and men behind them, and marched up and down, playing a wild northern tune called "Zakhme Bagan," and through the insolent blaring of the pipes and the high-pitched native yells you could hear the Archangels' band hammering, "For they are all jolly good fellows," and then reproachfully to the losing team, "Ooh, Kafoozalum! Kafoozalum! Kafoozalum!"

Besides all these things and many more, there was a Commander-in-Chief, and an Inspector-General of Cavalry, and the principal veterinary officer in all India, standing on the top of a regimental coach, yelling like schoolboys; and brigadiers and colonels and commissioners, and hundreds of pretty ladies joined the chorus. But the Maltese Cat stood with his head down, wondering how many legs were left to him; and Lutyens watched the men and ponies pick themselves out of the wreck of the two goalposts, and he patted the Cat very tenderly.

"I say," said the captain of the Archangels, spitting a pebble out of his mouth, "will you take three thousand for that pony—as he stands?"

"No, thank you. I've an idea he's saved my life," said Lutyens, getting off and lying down at full length. Both teams were on the ground too, waving their boots in the air, and coughing and drawing deep breaths, as the saises ran up to take away the ponies, and an officious water-carrier sprinkled the players with dirty water till they sat up.

"My Aunt!" said Powell, rubbing his back and looking at the stumps of the goalposts, "that was a game!"

They played it over again, every stroke of it, that night at the big dinner, when the Free-for-All Cup was filled and passed down the table, and emptied and filled again, and everybody made most eloquent speeches. About two in the morning, when there might have been some singing, a wise little, plain little, gray little head looked in through the open door.

"Hurrah! Bring him in," said the Archangels; and his sais, who was very happy indeed, patted the Maltese Cat on the flank, and he limped into the blaze of light and the glittering uniforms, looking for Lutyens. He was used to messes, and men's bedrooms, and places where ponies are not usually encouraged, and in his youth had jumped on and off a mess table for a bet. So he behaved himself very politely, and ate bread dipped in salt, and was petted all round the table, moving gingerly; and they drank his health, because he had done more to win the Cup than any man or horse on the ground.

That was glory and honor enough for the rest of his days, and the Maltese Cat did not complain much when his veterinary surgeon said that he would be no good for polo any more. When Lutyens married, his wife did not allow him to play, so he was forced to be an umpire; and his pony on these occasions was a flea-bitten gray with a neat polo tail, lame all round, but desperately quick on his feet, and, as everybody knew, Past Pluperfect Prestissimo Player of the Game.

THE FIGHTING HORSE

CRUSADER

by Stuart Cloete

Crusader was probably the handsomest little horse I ever owned. A six-year-old chestnut Basuto stallion with a blaze and snip who stood thirteen hands. I suppose this is his story, but it's the story of Joan and her mother, too. Joan French was eleven and her mother was my neighbor. If Joan had a passion in life it was horses, and I shall never forget her expression when she saw Crusader. She was a leggy girl—all legs and big light brown eyes. "Oh," she said. "Oh, Mr. King, where did you get him?"

"Up from Basutoland, Joan," I said.

She said, "Oh!" again, and put her finger into her mouth like a child of three and stood staring. I thought her eyes would pop out. She just stood frozen on her long spindly legs, staring and "Ohing." It made me smile. Love at first sight, I thought, and not so funny either, as things turned out.

But the odd thing was that her love seemed to be reciprocated. The horse, that first day, stared back at her and tossed his head. His nostrils flared as he blew air out of them the way stallions do, and then suddenly, as though he had got wind of her, as though her scent told him something, he quieted. The fire went out of his roving eye; he stopped tapping at the ground with his foreleg.

So there you are, horse and girl; they met on the veld outside my house, and something happened between them. As I say, at the time I laughed. Perhaps I was even a little embarrassed at being so stupid—at having such a silly idea. Laughter is a defense mechanism; besides, I was a little in love with Joan myself. She was so pretty, with her yellow hair, like a little daffodil on a long, thin stem. And I was very much in love with Muriel, her mother. So that here, in this meeting, there were a lot of factors. Not that

I thought of them then. . . . The girl, the horse, Mrs. French, my job—I was managing a small gold mine at the time. It was, in fact, looking back on it, one of those golden moments when your life takes a turn, when you are actually one with it—which you never notice at the time and only see long after it has passed. I see the picture now in my mind's eye: the chestnut stallion flicking the flies with his long tail and shaking his head as the boy holds him, and the little girl staring, shading her eyes with her hand in the sunshine, and standing on one leg rubbing the calf of the other with her bare foot. . . .

When we saddled Crusader he turned round to nip me as I girthed him; and blew himself up; but even when he let the air out of his barrel he was very deep through for such a little horse. The boy was still at his head when I mounted. "Let go," I said.

Crusader stood still for a second. Absolutely still like a statue. But I could feel him living under me. I even knew or thought I knew what he was thinking: Should he fight or give in? He was a trained saddle horse, but it is the character of a blood entire to make up his mind like this. Sometimes they take an objection to a man and will not let him near them. Then the horse stretched his neck a little to feel the bit. As he reached I gave. I leaned forward and patted his neck. It was arched, firm as a board with muscle and curded with white sweat already.

Moments passed, the horse standing motionless. Slowly then, as if it was a ballet, he raised one foot and put it down exactly where it came from. He raised the other foreleg and did the same thing. All the time I could feel him boiling under me, like a kettle. And all the time I spoke to him. I think his name came to me then. I think I said, "Crusader . . . good boy, good boy." His ears flicked back and forward again together; then he turned one ear back and played with the bit on his tongue, feeling it on the bars of his mouth. I did not want to touch him with my heels, so I just tightened my calves on him and slacked the reins.

He began to walk . . . beautifully, like a dancer, like a cat on hot bricks. Looking over his shoulder I could watch his white hoofs come down; they hardly touched the ground before he picked them up again, and he had a long free stride. I pushed him a little and he broke into a trot; from that into a flying trot. Tightening the reins, I touched him with my heels and he trippled, moving first both near legs and then both off, with the whole of him balanced under me. Slacking the reins I let him out into a canter and bent him this way and that—a circle, a figure eight. He changed legs without any hesitation and seemed to be enjoying himself.

Then—by now we were on a nice piece of veld where there were no loose stones or rocks—I let him out. He broke from a canter into full gallop with one bound and progressed in what seemed to be a series of tremendous leaps, hitting the ground and raising himself over it as if he took pleasure in his strength; and yet as soon as I started to pull him up he stopped dead. I dropped the reins on his withers, letting go of them entirely, and he never moved. He was, I think, the most superbly trained horse I had ever ridden.

I turned him and cantered him back to the groom and Joan. She didn't seem to have moved and only said "Oh!" again as I threw my leg over his neck and dismounted. I remember feeling I should do something about Joan; she was upset by the horse—nervously. She was very white and a bit trembly. If she had been a man I'd have said: Come on in and have a drink. But you couldn't say that to a little girl, so I took her by the hand and said, "Nice, isn't he?"

"Yes, he's nice," she said. "He's . . . he's beautiful!"

Get her into the house, I thought—give her a glass of milk and something to eat, and then drive her back in the Cape cart. It would give me an excuse to see Muriel, too. We might have a game of tennis or a swim, and she might ask me to stay to supper. Almost have to, as a matter of fact.

I had never known Jack French, her husband. He had been killed by a lion before I took over the mine, and she had carried on after his death with the farm. As a matter of fact I, or rather my boys, were her main market for mealie meal—she had her own mill, a little one—and meat. So our relations were pretty close, but still had not reached the point of closeness that I desired. I wanted to marry her and she knew I did, but I think we both felt that there was plenty of time.

I gave Joan her milk and she gulped it down and held out the glass for more. Then she sat, not drinking, but just holding the full glass in her right hand and sucking the index finger of her left.

I don't remember if Joan ate well when we had lunch—probably not. Anyway, afterward I made her lie down and rest. At first she wouldn't and I only persuaded her to by saying she could come over and see Crusader whenever she wanted to; and then, later in the afternoon, I drove her back to the farm.

Muriel, as usual, was charming; thanked me for bringing Joan back and said:

"Dick, I really don't know what to do with Joan. She's horse mad."

"Might be worse," I said. "She could be boy mad, or crazy to go in the pictures or something. Horses have never hurt anyone yet, except when they bet on them."

Muriel smiled at me the way women do when they know something that men can't understand. But when she smiled I really didn't mind if she did know more than I did about some things. She was a truly lovely woman, her fair hair was really honey colored and she had very light brown eyes, almost topaz, flecked with little lights. They reminded me of Danzig Goldwasser, that liqueur which is golden brown and has specks of gold leaf floating in it; I had told her so once and it had made her laugh. She had pretty laughter like that of a girl. At that time it had been hard to make her laugh, what with her husband's tragic death and the fact that she had a child to bring up, and the farm— it was a big one—her only asset. The gold mine, by the way, was on her property, and my house only a couple of miles from the homestead.

This afternoon, the one I am speaking about and that I remember so clearly, Muriel looked even prettier than usual. We played a couple of sets of tennis and bathed in the dam—Joan could swim like a fish—and I stayed to dinner. It was just one of those very pleasant afternoons and evenings I had spent there.

The next few weeks were passed in work, going to see Muriel and Joan, and in Joan drifting over to my place to see Crusader. I don't know that I thought of it consciously, but I think I felt something odd about the relationship between the child and the stallion. He was, as I have said, a very small horse and Joan a long-legged, active child. But even taking these facts into consid-

eration it was extraordinary the way he would let her mount him
and ride him bareback without even a rein in his mouth. She
would guide him by leaning forward and covering his eye with
her hand—the near eye if she wanted him to turn to the off side
and vice versa. She talked to him all the time whether she was on
his back or not, and he seemed to answer her. Puffing and blowing, stamping his feet and neighing shrilly the trumpet blast of a
stallion when he saw her coming. The girl and the horse were
friends.

As far as I was concerned Crusader was a very good horse
and a very comfortable ride. A bit fidgety to mount, but that was
all. At least it was all until one day when he played up badly and
I lost my temper with him and thrashed him with a sjambok. This
was inexcusable even though I had been working all night the
night before and was tired. It was the end of things, too, as far as
the horse was concerned. Twice after that, he charged me, his
mouth open, his forelegs raised to chop me; and I could only
mount him if he was blindfolded and two boys held him. I still
kept him because I hate to be beaten, but no amount of gentleness
on my part now could make up for the indignity he had suffered.
It went on like this for another month or so and then one day I
went too near him and he picked me up with his teeth and shook
me the way a terrier shakes a rat. He would have killed me if
Sixpence had not beaten him off.

Now I was really afraid of him and he knew it. I had lost the
battle and he had won it. He knew this, too. He was turning into
a man-killer. It was not only me; he had savaged Sixpence, too,
taking a piece out of his arm. It seemed a terrible thing to do but
I decided to put a bullet through Crusader.

Oddly enough, the next day was mail day and a friend of
mine, Bill Saunders, wrote from Bechuanaland to ask if I had
heard of a small chestnut stallion, a man-killer, up my way. He
had heard indirectly that he had been sent up to Rhodesia after
having killed two men, both of whom had won races on him. So
that was it. If anyone hit him he killed them. Now why should the
horse dealer have sent him up to me and not said anything about
it? Then I remembered: Long ago—ten years at least—the dealer
had had a row with me, saying I had done him out of a job he
wanted. He had been mining then and accused me of sending a

bad report to the company about him. The thing had blown over, and later I had bought some horses from him. But evidently he had not forgotten his old grudge.

Next morning I had just finished breakfast and was pouring myself out a stiff whisky and soda before I went out to shoot Crusader—it's not easy to bring yourself to shoot a horse or a dog —when Joan burst in. She looked wildly about the room.

"You can't," she said at once. "You can't!"

"Can't what?" How the devil had the child heard? I had not even told Sixpence.

"You can't kill him," she said. "You shan't, either." She stood straight as an arrow, her eyes flashing. She was trembling like a leaf.

"He's dangerous," I said.

"Only to you, because you hit him."

"He's killed two men," I said, "and I'm going to shoot him." I expected her to cry. Her eyes were wide, bright with tears, and her lower lip trembled. Instead she picked up the coffeepot, threw it at me and ran straight for the stables. Wiping the coffee out of my eyes I followed her. By the time I had got onto the stoep she had reached Crusader's box and opened the door.

The horse was screaming with excitement as he saw her. When she got him outside, instead of galloping off, he stood. With a flying jump she was across his back, her left hand on his mane. She wriggled forward and got her right leg over him. Then she slapped him with her open hand and they were off, tearing across the veld, her yellow hair flying behind her all mixed up with Crusader's mane as she leaned over his neck.

This was a fine mess. . . . Muriel's kid having stolen my man-killing horse. And how had she known I was going to shoot him? Why, the rifle was out on a chair. I got up to put it back in the rack and decided to go over and square things with Muriel, if I could.

Of course Muriel knew why I'd come. "I suppose it's the horse," she said.

I said yes, and that if Joan wanted him she'd better keep him if she, Muriel, thought it was safe.

"He's safe enough with her," Muriel said, "and I told her she could keep him if you agreed"—she had known that I'd agree to anything if she asked me to—"but that she must look after him herself," Muriel went on. "I don't want any of my boys hurt." So the matter was settled pretty easily.

Muriel called the houseboy to bring tea, and while we drank it she told me about what had happened. It seems that Joan had jumped up in the middle of her breakfast and had said, "Something is wrong with Crusader—I know it." Leaving everything she had run out; she must have run and trotted the whole two miles to my place. The next thing Muriel had known was the thunder of Crusader's hoofs as he came dashing into the yard, and the yells of the boys who had scattered in front of him. Joan had taken him straight to the old dairy, where there was a good stall for him, had watered and fed him and bedded him down with veld hay before she came into the house. She had said practically nothing to her mother except, "He's mine now and I'm going to keep him." Then she had burst into tears and had been sick.

"I've never seen anyone so upset," Muriel said.

We had another cup of tea and we both agreed it was all most extraordinary but that with a girl as high-strung as Joan there was very little to do about it. She might have become seriously ill if the horse was shot.

I left Muriel a little later and in the course of the next few weeks everything went well, from what I heard. Joan avoided me, which I was sorry about as we had been good friends; it appeared she spent all the time she wasn't in the house either in the stable with Crusader or out on the veld with him riding him or just walking, with the horse following her like a dog.

Muriel was quite pleased about it because she said he was better than a dog as a protection. He would let no one come near the child and on one occasion killed a big ringals—a South African cobra—that she had disturbed.

And then it happened. Suddenly, the way things do happen. On the mine we worked a couple of hundred boys, Mashonas, and we never had any trouble from them. Not that we expected it, either. We thought of them as the Matabele who had first conquered and then enslaved them did—*as dogs*. Workers who, if they were inclined at times to be sullen, were also spiritless. Anyway, the first thing I knew was my houseboy John, who was a Zulu, waking me in the night, saying:

"Master, the Mashonas are up. They are killing the white people."

"Bailey!" I said. He was my assistant and had a small shanty near the boys' compound.

"He is dead, *Baas*. His house is burned."

"Where are they now?" I asked. By this time I had on my trousers.

"They've gone to the big house."

Gone to Muriel's house! Why in God's name they left me I never found out. Perhaps because they thought a woman and child easier to kill; perhaps they wanted a white woman, which was not a pleasant thought. John, without a word from me, had brought a rifle and bandolier into the room.

"What boys have we got who'll fight?" I asked.

"Sixpence," John said. "He is saddling the horses for us."

"For us?"

"*Ja, Baas*. I knew the *baas* would ride to the missus, and Sixpence and I ride with him." John was a good horseman.

"*Baas*, can we have guns?"

"Can you use them?" It is illegal to arm natives but this was no moment to worry about the letter of the law.

"*Ja*, we can use them." How they had learned I never found out, but a minute later we were out and mounted—a little commando, as the Boers would call it—and galloping toward Muriel's place. There were fires burning there already. I prayed it was only the outbuildings. As we got closer I heard rifle fire from the house. At least, the Mashonas had not caught them asleep. Muriel had some good boys, and both she and Joan were good shots. As we got nearer we could see the Mashonas dancing about and yelling blue murder in the light of the burning buildings.

Shouting as loud as we could, we charged. I was a bit ahead with Sixpence on my left and John on my right. With the reins looped over my arm I fired two shots into the brown mass and saw one Mashona throw up his hand—he had an assegai in it—and fall.

Then we were through. It was my intention to charge back again. There were fewer Mashonas than I had thought there would be. Either they had divided into several parties or some of them had no stomach for this kind of thing. But I had hardly swung my horse round when Sixpence shouted:

"Look! Crusader!"

And there he was. The dairy was alight but he must have kicked down the door. The red horse in the red light of the fire, his mane and tail flowing, was into the Mashonas like a great dog, kicking, savaging with his forelegs, biting and screaming as he cleared the road to the house. He was making no effort to bolt but was literally attacking the Mashonas, who were running from him as if he were the devil himself, which is what he looked like.

As he got to the stoep, Joan and her mother ran out. The child held Crusader's forelock in her hand while her mother mounted, and then jumped up behind her. Crusader wheeled in a rear. I was afraid they'd fall, but Muriel held onto his mane; and still squealing with rage Crusader broke through the last small group left near the house. We fired a volley at them and, turning, followed Crusader and the women. As we galloped I could hear Sixpence swearing to himself: *The horse is a devil . . . the horse is a devil.* Fortunately it was nearly daylight or we should have lost them.

"So it was you," Muriel said when we caught up with them. "I thought it was them. . . . I thought they'd got hold of horses and were following us."

Leaving Joan and her mother at the salt pan where the white people had made a *laager,* I joined the other men who went out to put the rebellion down. And it was only when I got back that I heard the rest of the story.

Like me they had been warned by their house servants and were ready, but though they had killed and wounded quite a few of the Mashonas they thought they could not hold out much longer, till Joan had called to Crusader and he had kicked himself loose. My coming had helped them, but even without us I think they would have got away.

This is the story of Crusader. Explain it if you can. I can't, nor can Muriel. Muriel King she is now. Joan is a big girl who promises to be as pretty as her mother. And Crusader is an old horse and the father of most of the good horses near Gwelo. They're all small chestnut horses with a white blaze and a snip on the nose. "Crusaders" they call them round here. And another funny thing: after the battle Crusader was as quiet as a lamb. Perhaps he knew he didn't have to fight any more and that no one would ever hit him again.

THE JOYOUS HORSE

SONG OF THE HORSE
Translated from the Navajo
by Natalie Curtis

How joyous his neigh!
Lo, the Turquoise Horse of Johano-ai,
　　How joyous his neigh!
There on precious hides outspread standeth he;
　　How joyous his neigh!
There of mingled waters holy drinketh he;
　　How joyous his neigh!
There he spurneth dust of flittering grains;
　　How joyous his neigh!
There in mist of sacred pollen hidden, all hidden he;
　　How joyous his neigh!
There his offspring may grow and thrive for evermore;
　　How joyous his neigh!

JUSTICE FOR AN ARISTOCRAT
by Mazo de la Roche

There was a group of men about a charcoal stove in the street outside the military barracks. The men were digging a drain, and half-frozen earth lay in drab lumps in the roadside. Snow was beginning to fall and the air had that peculiar harsh grayness which takes the color from the face and intensifies every line and blemish. The men's faded clothes, their lumpish shapes, their thick irregular features, seemed a mere gathering together and enlivening of the earth itself. Only the fiery glow of the charcoal gave a soul to the scene.

But the men were the reverse of depressed. They were strong in belief in the superiority of their position as compared with the laborers of other countries. They knew that the workers owned their country and that, at last, the workers had justice and administered justice. They were free. They were strong. It was not like the old Czarist days of injustice and oppression.

"It's terrible to think," said Ivan Popoff, unwrapping his packet of half-frozen bread and taking an enormous bite, "how other countries are still under the heel of capitalists and tyrants."

"The workers of Russia own everything," said Peter Rakatin, his words struggling to utterance against a chunk of gristle.

Mitya Grushinka, a gaunt, curly-headed boy, stared into their mouths enviously. His scrap of food had been swallowed up in a moment. "Just the same," he said, "there must have been some pretty sights in the old days. I am too young to remember."

"Pretty sights won't fill your belly," returned Peter, champing the gristle. "The workers of Russia own everything."

"I know we do," said Mitya. "My father has told me how, in the old days, the sleighs of the nobility used to go gliding over the snow, with fur rugs hanging from the back and silver bells jingling. Once, my father says, a lady dropped her muff out of the sleigh and he picked it up and ran after and returned it to her. The gentleman gave him a silver piece and the lady, who was very beautiful, waved her muff and laughed."

"Well, it's our turn to laugh now," said Ivan grimly.

Peter shifted the gristle to the other side of his mouth. "The workers own everything," he said.

"My mother," went on Mitya, spreading his thin young hands to the heat of the charcoal, "says that the processions on holy days were beautiful. They made you forget all your worries."

"Religious ceremonies! Drugs! Drugs! Drugs—to make you

MAN O' WAR. Joseph A. Phetteplace. *Intarsia.*

forget!" said Ivan. "We have sent God packing. We have no more use for God."

"We don't acknowledge that he made the world." said Peter. "We made it ourselves. We made our own world. It's ours."

"My grandfather," said Mitya, "still keeps an ikon in a corner of the room. He burns a bit of candle in front of it. It looks pretty in the corner when one goes home cold and tired."

"Pretty be damned!" said Ivan. "Your grandfather ought to be ashamed of himself. But then, he is an old fool."

"He knows that. But he says he's too old now to give up God. He's got so used to God that he wouldn't know how to get on without him."

Peter bolted the gristle. "I get on without God, and look at me!"

"You look just like a frog," said Mitya.

They were ready to quarrel when their attention was caught by a man coming along the road leading a horse. On either side of the horse walked a soldier with his bayonet over his shoulder. Motor cars and lorries moved aside to make way for them and people walking on the pavement stopped to stare in curiosity at the beautiful beast.

His approach, through the mechanical drabness of the traffic, seemed the approach of a conqueror. He lifted his hoofs and put them down again with the precision of a musician's fingers on the keyboard. There was majesty in the moving lines of his superb body, and the elegance of his raised head annihilated the pretensions of what moved about him. He wore no saddle, but his bridle was held in the hand of a groom whose face bore the stamp of grief.

The group stopped outside the courthouse and at once the gate of the yard was thrown open by a porter who called out:

"This way with the prisoner!"

The porter was fully conscious of the effect of his words on the men about the charcoal fire and on the loiterers that were already gathering about the gate. He showed his yellow teeth proudly under his enormous mustache and gave a mock ceremonious bow to the horse.

Led by the groom, guarded by the soldiers, he passed through the gate, and it was shut with a frozen clang behind him.

But the porter remained on the outside and stood, his back against the gate, waiting for questions.

They came fast enough. What was taking place? Who owned the horse? Was the Court turning into a circus? Was the judge going for a ride? Mitya was the only one who did not ask questions. He stood, with his eyes fixed blankly on the closed gate, as though his soul had mounted the horse and passed through with it.

"It is a court-martial," answered the porter, mouthing the words in zest under his frozen mustache. "It is as true a court-martial as ever you saw. All the ceremony is there—the officers in full uniform, but—it is held outdoors, for the benefit of the prisoner, who is not accustomed to rooms and their furniture."

"But who is the prisoner?" asked Ivan.

"He is the horse you saw."

"The horse!" cried Mitya. "But what can he have done?"

"In the first place he is an aristocrat. The son of a famous sire, Sunstar. That is bad enough."

"It is certainly bad," said Peter. "He should be put to work —made to draw a dung cart."

"No. He is to be given a fair trial, with witnesses for and against. If he is found innocent of the crime he will be set free."

"But how can a horse commit a crime?" asked a woman with a child in her arms.

"I will tell you. This horse won a silver cup at the Royal Horse Show. And who offered this cup? Who offered it?" He glared into the faces about him.

No one knew.

"Then I will tell you. It was the late Czar! He offered the cup and this horse, Moonstar, won it! If you want my opinion, I will tell you that I don't think that he has the ghost of a chance of acquittal." He looked about him proudly.

After a little the group by the gate scattered, the laborers returned to their work. Mitya could think of nothing but the beautiful horse—the way he had lifted his feet, as though he knew the beauty of his every movement; the way he raised his head, as though a wind were in his face; the glance of gentle pride he had cast as the porter when he threw open the gate. Above the sound of the picks in frozen earth Mitya listened for the sound of horse's hoofs.

At last they sounded on the pavement of the courtyard, rhythmic as music, drawing nearer with every beat. The porter threw open the gate with a flourish, as though he had himself created a tableau, and there again stood the horse, the groom, and the armed soldiers on either side. But now there were six soldiers instead of two.

"Found guilty?" questioned the porter.

"Found guilty," answered the groom, his mouth twisted in pain. He led the horse into the road.

The gate clanged shut. The soldiers marked time on the freezing ground. "Right wheel!" shouted the one in command. "March!"

Mitya threw down his spade. "I'm going after them," he said. "I want to hear more about the horse."

"You can't do that!" cried Ivan. "You'll lose your job."

But the boy did not care. He followed the horse through the streets, marching in step with the soldiers till they turned into a row of stables belonging to the army. But when Mitya would have followed, a soldier barred his way.

"You can't come in here," he said.

"But I want to touch the horse."

"Is the fellow a fool?" asked another soldier, coming up.

"No, I'm not a fool," answered Mitya for himself. "It is only that I've never seen such a beast before and I'd like to stroke him."

The new Bolshevik Army had not a strict discipline. Mitya was allowed to follow the horse and groom into the stable.

He stood there astonished, staring at the rows of rounded, muscular flanks projecting from the series of stalls. He was used to motors of all sorts but he had never given a thought to horses. Their primitive power, their strange beauty, gave him a feeling of sadness, as for something unattainable.

The groom had led the condemned horse into a loose-box and was taking off the bridle. Mitya could see that he was crying.

"Do you think it was a fair trial?" he asked.

"Be careful," answered the groom, "that no one hears you. Yes, I suppose it was a fair trial, though the poor creature couldn't know he was doing wrong."

"Can I come in and stroke him?"

The groom nodded and Mitya went into the loose-box. The

smell of clean straw rose to his nostrils, the smell of polished leather, and a strange sweet animal smell from the horse. Free of his bridle he flung up his stark head, the whites of his eyes showing above the lustrous iris, the rosy nostrils spread as though to drink in the very fountain of life. He danced sideways from Mitya, as elegantly as a tightrope walker, then bent his head, bowing until his mane fell into his eyes.

"He's full of fun," said the groom. "He doesn't realize how things are with him."

"What are they going to do to him?"

"Shoot him. Tomorrow morning."

"Oh. . . . Do you think he'd let me stroke him?"

"If I say. He does what I tell him. You've no idea how glad he is to be alone with me again. He didn't like that trial, I can tell you. There they stood in their uniforms, looking solemn—talking, talking, and everything strange to him. When the sentence was pronounced he reared and lifted his forehoof, as though to strike, but it was just because he was angry at standing there so long."

"Perhaps he didn't like the looks of them."

"Perhaps not. They laughed and one said—'Well, at this time to-morrow, you'll be only horse meat!' "

"Will you tell him to let me stroke him?"

"Quiet, Moonstar, quiet, my pet! This young boy won't harm you."

The horse stood gentle while Mitya passed his hands over his sides, which were the color of a newly split chestnut, and his neck, which had the lovely curve of a harp.

"How firm he is! You'd think he was a different kind of flesh."

"I shouldn't mind if they shot me with him tomorrow."

"Well, I don't understand. What was he for? What use was he?"

"God help us! Did you never see a gentleman riding? Did you never hear of a horse show? I wish you might have seen his owner mounted on him. He was as fine a man as this is horse."

Mitya ran his fingers through the strong silk of the mane. "Is the owner dead, then?"

"Yes. They shot *him* six months ago. I've cared for the horse ever since. I never thought they'd be after him."

"It's a good thing he doesn't understand, isn't it?"

"I shall bandage his eyes, so he won't see the muskets raised. . . . Why, when I look at him standing here I can't believe in it all. If he chose he could jump over their heads as if they were rats. You ought to see him jump. He gathers himself together like a cloud. He looks at the barrier. He clears it like lightning—then skims on to the next one. He shows himself off like a prince. Aye! That's the trouble! Like a prince!"

"Might I have a few hairs of his mane to keep?" asked Mitya.

"Yes! Yes! I'll give you a lock of his mane. I'm glad you thought of that. I'll cut a lock for myself, too."

The horse stared, with a kind of glowing wonder in his eyes, as with a pair of clippers the groom cut a thick lock from the richness of his mane and divided it between Mitya and himself.

All the rest of the day Mitya was conscious of the lock of hair in his pocket. Now and again he would put in his fingers to make sure it was there. When evening came he sat in a corner of the room with his grandfather and told him about the horse. The candle before the ikon cast a glow on their faces, making each in his way beautiful.

Mitya was early at work. He kept looking down the road for the approach of the horse. It was very cold and red sunlight flamed on the windowpanes of the barracks when at last he saw him coming.

"Here he is!" he cried, and he straightened himself and ceased digging.

"Who?" demanded Ivan.

"Him—who's going to be shot."

"We workers own the country," said Peter, "and we must see that justice is done. He will make good meat, that beast."

"Don't!" said Mitya, beginning to cry.

The hoofbeats sounded muffled, for there had been a light fall of snow. The groom walked in his best clothes, very upright, but looking as though he had not slept. His mouth had sunk into his gray face in despair.

But the horse moved in the red sunlight as though he were a god of the sun. In purity of rhythm his muscular neck moved against the noble arch of his shoulders. His eyes beamed in proud confidence as he followed the groom.

The porter was there to throw open the gate. A second group

of soldiers was waiting inside. At the end of the barrack yard
Mitya had a glimpse of the firing squad. The three laborers leant
on their spades listening.

The frosty air was shivered by an explosion, as though the
fiery ball of the sun had burst.

"That's the end of him," said Ivan.

"As of all enemies of the State," said Peter.

Mitya began to dig wildly, throwing the earth about. He
kept his eyes fixed in the hole he was digging and would not look
as the sledge bearing the body of the horse passed through the
gate.